DREAMS
and the search for meaning

PETER O'CONNOR

Paulist Press
New York/Mahwah

Cover: Lawrence Daws b. 1927
Australian Dream V 1969
Gouache & Collage on Paper
52 x 52 cm
Private collection.

First published in 1986 by Methuen Haynes, an imprint of Methuen
Australia Pty. Ltd.

Published in the United States by Paulist Press
997 Macarthur Boulevard.,
Mahwah, N.J. 07430

Library of Congress Cataloging-in-Publication Data

O'Connor, Peter
    Dreams and the search for meaning.

    Bibliography: p.
    Includes index.
    1. Dreams. I. Title.
BF1078.027 1987   154.6'34   87-2234
ISBN 0-8091-2870-5

Printed and bound in the
United States of America

CONTENTS

To those who have shared
a dream.

And one day there will
come a great awakening,
when we shall realise that
life itself was a great
dream.

Chuang-tzu, 350BC

PREFACE

This book emerges out of several primary and related sources. At the personal level, I have been fascinated, frustrated, intrigued, and mystified by my own dreams for a period of over twenty years, throughout which I have kept a written record. My introduction to the world of dreams and the unconscious mind was due to an outstanding and inspiring teacher at the University of Melbourne in the early 1960s, the late Dr Allan Jeffries. His respect for and knowledge of the unconscious mind was indelibly imprinted upon my psyche, because, unlike so many academics, Dr Jeffries lived what he taught. This experience influenced my professional life, where for many years I have been interested in and respectful of the world of dreams and their capacity to provide rich insights into ourselves.

More than three years ago this interest culminated in my beginning dream analysis groups, where a small number of individuals meet weekly to share, explore, and participate in a dream. For each of us involved in these groups the learning has been rich, and it is to the members of my dream groups that I owe an enormous debt. They have not only facilitated and stimulated my own knowledge of dreams, they have also provided me with an opportunity to participate in a unique and rewarding experience. It is, therefore, appropriate that this book be dedicated to the members of these groups.

A third influence has been the inspirational writings and teachings of Dr James Hillman, an outstanding, contemporary Jungian analyst. Although I have acknowledged him by numerous references to his work throughout the text, I would like to declare formally my appreciation of his work. Much of my experience would have remained elusive and incomprehensible had James Hillman's writings not provided the vital and necessary framework.

The writing of this book has at times felt as frustrating as trying to provide a written description of a Picasso painting, since dreams are of that order. When I finished writing, it occurred to me that I had unwittingly produced a trilogy, for this book ties together my two earlier works: on the mid-life transition and on Jung. In the first I attempted to establish the pattern of mid-life and argue the necessity for undertaking the inner journey. In the Jung book I was trying not only to convey to the general educated public the basics of Jung's ideas, but also to place the mid-life transition in a broader context of individuation. This book, like the symbolic mercury that it is about, joins the salt of the mid-life with the sulphur of Jungian theory. It is concerned with the middle ground between experience (or body) and mind (or theory). This is the middle kingdom, where one finds soul; and dreams are the language of the soul.

Thus the aim of this book is not to provide some comprehensive or authoritative study of dreams and their interpretation. Indeed it is as much to do with psyche, or soul, as it is with dreams. It is fundamentally about the middle kingdom of dreams and the restoration of this realm of imagination to a legitimate position: the overriding concern is one of restoration, not interpretation. The meanings in any one dream are inexhaustible, and the point of a dream is not to get the 'right' interpretation, but to participate in the dream in the right way, to engage in an act of imagination, not rationality. If others, as I sincerely hope they do, find themselves having different thoughts and imaginings about the dreams discussed in this book, then it would have achieved its aim. The book is basically concerned with how to approach a dream and thereby one's unconscious mind, rather than how to interpret a dream. The latter act is very often motivated by a desire to control the unconscious out of a fear of the unknown. While an obsession with the 'correct interpretation' may temporarily ease our anxieties, whether professionally or personally, I doubt whether it advances understanding.

Some readers may well get both impatient and frustrated with some chapters in the book and want to concentrate solely on dream analysis. My experience tells me that one must approach dreams as though they are pieces of art, and thus dream analysis itself is a work of art. It is therefore appropriate and desirable that one should work slowly and patiently, spending considerable time in preparation for the task of analysis, just as the ancient Greeks did when they visited the temple of Asclepius, the god of healing. Some chapters, then, prepare the ground, and others explain techniques, so that the reader comes to dream analysis in the most receptive frame of mind.

No doubt this book will, like my two previous ones, draw some criticism from my more academically and rationally orientated colleagues, who may once again criticise my lack of an empirical and scientific base. To these colleagues I again say that, in the realm of the unconscious, art provides a more appropriate model than some hard-nosed empiricism. There are severe limits to rationality and logical positivism, and dreams are a phenomenon that highlights these limits. I have not written this book to prove anything. Indeed, I would consider such a task irrelevant. I have written it only to share some of the thoughts and experiences that I have had the opportunity and the privilege of participating in. My hope is that this sharing will be helpful to others in their inner journey and will provide a map for some of the path. Other colleagues may wonder about the wisdom of discussing dreams out of the context of an ongoing therapeutic relationship, where one has a much deeper and broader knowledge of the dreamer. This concern is a valid one, and I am acutely aware of it. However, I feel over all that there is more to be gained from the sharing of some dream material than there is to be lost by the omission of extensive biographical material. The omissions, of course, have meant a necessary restriction to possible associations and amplifications of any particular dream. However, the purpose of the book is to engage the reader in an imaginative act, not to undertake a full-scale analysis.

I record my gratitude to those individuals with whom I have had a psychotherapy relationship, and whose dreams form part of this book, especially for their permission to use the dreams. I perhaps need to make the point here that the dreams as such do not belong to us as individuals, since similar motifs and types of dreams occur to many different persons. So none of the dreamers ought to identify too closely with the discussion, as the dreams are presented and discussed solely for the purposes of illustration. To the members of my dream groups whose dreams I have used, the same gratitude and comments apply.

Two other people deserve my specific thanks. The first is my publisher, Susan Haynes, who saw the gleam of another book in my eye long before I did. Susan has been, and continues to be, a major source of encouragement, support, and stimulation; a rare combination indeed amongst publishers. To Marilyn Rowntree I owe my sincere thanks for her tolerance and skill in typing the manuscript.

Melbourne, 1986   Peter O'Connor

ABBREVIATIONS

CW – C.G. Jung, **Collected Works**, 20 vols (see Sources, p. 232 for details. **MDR** – C.G. Jung, **Memories, Dreams and Reflections**, Routledge and Kegan Paul, 1963.

1
SETTING THE SCENE

At the turning-point of this century, Sigmund Freud, the founder of psychoanalysis, published a revolutionary book for the times, on dreams: it was entitled *The Interpretation of Dreams*. The first edition consisted of only 600 copies, and it took eight years to sell them. The tardiness of sales can scarcely reflect upon the quality of the book, which as time has elapsed has come to be regarded as a classic work on dreams. It reflects more upon the resistance of both the lay and professional public to the discussion of dreams and dreaming. This unwillingness to admit the significance of dreams still persists, although there is every indication of change, change that is long overdue as we reach the limits of our Western, post-industrial obsession with rationalism and materialism.

However, dreams themselves evoke a reaction: either negative, in the form of resistance; or positive, often in the form of over-idealising them; but rarely neutral. One often hears a person say, 'Oh, I had a weird dream last night', and an immediate response from someone near by. The response is either in a denigrating form, such as, 'Oh, dreams are a lot of bunkum', or receptive, such as, 'Tell me more. Dreams

1

can contain very important messages from our unconscious mind, and always tell us the truth.' Sometimes the response to me personally is one of a sort of cynical disbelief, such as, 'You don't really believe dreams mean anything, do you?' Underlying this quasi-question-cum-statement is the surprise that anyone who is reasonably intelligent (and by the rules of our society a Ph.D. legitimates one as intelligent!) could possibly believe in dreams. By way of contrast, other people approach me with a burning fire of enthusiasm in their eyes, true seekers of 'truth', urgently wanting to tell me about their most wonderful and amazing dreams, convinced that I will be interested in them. Underlying this latter approach to dreams is a naive and childlike belief that there is actually a single meaning of a dream and, furthermore, that a 'expert' or modern-day Delphic oracle can infallibly decipher it.

The truth, as so often happens, lies somewhere between the extremes of disbelief and *naiveté* . What is very clear is that dreams do have meaning, they are not simply randomly arranged images. But rarely is this meaning a single one, and the meaning is by and large peculiar to the individual who has the dream. If dreams appear meaningless, that is a judgement of our rational minds. They certainly are meaningless in a logical, rational sense, since logic and reason are not part of the language of dreams. Dreams are a symbolic language, and what we know from Carl Jung is that a symbol is the best possible expression of something that we have not yet understood; that is, not understood in a conscious, rational manner. In other words, dreams are pictures, images, not thoughts, but it is important to note that being in images does not render the dream any less real. One often hears someone say about a dream, 'It was as if it was really happening' or ask, 'Did it really happen, or was it a dream?' So, within our own everyday phrases we reflect the wisdom that dreams are real,

2

even though in a different way from the way we ordinarily perceive or think of as real. Indeed, our present age and its cynicism towards dreams is reflective of a much broader cynicism about the entire imaginal realm. Thus we have relegated fairy-tales, for example, to children, an act indicating that we collectively regard them as childish, and thereby lose a powerful and important link to profound wisdom and insights that they so very often contain. The entire world of mythology has been subjected to this active denigration or, alternatively, to dismembering by a harsh form of logic, which fails to appreciate that myths are written in an imaginative or mythopoetic style that tells a story. In the final analysis the story or series of stories are about ourselves and the inner forces, images that move us collectively.

We have come to regard our waking state as the state of existence where reason and rationality prevail, and if we cannot explain it, touch it, point to it, predict it, and hopefully control it, then it 'does not have meaning, does not matter, is mere fantasy'. How odd, when one reflects for a moment upon the fact that we spend an average of eight hours a night sleeping and, for the average person living until seventy or seventy-two years of age, this means that one-third of these years will be spent asleep: that is approximately twenty-four years of sleep! Further, what we know nowadays from the experimental work in sleep laboratories is that approximately 20 to 25 per cent of our sleeping time is spent dreaming, hence we dream for approximately six full years of our life. Perhaps there is more truth than one at first realised in the old expression about somebody who is 'dreaming his life away'.

The sleep research that commenced with the outstanding pioneering work of Aserinsky and Kleitman in 1953 and continues on until the present time has also established, using rapid eye movements (REM) as the objective indicator, that we all dream.

What distinguishes us is not whether people dream or not, but whether we can recall our dreams or not. So, each and every night we are subjected to another reality, different from our waking reality, another form of existence, where we invent stories, some about people, places, and things we know from our waking reality, others about events that we have no precedent for in our waking reality. In short, we dream, during which time we ignore the usual restraints of space and time. We can be far away in another country, or alternatively we can find ourselves doing two totally contradictory things at the same time. We can also alter people's ages, alter their size, alter their appearance, etc., etc. It is an entire world of invention, fiction, and imagination. Also we can find ourselves remembering people, events, places that we have no recall or memory of in our ordinary waking state. Above all else, we seemingly cannot control our dreams. Given, then, that the dream world so blatantly violates our preferred notions of 'reality', it is not surprising that some people dismiss the dream world as stupid.

Yet we equally must know, at some level, that it is an important part of our existence, because, as we shall see in the next chapter, human beings throughout time have known of and paid considerable attention to dreams. Our problem is, as Erich Fromm so adequately states, that symbolic language, the language of dreams, 'has been forgotten by modern man. Not when he is asleep, but when he is awake.' This 'forgetting' has, I believe, created a profound sense of loss in modern man, in so far as he has 'forgotten' that he is far more than his ego-conscious self. He is also an imaginative, reflective being, and this 'forgetting' has separated him from a source of wisdom that lies within him and distinguishes *homo sapiens* from the animal kingdom. By 'forgetting' the symbolic language, he is disconnected from his own myth, his own plot, his own *raison d'être*, and is thus

4

vulnerable to living out others' pre-formed, stereotyped, and pre-packaged myths or plots. In so doing,
he is turning his back on his own individuality and,
ironically, on his own depth of being, which
inhibits his awareness of others' individualities.
Dreaming is the most natural, obvious, and readily
accessible means for remembering a symbolic
language and thereby remembering our imaginal inner
world. It balances the proliferation and domination
of our existence by our outer reality. Not to listen
to and be attentive to dreams is to choose to be
psychologically amnesic, at best, and psychologically
dead, at worst. Since imagination can be seen as
breath to the psyche in the same vital way as oxygen
is to the body, thus dreams are essential to life, not
peripheral. As the medieval author Synesius of Cyrene
states in speaking of the heightened capacity for
insight during sleep: 'We do not sleep merely to live,
but to learn to live well.' And a little further on he
says: 'Sleep offers itself to all: it is an oracle always
ready to be our infallible and silent counselor.'

It is a truth known since antiquity and clearly stated
in classical Greek times that dreams contribute to our
well-being. When patients visited the temple of
Asclepius the god of healing, and slept there over-
night, he revealed to them through dreams the
remedies that only he knew. Asclepius can be seen
as an image or personification of our own healing
capacity. We also can visit his temple each night when
we sleep. But how many listen to the 'remedy' or ask
the gods within? Rationality denies us this visitation.
As Max Zeller says:

> I believe that the frequently occurring earthquake
> dreams use their language and imagery to shake
> us from an unconscious state of existence in order
> to arouse the sleepers who sleep too tightly.
> 'Sleepers awake!' calls the watchman's voice
> through the night, to arouse man drowned in
> unconsciousness, to awaken him to a greater real-

ity and to penetrate his very being. But who listens to this calling, though it would point the way?

It is, to return to Fromm's thought, that we forget the symbolic language, the world of images, when we are awake, but it seems that we do not forget when we are asleep. The following short dream from a forty-two-year-old male, struggling to reawaken his imagination from a prolonged period of loss of contact with it, demonstrates the problem of being asleep.

*A dream, very vague, elusive, but a sense of being heavily asleep and quite unable to wake myself up. I had a gross sense of disorientation, of not being able to open my eyes no matter how hard I tried. I think by not being able to wake up I missed a very important seminar being given by a creative person. ***

This dream, brief as it is, draws the dreamer's attention to the fact that the problem in his life is that he is asleep. Indeed, the only time he is awake is when he's asleep, and his imagination reminds him that it's time he woke up. This is often the case with men passing through the mid-life transition. They are short of breath, psychologically speaking, a shortness that is not cured by physical exercise, but only by the evocation and stimulation of their imagination. This task is most easily and naturally accomplished by paying attention to their dreams. As Erich Fromm says:

Not only is our power of imagination greater in our sleep that in our waking life, but the innate strivings for health and happiness often assert themselves in our sleep more forcefully than when we are awake.

The Old Testament records the truth of this view when in the Book of Job we find the following thoughts:

---

*All dreams quoted in this book are set out in the exact form in which the dreamer recorded the dream, with no corrections of grammar, spelling, etc.

For God speaketh once, yea twice, yet man perceiveth it not. In a dream, in a vision of the night, when deep sleep falleth upon men, in slumberings upon the bed; then he openeth the ears of men, and sealeth their instruction . . . (Job 33:14–16)

But to turn inward, particularly at times of transition, such as mid-life, seems very difficult for most people. It is as if the price we have paid for 'progress' has been a severing of our belief in the inner world and the projection of healing onto outside experts, whether they be yogis, medical practitioners, natural healers, masseurs, psychologists, or whatever. In my own personal and professional life I have been repeatedly struck by the inner healing force, the inner Asclepius, who is for ever available to us. People initially seeking psychotherapy tend to believe that the therapist will help them, when the truth is that the therapist is, or ought to be, a catalyst to stimulate their own inner healing. For me, that healing lies in one's dreams, the healing of the great chasm in our psyche between our conscious and unconscious self: a chasm into which we fall with depression, jealousy, anger, despair, hopelessness, anxiety, etc., etc. Yet each night we lower the drawbridge between consciousness and unconsciousness, only to forget, when we wake, that we have done it. Or, even worse, we deny that we have done it and persist in clinging to the conscious rational end of the bridge in the false belief that it is the whole bridge.

James Hillman has this to say about a dream: 'The dream itself is a symbol; that is, it joins in itself the conscious and the unconscious, bringing together incommensurables and opposites.' It is this struggle to reconcile the opposite forces within us that forms the cornerstone of Jungian psychology, the instinctual journey towards completion. The thwarting of this instinct, like the thwarting of any instinct, produces dis-ease and results in the filling of

7

psychologists' and psychiatrists' consulting rooms. This process of moving towards completing oneself Jung called individuation, and dreams are intrinsically linked to it through their capacity to help us to recognize parts of ourselves that we may normally be unaware of, thereby facilitating their integration into our conscious view of ourselves. Each re-cognition builds another link between consciousness and unconsciousness, and in so doing each time narrows the gap within ourselves. This gap is narrowed by reflection and awareness, and in so doing we are heeding the admonition inscribed on the temple of Apollo at Delphi: 'Know thyself.' This admonition takes on even more precise meaning when one remembers that Asclepius was the son of Apollo, so perhaps we can imaginatively say that the offspring of 'Knowing thyself' is health, and the *via regia* to health is the world of dreams. We need to rebuild our own temple to Asclepius by taking our dreams seriously, reflecting upon them, and incorporating their wisdom into our everyday life.

If we are to be healed by our dreams, then what is this sickness from which we suffer? While I think it true to say that dreams play an important part in physical health, the ill health that I see dreams being therapeutic for is psychological ill health. Again, one might be tempted to assume that what I mean by this is the usual well-known and often overly well-recited ills of anxiety, depression, conflict, marital and family breakdown, etc., etc. However, all of these commonly regarded psychological ills are, in my view, symptoms that point towards a deeper and more pervasive disease in our present society. This I see as the dis-ease of literality. As James Hillman, who has done more than any other contemporary Jungian to tackle this dis-ease, says:

'Literalism is sickness.' Whenever we are caught in a literal view, a literal belief, a literal statement, we have lost the imaginative metaphorical perspective to ourselves and our world.

We have, in other words, been adult-erated with literal rationalistic explanations of the world and ourselves, to which modern-day psychology has been a major contributor with its ever-increasing obsession with measurement and behaviourism. This adult-eration has meant the loss of the imaginative, spontaneous, playful, childlike (but not childish) quality. We find it harder to play imaginatively and instead ask the television or movie theatre to play at us, for us and renegue on our own responsibility and capacity to imagine. Fixed, stereotyped images hounding us every day are atrophising our capacity to imagine, to let the inner world speak and breathe, and this has resulted in the dis-ease of literality. We are swamped by massive amounts of information, photostatted at an alarming rate, or tape-recorded to play in our cars, just in case we suffer withdrawal symptoms from a lack of information. Literality abounding has drawn our psyche out into the world and away from its inner source, we seek cure from this dis-ease in high-pressured, so-called 'growth weekends', where we can take your dis-ease and treat it in any number of literal ways from massaging it to having the Tarot read it, to meditating upon it, through to the penultimate case of literalising, re-birthing it, re-birthing it . . . be a born-again person! Such are the fantasies and images we create in our literal world to attend to this dis-ease of the soul. Yet, paradoxically, all these literal forms of attending to self seem to me to simply compound and perpetuate the problem, condemning us to believing that an answer lies outside in the literal world, rather than in the metaphors and images that move behind this literality.

It is the dream world that resides between these flights into mind therapies or body therapies, it is the dream world that is truly the middle kingdom, that ancient Celtic land of fairies, leprechauns, and other mythical characters. We need to reflect upon the middle kingdom and see what psyche is endeavour-

9

ing to get us to see through these external manifestations, whether they be symptoms or espoused cures. So each of these varied 'cures' contains an underlying image, and that image is where real cure lies. So re-birthing in an imagistic sense, not the simplistic literal sense, is an image of a new beginning, new growth, the emergence of a new child from within ourselves, the need for spontaneity and restoration of *puer* over *senex*. But to literalise the image is to restrict its possibilities and place the process outside of oneself into the hands of a 're-birther'. Past lives or regression therapy can be seen as having an underlying metaphor of understanding or coming to grips with the plot or plots that form our lives; ways to uncover the mythical images that move us from within ourselves. To literalise these in past lives as such is to render them sterile and impotent in their capacity to alter our everyday, conscious behaviour.

To be told that one was a 'princess' in a past life is a clear image of the higher or special qualities within oneself that we need to realign with. To literally believe it is an act of psychological suicide, destroying the metaphorical and imaginative possibilities that lie within the very image itself. One could go on and on exploring these literalised images; but, to return to the central point, it is the dream world that enables us and assists us to stay literally in touch with the imaginal world and helps us to see through literality and concretism, so that images become available for integration into consciousness, thereby moving us slowly but systematically towards completing ourselves. The dream provides a pathway for individuation that is available to us all.

If we now turn from the varied 'cures' as ways of imagining ourselves, we can also see the same forces operating in relation to psychological problems. The underlying assumption in so much of contemporary counselling is that the problems individuals have are brought to counsellors to be solved. We can see this no

10

more clearly than in present-day marriage counselling, where the counsellor works on the shared, albeit collusive, assumption that a couple seeking marriage counselling actually have a problem *in* their marriage, *in* that elusive, non-tangible quality that lies between them. This view of 'having a problem' is a grand step into literality, and a counsellor attempting to solve *the* problem is taking one further step into the quagmire of literality. In this particular spot, no one is really held responsible, since after all the couple 'have' a problem, like you 'have' influenza.

The proliferation of counselling services and training programmes tends to create shrines to this literalisation and to encourage more and more 'experts' in human relations to be cleverer and cleverer in their treatments. Each claims a bit of the proverbial elephant as the entire elephant. Such counselling is increasingly built on the blatant literalisation within psychology called behaviourism. Such a drift in psychology lends itself well to the growth of the professional expert who will treat the problems *we ostensibly have* with the appropriate information or behavioural schedules. Either way, it will probably not dawn on the counsellor that in his helpfulness he has colluded with the client in sharing the belief that something outside will alter how we are within ourselves. Whatever limitations the broad psychoanalytic world might have, whether it be Freudian, Jungian, Kleinian, or whatever, one thing they do not do is to take the clients at face value and reinforce their literality. Because the psychoanalytic world holds to the view that the unconscious mind is what determines our behaviour, it quite naturally holds to a symbolic rather than literal view of problems, and therefore is less likely to be caught in 'helpful', problem-solving behaviour. Such behaviour can in the long run serve only to sever the individual from the inner self and send her or him in ever-increasing circles to find a 'solution' to her or his problems, rather than stopping and asking the simple question: 'What does the problem mean?'

James Hillman reminds us that 'Problems in psychology are not something people *have* but something people *are*' (italics mine). 'Something people are' implies that psychological problems are the literalisation or externalisation of how we imagine ourselves. So a marital problem becomes an external representation of an internal image of ourselves as not being able to relate to the opposite aspects of ourselves. The problems that we so fervently want to believe we *have* are, in the final analysis, representations of an underlying myth or plot, images stemming from our own imaginative story or fiction, which we call our life. As Hillman says, 'History is a way of musing upon oneself.' The danger, when the images become problems, lies in the risk of losing sight of what is really troubling us as we distance ourselves from the image by projecting it out as if it was a problem. Behind each and every psychological problem lies an image, and unless we understand the image I suspect we are condemned to go on creating problems for ourselves as a psychological mechanism for drawing attention to the image.

The dream world can provide a very clear picture or X-Ray of the problem, and it is well established in the psychotherapy field that the dreams an individual has the night before a first appointment is usually a very precise diagnosis of the problem. For example, a forty-two-year-old professional man consulted me for his acute mid-life transition, in which he had lost all sense of purpose and, in his own words, 'could see no point to anything'. Life for him had been one constant exercise in achievement, and he had built up a substantial professional practice, but his personal life, his emotional life, was non-existent. In short, he was acutely depressed, and this was coupled with very angry feelings towards the world and everyone else.

Here, then, is the initial dream he dreamed the evening before he saw me for the first time:

I am watching a game of poker. A male player arises from the table after having discarded one card after the deal. He passes the four remaining cards to me to hold while he is absent from the table. I constantly move around the room holding his cards and am requested by a male at an adjacent table to show him the cards. I refuse and he attempts to remove the cards from my grasp forcibly. His attempts are unsuccessful and he is joined by a woman who bends my fingers back, my wrists are wrenched from side to side but I hang on to the cards with determination They are unsuccessful.

It takes very little expertise to see some of what this dream may be about. The image throughout the dream is one literally of 'not showing his hand', of not really revealing the value of his cards, or in a psychological sense not revealing his feelings. Yet there is an additional interesting point in the dream: they were not his cards in the first place! So, whose hand or cards is he holding, and why? Given it is a game of poker, why did he not call for the additional card after the original male player had discarded one? From this man's history it became clear that the hand he was playing or holding was his father's hand, and his father passed on to him the game of never revealing his feelings. Perhaps if he had called for the additional card following the discarding he may have been able to add something, at least one card, of his own. But no, we notice in the dream that he faithfully, indeed relentlessly, holds onto the cards passed on to him.

This image persists throughout the dream, despite the request from another man (a warning to me as the therapist not to force the pace or expect too much too soon) and a female (perhaps his feminine self).

Defiant and triumphant he is to the end in his determination not to reveal his hand. Given this image and given the view that as we image ourselves so we are, then it becomes clear why this man's personal life was in tatters. To share feelings, an essential ingredient for any relationship, was not an image he was moved by. He had long ago learned to 'play his cards close to his chest', a lesson that, regrettably, so many males in our society have learned at a very early age.

But feelings have a way of finding their way out, and dreams have a way of picturing the escape. Somewhat amusingly, the same man had a dream a month later, which, following on from the initial diagnostic dream, provided us with a sense of direction as to how we might go about altering the card game, and what was behind the fear of showing his hand. This was the dream:

I am inspecting a building construction site. At the first floor level there exists a precast concrete end wall and a steel column. Both of these are free-standing, unbraced and unsupported. Prefabricated plumbing stacks are being delivered to a different construction site, one such conglomeration of pipes requires a waste outlet which has not been provided for in the building. A decision is made to simply connect the waste outlet to an adjacent fire hydrant!

Here one is struck by the image of unsupported walls in the first part of the dream, a sense, perhaps, of internal instability, just a free-standing concrete wall, no bracing, no sense of inner strength. The second image becomes poignantly clear when one extends the image of the dream to ask the question, 'What happens if you turn the fire hydrant on?' The answer is obvious: one large amount of waste-matter sprayed all over the place. This image allowed the man to see that his only imaginative way of expressing his negative or waste feeling was to connect it in some way that will result in spraying or spreading it all over the place. In short, he needed a re-plumbing

14

job, psychologically speaking, which would allow him a more effective and efficient means of disposing his waste or negative feelings. He also had alerted me to his fear of an internal collapse should he get in touch with his feelings, so in addition to some plumbing, some strengthening or bracing of his internal walls or defences was also necessary.

Now, one may find oneself saying or musing that all my discussion to this point of the dream is fanciful, but not real. However, it is important to note that I have, apart from asking a question about the fire hydrant, not gone outside the dream. I have not so much interpreted the dream as let the images speak for themselves. The first dream spoke of 'playing his cards close to his chest', the second of unsupported walls and of an inappropriate and maladaptive form of waste-disposal. To have focused solely on the literality of this man's problems would have meant missing his own inner wisdom about what was troubling him. His dream images provided the diagnosis, the precautions that are required, and the treatment plan. This is not to say that he didn't want to stay in a literal mode; on the contrary, he frequently reminded me when I focused on his dreams 'that it is all very well talking about dreams, but I have a professional practice to run that is deteriorating because I can't get going'. He wanted to feel better, have the problem that he 'had' removed, as though it were his appendix or tonsils. He resisted facing his images, because over these he could not exercise the control he did over his outer world. He resistance recalls the earlier words of Max Zeller: 'But who listens to this calling, though it would point the way?'

So, whether we focus on the plethora of modern-day, wonder cures for our dis-ease, or the problems that reflect this dis-ease, what is apparent is that behind both of these lies the imaginal world seeking recognition, or more precisely re-cognition. To reconnect to the world of dreams is to remind ourselves, once again, that life is a symbolic act, and that man is a symbol-forming creature. To attend to our images is to attend to life, since it is in our images that we can discover our own myths or plots. In so doing we can begin the task of making sense and order of our existence from within ourselves, transcending the limited horizons of our egos. For it is the imaginal world, as Blake would surely agree, that allows us

> To see a World in a grain of sand
> And a Heaven in a wild flower
> Hold Infinity in the palm of your hand,
> And Eternity in an hour.

2
DREAMS THROUGH TIME

If dreams are so vital to our well-being, how have our forefathers seen the role of dreams and the art of dream interpretation? A full history of dreams and dreaming is beyond the scope of the present book, however some time spent in perusing the history, albeit briefly, is necessary, if for no other reason than to realise that dreams have intrigued mankind since the dawn of time. Explanations of dreams are as varied as historical times themselves, however three broad categories of explanation can be detected. Sometimes these are exclusive of each other, and at other times there is an overlapping of categories. Broadly speaking, they can be seen as deriving their explanation from the gods, from man's psyche, and/or from his body.

I would now like to discuss briefly each of these categories, which more or less line up with specific historical periods. The reason for discussion is that I believe we have come a full circle today and are once again returning to older and more ancient views of dreams, only this time with an expanded sense of consciousness. However firstly we need to look at pre-literate man's view of dreams.

PRE-LITERATE MAN

Primitive man or the primitive man in pre-literate societies believed in dreams most of all because his belief in dreams was intrinsically linked to his belief in his soul. He believed that his soul left his body in sleep (a modern-day version can be seen in the belief of astral travelling), and hence dreams were not a psychological phenomena, but a *real* experience of the disembodied soul. According to Landtman, the Kiwai of Papua New Guinea believed that if a sorcerer managed to catch the soul of somebody in the state of dreaming, the sleeper never woke up. One can't but help wondering whether this is a mythological explanation of a psychotic state, in which the person is captured by the sorcerer in the unconscious mind and thereby loses a grip on his or her waking reality. The Ashanti tribesmen of Africa, concerning a topic close to the twentieth-century man's dreams, assume that if a man dreams of having sexual intercourse with another man's wife, he will be fined the usual adultery fee, for his soul and hers have had sexual intercourse. One is left wondering why he would ever own up, and the mind marvels at the prospective revenue for the government if such fines were instigated in our own society! Parking meters would become a very poor second as revenue-raisers!

Primitive man believed in his dreams even more than he did in his own conscious perception, and he relied on them for guidance in his everyday affairs. And not only was a person held responsible for what he or she did to others in dreams, but a person was ready to accept responsibility for what another had dreamed he or she was doing.

An often-quoted and classic example of the role of dreams in guiding one's relationships with fellow man can be seen in the Senoi people of Malaysia, some-times referred to as the 'Dream Culture'. They were originally studied by the anthropologist Kilton Stewart, who visited the Senoi in 1935. Reportedly, they were a primitive tribe, consisting of approximately 12,000 individuals who were living in the mountainous jungles of Malaysia. Stewart was obviously greatly impressed by them, and by the fact that they lived together without a police force, psychiatric hospitals, or the equivalents of these institutions. He concluded that the key to their harmonious life lay in the way in which they dealt with dreams. Despite the fact that some questions have recently been raised about the validity of Stewart's study, the main observations are important and relevant to our understanding of dreams and their role in our lives. Dream interpretation in a Senoi tribe belonged to everyone, although it is also true that there were specialists in dreams who were called the Halaks. 'Breakfast in the Senoi house' Stewart wrote 'is like a dream clinic.' People listened to and discussed the dreams of children, husbands, wives, and friends.

Basically the Senoi believed that hostile images that appeared in their dreams had a negative effect on the dreamer and on others, and unless the negative dream images were dealt with, the negativity would be reproduced in outer society. The dream figures to the Senoi represented real spiritual forces, which a person could and indeed should relate to. Patricia Garfield states that the first general rule of the Senoi approach to dreams was to 'confront and conquer danger'; that is, to relate to the negative images and call on other dream figures to help in the confrontation and conquest. Negative personal behaviour in dreams was seen as needing to be compensated for in the outer life by positive interaction with those images that had appeared negatively in the dream. So inner and outer world were not divided by the Senoi, and dreams were seen as the internalised expression of external forces. Thus by harmonising these internal forces and figures the Senoi believed that their outer world would also be harmonised. They saw death of a dream enemy image as a positive thing since, according to Stewart, such a death released positive forces from that part of the dream that had formed the negative dream image.

Those familiar with Jungian psychology will readily appreciate the sophistication of the Senoi view and its mode of facing one's shadow in Jung's terms. Psychologically repressing or keeping one's shadow — that is, negative and unacceptable aspects of ourselves — out of consciousness requires psychic energy, and hence, just as the Senoi suggested, the death or ending of the shadow released the energy previously tied up in the repression. Perhaps the distinguishing feature of the Senoi is the very deliberate act of carrying actions over into waking life by making amends with the person that one has negatively dreamed of. Mattoon claims that taking dreams literally and acting on them is very characteristic of several pre-literate tribes, and that people often apologise for injuring a neighbour in the dream.

In a contemporary psychological sense, coming to grips with our shadow also facilitates our withdrawal of projections, thereby enabling us to interact with less acrimony. Hence, by paying attention to our dreams, we, like the Senoi, can prevent the acting out of negative behaviour towards our neighbours. Since, as James Hillman so simply says, 'The way we imagine our lives is the way we are going to go on living our lives.' By facing and confronting our negative images we are continuing an ancient primitive art seen to perfection in the Senoi people.

MESSAGES FROM THE GODS
In this category of explanation we can ascertain two major sources, one biblical and the other from classical Greece. Another example of dreams as part of spiritual life comes from the American Indians, for Chief Seattle said that dreams 'Are given to men in the solemn hours of the night by the Great Spirit.' The American Indians believed that the soul was an

individual expression of the Great Spirit, but the soul needed guidance, and dreams from the Great Spirit was one form of guidance. In this sense, one can see that the American Indians thought of dreams as messages from the gods.

The Bible has an ambivalent attitude to dreams. They are, however, taken seriously. John Sanford, a Jungian analyst and Episcopal priest, maintains that 'Dreams, or similar experiences, are recorded or mentioned in almost every part of the Bible from Genesis to Revelations.' Almost without exception, such dreams are believed to be a message from God or from some other divine or spiritual source. That is, the dreams are not seen to be psychological in origin. So one can readily see some connection to primitive tribes who attribute the source of the dream to an external force. There seems to be little difference between the significance of biblical dreams and those coming from the American Indian 'Great Spirit'.

There is, as I have said, some ambivalence to dreams in the Bible. For example, in Numbers 12:5-6 we find the following thought:

> And the Lord came down in the pillar of cloud, and stood in the door of the tabernacle and called Aaron and Miriam: and they both came forth. And he said 'Hear now my words: If there be a prophet among you, I the Lord will make myself known unto him in a vision, and will speak unto him in a dream.'

On the other hand, in Deuteronomy 18:10-12, we find the following warning concerning divination and other methods for determining the will of God:

> There shall not be found among you any one that maketh his son or his daughter to pass through the fire, or that useth divination, or an observer of times, or an enchanter, or a witch. Or a charmer, or a consulter with familiar spirits, or a wizard, or a necromancer. For all that do these things are an abomination unto the Lord . . .

Here one can see a general resistance to and perhaps fear of the unconscious world and an attempt to maintain the externalised authority and presumably order of organised religion. As I have already indicated, we find in the Book of Job an unequivocal assertion that dreams are messages from God, who is seen to be speaking to men 'In a dream, in a vision of the night' (Job 33:15). As to practical applications of dream interpretation or reading of the messages from God, perhaps none stands out more vividly than Joseph's interpretation of the dream of Pharaoh. Joseph, when requested by Pharaoh to interpret the dream says, 'God has shown Pharaoh what he is about to do.' This statement leaves no doubt that in this biblical view dreams were messages from God, from the divine spirit. Here then is Pharaoh's dream.

. . . Pharaoh dreamed: and, behold, he stood by the river. And, behold, there came up out of the river seven well-favoured kine and fat fleshed; and they fed in a meadow. And, behold, seven other kine came up and after them out of the river, ill-favoured and lean fleshed; and stood by the other kine upon the brink of the river. And the ill-favoured and lean-fleshed kine did eat up the seven well-favoured and fat kine. So Pharaoh awoke.

And he slept and dreamed a second time: and, behold, seven ears of corn came up upon one stalk, rank and good. And, behold, seven thin ears and blasted with the east wind sprung up after them. And the seven thin ears devoured the seven rank and full ears. And Pharaoh awoke . . . (Genesis 41:1-7)

Joseph's interpretation is:

The seven good kine are seven years; and the seven good ears are seven years; the dream is one. And the seven thin and ill-favoured kine that came up after them are seven years; and the seven empty ears blasted with the east wind shall be seven years of famine. This is the thing which I have spoken

22

unto Pharaoh: What God is about to do he sheweth unto Pharaoh. (Genesis 41:26-28)

Joseph continues by explaining that seven years of plenty will be followed by seven years of famine and the need to store food to protect the land from the famine. The rest of the story is well known. Joseph's interpretation proved to be correct, resulting in him being elevated to a powerful position in the land. The Bible leaves us in no doubt that the dream was a vision shown to man by God.

In short, it would be clearly classified as a prophetic dream, although personally I think one can also make a case out for its potentional psychological meaning. Here one would profitably reflect upon the reason why Joseph was in prison in the first place. This was because he had thwarted the seductive attempts of the Pharaoh's wife, and, out of spite, she had falsely accused him of molesting her. One wonders what sort of person she was and even further what it tells us about the feminine aspect of the Pharaoh himself, if his wife represents that part of him. At a psychological level one could also speculate that the river is a point of transition in Pharaoh's life and the cow obviously an animal we would normally associate with nurturance and the feminine spirit. Likewise, corn grows out of mother earth, and again could be associated with the feminine side of the Pharaoh. The number seven is usually considered to represent the perfect order, or sometimes the spiritual year. Putting these thoughts together, at the psychological level, it may be that the Pharaoh was struggling with the negative side of his anima or feminine self, which was threatening to destroy his positive aspects. His throwing of Joseph, along with the baker and the butler, into prison could be indicative of negative moods and anger, traits that are normally associated with the dark side of a man's anima or feminine self. Seven also represents the union of three, the masculine principle, with four, the feminine principle. So perhaps the dream also represents the need to integrate the masculine and feminine aspects of his psyche. However, this aside is merely to establish that one can explore a dream at many different levels, both archetypally (that is, as messages from the gods) and psychologically (messages from one's own conscious mind). While biblical interpretation, as I have already said, does not allow for personal meaning in dreams, we shall see that from the time of Classical Greece through to the Middle Ages dream interpretations combined both these points of view.

Other dreams that are frequently referred to from the Old Testament are Jacob's famous dream involving a ladder that stretched down from heaven above to earth below. The Lord is seen as standing above it and saying

I am the Lord God of Abraham thy Father, and the God of Isaac: the land whereon thou liest, to thee will I give and to thy seed . . . (Genesis 28:13)

Nebuchadnezzar, the King of Babylon, is another biblical dreamer, for whom Daniel acts as an interpreter (Daniel 2:31-45). When one turns to the New Testament, dreams are fewer than in the Old Testament, but are still perceived to be strictly nonpsychological, non-personal in meaning, as we have seen to be characteristic of the Old Testament. One recalls that in Matthew 1:20 it was an angel, a divine messenger, who appeared in a dream to Joseph and gave him the message concerning Mary.

Joseph, thou son of David, fear not to take unto thee Mary thy wife: for that which is conceived in her is of the Holy Ghost.

An example of a dream that foretells danger is in Matthew 2:13. We find Joseph receiving the following message from a divine source, an angel of the Lord.

Arise, and take the young child and his mother, and flee into Egypt, and be thou there until I bring thee word: for Herod will seek the young child to destroy him.

24

And finally, upon Herod's death, an angel again appears in a dream to Joseph in Egypt (Matthew 2:20).

> Arise, and take the young child and his mother, and go into the land of Israel: for they are dead which sought the young child's life.

As recorded, these New Testament dreams unequivocally confirm that at this time and place in history dreams were seen as messages from God. But one is left wondering whether this is necessarily so, or whether dreams recorded in the Bible represent profound turning-points in the history of mankind and this is why they are recorded and why they are given divine status, since they are truly transpersonal dreams. Pharaoh's dream and Joseph's interpretation of it resulted in the reuniting of the twelve brothers, culminating historically in the reuniting of the twelve tribes of Israel. Without the interpretation that resulted in the storing of food, Joseph would not have been reunited with his brothers, who came to Egypt for the food.

Likewise one wonders what would have happened to Christianity if Herod had destroyed Christ or if the family had not returned to Israel as directed by the dreams.

What we do not know, or have any evidence of, is the role played by personal dreams in this time and place in history. Perhaps in the quotation from Deuteronomy we have some evidence of the prevailing attitude towards personal dreams; that is, that they were false and demonic and belief in them was offensive to the Lord. When we turn to the Classical period of Ancient Greece and to Rome and then through the Middle Ages, we shall find that this dilemma of whether dreams were divinely or demonically inspired is a continuing theme.

CLASSICAL PERIOD OF GREECE AND ROME
The Ancient Greeks seem to have taken what they regarded as valuable or useful from Egyptian and

Babylonian sources, and one finds discussions on dreams in both Homer's *Odyssey* and Hesiod's *Theogony*. In Homer's *Odyssey*, for example, the distinction is made between true and false dreams. He assigns two gates to dreams, the Gate of Horn through which true dreams come, presumably ones that are divinely inspired messages, and the Gate of Ivory, through which false dreams come. The latter gates refer to the transparent quality of ivory when compared to horn, and false dreams will therefore be seen as those emanating from the irrational and delusional desires of the dreamer, not from God.

In Homer's *Odyssey* the theme of communication from the gods is apparent. For example, when Athene comes in a dream to the maiden Nausicaa and in the form of one of her friends tells her it is time she gave up her slovenly ways and began to wash her linen:

'Look at the lovely clothing you allow to lie about neglected, although you may soon be married and in need of beautiful clothes . . . It's this kind of thing that gives a girl a good name in the town . . .'

Athene urged Nausicaa to collect her clothes up the next day and cleanse them in the washing pools, where she then met Odysseus. Apart from this being a message-from-the-gods type of dream, it could also have been seen psychologically as a transitional period from adolescence to adulthood. There are no doubt many parents of adolescent girls who can only lament the fact that Athene has not appeared to their daughters in a dream!

Without doubt the most well-established use of dreams in the Ancient Greek world can be seen in connection with the cult of Asclepius, the god of healing. I have already mentioned this cult in the preceding chapter, however I would now like to consider it in greater depth, since it seems to me that as a model for approaching dreams it has much to commend it in this latter part of the twentieth century.

The principal sanctuary of this cult was at Epidaurus, near Athens, although there appears to have been about four hundred Asclepian temples, these satellite temples being established by installing an image of the god, often in the form of a serpent. The cult, as such, seems to have been active between the sixth century BC and the third century AD. An ill person slept at an Asclepian temple in the hope that a significant dream would occur, which would reveal either the cure or directions for the treatment of the ailment. So, the purpose of dreams was seen as a means of determining the will of the gods and of receiving divine instructions. The seeking of dreams that would invoke the powers of the gods is a process known as incubation. This can be broadly defined as sleeping in a sanctuary with the specific intention of receiving a dream reply to a question asked of a god or goddess, having first performed prescribed rituals. These included abstinence from sex, from eating meat, from drinking alcohol, and the giving of an offering to the deity to be invoked.

The incubation rituals were designed to transform one's usual state of consciousness, where the identity is tied to the ego, to the level where the incubant was able to receive a vision or dream from the gods. Mary Watkins says:

> The outer symbolic actions of the ritual were able to create a state of awareness and certain inner attitudes that allowed the incubant to gradually separate himself from the usual frame of consciousness in order to be able to participate in the visionary realm with the god.

In psychological words, the rituals were designed to help the seeker to be receptive to his inner world and to disconnect himself from his outer, distracting thoughts. This meant that the patient was at the mercy of the god, and that he would be acknowledging his humility in the face of a far more powerful force than himself.

This question of the right or correct spirit with which to receive the messages from the gods seems to be critical in all incubation rituals. In the Mysteries of Isis, the person seeking guidance had first to be invited by the god to come and sleep in the temple. It was believed that if he tried to sleep in the temple's adytum (the innermost part of the temple, not to be entered by the unbidden) without first being invited, then he would die. Presumably this part of the ritual reminded the incubant, or patient, that his ego could not decide whether to participate with the gods or not. One can readily see in these rituals the stark reminder to modern man of a need to subjugate his ego if he is to hear the gods within himself. He must, in other words, suspend his rational, critical, and ego-centred self if he is to hear and appreciate his own dreams.

At all the Asclepian sanctuaries the incubants were also required to pay fees and to write down or dictate their dreams, a practice that is of vital importance today if we are to benefit from paying attention to our dreams. The act of writing the dream down is an act of commitment to the reality of dreams themselves, and therefore is vital in the building of a working relationship with our own unconscious mind. I have repeatedly observed in my own professional experience that the failure of certain individuals to write their dreams down reflects a failure to dedicate themselves to this task. More often than not, these persons are heavily orientated in an intellectual way and unconsciously resist giving any real credence to the dream world, despite their declarations of such a commitment. It is interesting also to observe that until they *do* write them down, they do not gain any substantial benefit from the dream world. One is also tempted to say that, as at all Asclepian sanctuaries, paying for dream analysis strengthens the decision to take the dream seriously and to work at understanding it!

To repeat the point already made, with the healing cult of Asclepius and the process of incubation, humility was the vital aspect, since it prepared people to be receptive to the gods. Meier, a world authority on ancient healing rites, sums up the importance of this attitude in the following words:

> We want the god to help us to see more clearly what is going on in us. In this sense we are *aitematikoi*, disposed to ask, and so are our dreams. But [Artemidorus] added, we should never ask the gods undue questions! And if the answer has been granted, we must not forget to sacrifice and give thanks.

The dream was often interpreted by priests and priestesses; and if the dreamer was not healed, this was, interestingly enough, blamed on inadequate preparatory rites. Again, psychologically speaking, this serves as a reminder that we need to prepare ourselves if we are to have contact with the healing capacities of our dreams. Modern man's tendency to pump himself full of sleeping tablets, tranquilisers, anti-depressants, and alcohol before going to sleep can scarcely be seen as an adequate incubation preparation or ritual. Could this explain why he wakes feeling so fitful and unrested? And does it explain why the same 'busy', 'over-worked' individual is ready to denigrate dreams as sheer nonsense? It seems to me that there is much we can learn from the Asclepian temples and their rituals.

Apart from this well-established dream practice associated with incubation, the Greek philosophers also had various theories concerning the nature and interpretation of dreams. Socrates, as quoted in Plato's *Phaedo*, held the view that dreams represented the voice of conscience, and that it was important to listen to and follow this voice. Plato himself (427–347 BC), by contrast, held a personal view of dreams that is remarkably close to the one that Freud was to develop. For Plato, dreams were the expression of our inner, irrational urges. In *The Republic* he says:

> . . . the point which I desire to note is that in all of us, even in good men, there is a lawless wild-beast nature, which peers out in sleep.

Thus the visions of the night, for Plato, were not messages from the gods so much, but rather instinctual urges seeking expression, urges and passions that were prohibited and unacceptable during the normal waking days. So here, in Plato, we see the beginnings of the idea that dreams express the irrational in man.

Aristotle (384–322 BC), by contrast, although also rejecting the earlier view of messages from the gods, nevertheless held that there was a rational quality to dreams, in addition to coincidental phenomena, which others may have seen as divine messages or prophecies. Aristotle's account of dreams is written in his *Parva Naturalia*, and it maintains or asserts the view that dreams are illusions or images produced by the very subtle movements of the body during sleep. He also saw dreams as being occupied with the visualisation of plans of action related to the ordinary, day-time activities. It is in this connection that Aristotle made a most interesting and highly relevant observation for us today. He suggested that not only are images the outcome of the previous day's activities, but that the converse may also be true, the actions might be determined by the images themselves.

> For as when we are about to act [in waking hours], or are engaged in any course of action, or have already performed certain actions, we often find ourselves concerned with these actions, or performing them, in a vivid dream; the *cause* whereof is that the dream-movement has had a way paved for it from the original movements set up in the daytime; exactly so, but conversely, it must happen that the movements set up first in sleep should also prove to be starting-points of actions to be performed in the daytime, since the recurrence by day of the thought of these actions also has had its way paved for it in the images before the mind at night. (italics mine)

In this theory of Aristotle one comes the full circle

to the contemporary view of the role of imagination as personified in Jung's and, more recently, James Hillman's work. Here, both writers basically see images as the starting-point of reality. For example, James Hillman states:

Man is primarily an image maker and our psychic substance consists of images; our being is imaginal being, an existence in imagination. We are indeed such stuff as dreams are made on.

Or, in Jung's succinct words, 'The psyche creates reality every day' and 'Every psychic process is an image and an "imagining"'. We will return to this role of images and imagination and their relationship to dreams throughout this book, since, as already stated, images are the language of dreams and Aristotle seems to be adumbrating the development so clearly seen in the writings of Jung and Hillman.

A far more literal and concrete view of dreams and images can be seen in the views of Lucretius (95–55 BC), a couple of centuries after Aristotle. He taught that dream images were actual atomic combinations, 'Whether shed from the surface of solid objects or generated spontaneously in mid air'. According to McCurdy, Lucretius attributed dream images to chance, and he found it difficult to explain how supposedly chance images could have any meaning for the dreamer. In Lucretius we can see the beginnings of literalisation and the turning away from the belief in dreams having personal meaning. This literalisation grew in stature until, 1900 years later, when Freud began the return to earlier perceptions.

However, the transition into literalisation was not complete, and throughout the Middle Ages one can still find theorists believing in the personal meaning of dreams. Well before the Middle Ages there existed an outstanding and much-referred-to dream theorist, a Roman by the name of Artemidorus. He lived in the second century AD, and his book *The Interpretation of Dreams (Oneirocritica)* stands as one of the most impressive and systematic of ancient works on dreams. His writings had a great influence on the theory of dreams throughout the medieval period. According to Artemidorus there existed five kinds of dreams, each having a different quality. These ranged from dreams as such, through to visions, oracles, fantasy, and apparitions. But consistent with what he saw as a dream, Artemidorus's first category, it is clear that he assumed it to be a symbolic language that expressed various insights. So, for Artemidorus, Pharaoh's dream would not have been a vision sent to him by God, but rather a symbolic expression of the Pharaoh's own rational insight. He saw divine message dreams as equivalent to oracles.

Another important quality of Artemidorus's thinking, which establishes how relevant his theories are to the contemporary situation, was his insistence on interpreters knowing certain facts. In discussing these, McCurdy lists as the first one that Artemidorus felt it was important to establish which images were natural and customary for the dreamer. He also stressed the importance of the circumstances of the dream, along with the dreamer's occupation and personality. One can readily appreciate the importance of each of these aspects in contemporary dream interpretation, and this no doubt explains why Artemidorus has been so widely respected. Personally, I find the circumstances at the time of a dream an absolutely vital piece of information in terms of establishing a context within which the dream can be heard. Likewise, a modern version of establishing which images are 'customary and natural' to the dreamer could be seen in the need to encourage the dreamer to establish the meaning of the symbols to him or her within the context of his or her own life history. Here is an extract from Artemidorus, showing his capacity to explore varied interpretations and meanings and demonstrating the need to pay careful attention to the dreamer's life circumstances.

If a young woman dreams that she has milk in her breasts, it signifies that she will conceive, carry, and bring to birth a child. But for an old woman, if she is poor it prophesises riches; If she is rich, it indicates expenses. For a maiden in the bloom of youth, it means marriage, since she could not have milk without sexual intercourse. But for a girl who is quite small and far from the time of marriage, it prophesises death. For all things, with few exceptions, that are out of season, are bad. But for a poor man without a livelihood, it foretells an abundance of money and possessions so that he will be able to feed even others.

. . . But for an athlete, a gladiator, and for everyone in training, it means sickness, since it is the bodies of the weaker sex that have milk. Furthermore, I have known it to happen that a man with a wife and children, after this dream, lost his wife and brought up his children by himself, demonstrating toward them the combined duty of both a father and a mother.

Upon reading this series of interpretations one can readily appreciate the fact that Artemidorus obviously practised what he preached, since in his own words:

The rules of dreaming are not general, and therefore cannot satisfy all persons, seeing they often, according to times and persons, admit of varied interpretations.

In fact, his commitment to such variation in interpretation is a welcome antidote to the common tendency to want dream recipe books for interpreting dreams. Certainly, the emphasis is on personal meaning of the dream for Artemidorus, and this represents a major break in the tradition of seeing dreams as messages from the gods. Such messages obviously could not allow for the varied interpretation that Artemidorus is at pains to point out.

POST-CLASSICAL PERIOD
Despite his very able contribution to the thinking on

dreams, it seems as if the entire phenomenon of dreams witnessed a sort of stagnation after Artemidorus. This is no doubt in part reflective of the church's resistance to dreams and its discouragement of them as either messages from God or sources of wisdom. In its time, the medieval church was clearly the dominant influence on thought and behaviour, and experiences that were outside its doctrine were seen to challenge its authority. Hence the church regarded such phenomena with suspicion, if not outright condemnation.

The world of alchemy is a fine example of an entire field that threatened the church's authority and, as a consequence, its practitioners were persecuted and driven underground. This persecution has been given as a reason for the alchemists' use of chemical language as a cover for their mystical reflections. What discussion or reflection on dreams there was seems to have had as an underlying preoccupation the question of whether they were true or false dreams – to return to Homer's Horn and Ivory gates.

Within the period of history from Artemidorus to Freud, several figures nevertheless stand out. Among the earliest is a Christian called Clement, of the late second century. He believed that true dreams came from the soul's depth and revealed the relationship between man and God. His conclusion was that during sleep the soul, freed from the restraints of bodily impressions, had a heightened ability to reflect upon itself. This is clearly a very advanced notion of dreams, if one translates 'God' to mean that 'self' in Jungian terms and 'soul' to mean psyche. Here, then, in Clement's thoughts we have some profound ideas on the process that Jungians' would call individuation and the relationship of imagination to this task of moving towards completing ourselves; ideas that have more recently been elaborated and articulated by James Hillman.

For Augustine (AD 354–430), the church father, dreams were important in grasping the inner workings of his mind and his relationship with God. It is in the thinking of the somewhat unorthodox Bishop of Ptolemais, Synesius of Cyrene, that once again the notion of dreams stemming from a heightened capacity for insight appears:

> Sleep opens the way to the most perfect inspection of true things to the soul which previously had not desired these inspections.

Bartholomew of England, a thirteenth-century Franciscan monk, provides us with some indication of the ever-growing concern on the part of the church that dreams were potentially dangerous and that one needed to distinguish between 'good' dreams (prophecies or messages from God) and 'evil' dreams from Satan. He saw the origin of dreams as varying from divine inspiration and angelic activity to diabolic illusion (presumably a reference to personal fantasy) and, finally, natural bodily causes.

St Thomas Aquinas (1225–74) condemned most divinations. He argued that one could err in using dreams as a source of knowledge about the future, either by making a pact with demons or by trying to take divination too far. Here again we can see the church becoming anxious about the world of dreams, and its desire to distance itself and its followers from the inner world. Presumably the intent of this strategy was to reinforce the external authority of the church, an intent that could be seen as the assertion of the masculine as opposed to the feminine principle.

Thomas Aquinas must have felt in some dilemma about the entire issue of dreams and the inner world, since it is often suggested that he himself was an alchemist, responsible for a major alchemical text, entitled *Aurora Consurgens*. Furthermore, this text is generally regarded as being 'an extremely characteristic example of the mystical side of alchemy, affording deep insight into this extraordinary state of mind'. It could be said that Aquinas resolved what must have been a dilemma for him between his allegiance to the church and his own inner knowledge, by indicating that dreams could come from either an inner or outer source. Those dreams that he saw as stemming from man's soul were seen as the dreamer's imagination occupying itself with the same issues as those that had occupied him during the day. He also held, like Aristotle before him, that the body senses were an important aspect of dreams. Indeed, he suggested that certain bodily dispositions can be recognised in dream interpretation. It is particularly interesting to note that this view has recently been explored in depth by a contemporary Jungian, Arnold Mindell, in his stimulating and thought-provoking book *Dreambody*.

The outward cause of dreams that Aquinas spoke of were spiritual and corporal. The latter was seen as being related to the heavenly bodies, and the spiritual cause sometimes referred to the old theme of messages from God. So in a sense St Thomas Aquinas covered all his options, and seemingly preserved his relationship to the authority of the church and his own integrity.

In his book *Clinical Uses of Dreams* James Hall asserts that towards the end of the Middle Ages people began to lose interest in whether dreams were demonic or divine in origin. He sees the energy of the Renaissance being directed towards an exploration of the outer world, although he fails to take account of the role of alchemy in sustaining an interest, albeit secret, in the inner world. His suggestions lead one to conclude that there was a progressive turning away from the inner world of imagination and a redirection of mind towards experimentation in science and art, a pattern we can see continuing into the present day. Over all, it seems as if dream interpretation essentially remained a variation of those theories of antiquity and the Middle Ages until the arrival of Sigmund Freud. With Freud, there can be seen the beginning of the modern era of dream research and thinking, and also the restoration of dream interpretation as a legitimate and valid way to approach the unconscious mind. Jung, in his extensive writing, was to take this restoration one step farther. The essential difference between these two highly creative scholars is the old difference that we have seen as the connecting thread through the history of dreaming. That is, the true or false dream, the Horn or Ivory gates, restated in terms of whether the dreams are composed of irrational material (Freud) and therefore delusions (false: Ivory Gates) or whether they are a revelation of higher wisdom and important insights (Jung) and therefore of the Horn Gates. The answer would seem to be that dreams partake of both these features, and again history tends to confirm this observation.

3
THE MODERN ERA:
FREUD AND JUNG

Any book on dreams would be incomplete without some attention to the pioneering work of Sigmund Freud. After all, it was Freud who rehabilitated the dream after nearly nineteen centuries of almost total neglect. In his introductory lectures on psychoanalysis, Freud acknowledged this gap and proposed to 'embrace the prejudice of ancients' and to retrace the footsteps of 'the dream interpreters of antiquity'. Given the age in which Freud was writing and thinking, an age dominated by rationalism, his attempt to restore the sense of personal meaning to dreams can only be seen as a truly heroic act. However, unlike his ancient predecessors, Freud dismissed the issues of whether a dream was a message from the gods and whether it was true or false. He also distinguished himself from his predecessors in terms of how and why he came to study dreams. It is true to say that his work was linked to the ancient practice of the Asclepian sanctuaries in so far as Freud, like Asclepius, was concerned with the healing of the ill. However, in Freud's case, the 'ill' were mentally ill, neurotic personalities. This fact, I think, is vital in appreciating Freud's theory of dreams, since it is intrinsically and explicably tied to his general theory of psychology, which in turn is derived from his clinical practice.

The basic assumptions within Freud's theory, the bottom line, if you like, is that we have feelings, wishes, and needs that motivate our actions, yet we have no awareness of these: that is, they are unconscious. They are unconscious because we have repressed these needs, because, as Freud would maintain, they are unacceptable to our conscious view of ourselves, which is systematically shaped by our parents and by our basic need for parental approval. Consciously, we believe that we have got rid of all these unacceptable, usually instinctual feelings, which are predominantly from childhood; however, they are for ever threatening to re-emerge into consciousness. This fear of the return of the repressed material, thoughts, fantasies creates anxiety in us. If and when they do return, they must, so to speak, sneak past our conscious mind; and the manner, which Freud observed, in which they sneak past is by being distorted and disguised. This process is carried out by a sort of internal censor, which so alters the undesirable feelings that our conscious thinking fails to recognise them for what they are presumed to be. However, when we go to sleep, the 'censor' also has a rest, although not a complete rest, so our dreams, in Freud's view, allow and give expression to these undesirable and unconscious strivings. Indeed, these strivings are what Freud would call a dream. Therefore our 'Freudian dreams' are composed of irrational desires, and because Freud observed that sexual feelings were the specific feelings most commonly repressed during his time, then these, according to Freud, were the urges most commonly seen in dreams. He derived this theory from his clinical work, and he maintained that the repression of sexual feelings is central to neurotic disorders. All this may have been true in Vienna at the time that Freud was writing and working. How generally true it is today is doubtful, although it is important to state that it is most certainly not irrelevant for people who have been brought up in a strictly religious way. For them, the repression of sexual material is exactly the same as it was in Freud's time. Speaking of the content of dreams, Freud said:

> The more one is occupied with the solution of dreams, the more willing one must become to acknowledge that the majority of dreams of adults treat of sexual material and give expression to erotic wishes.

These sexual wishes from the unconscious, says Freud, have to be repressed in order for us to live in outer reality, so a conflict for ever exists between the reality principle and the pleasure principle. This conflict and the need for outlet of sexual desires create tension during the day, which is discharged during the night in the imaginal gratification of our dreams. This gratification, Freud further argued, allows us to sleep, since during sleep we imagine that our desires have been fulfilled and thus are left with a feeling of satisfaction rather than a disturbing frustration. This view of dreams as the guardians of sleep is now being seriously questioned, for the experimental work in sleep laboratories indicates that we may well sleep in order to dream, not the reverse, as Freud would have us believe. However, the sleep question aside (and whatever other qualifications that one may have about Freud's theory), it remains indisputable that, for him, dreams are unequivocally about wish-fulfilment.

> The fulfilment of a wish is its [the dream's] only purpose. . . . the dream therefore is the [disguised] fulfilment of a [suppressed, repressed] wish.

We shall return to this wish-fulfilment theory of Freud's later on, since I think one can perceive a link between Freud and Jung around the theme of wish-fulfilment, if we do not adhere to the rigid, hallucinatory quality that Freud appears to give it.

But first, let us look at some other relevant points concerning Freud's pioneering work on dreams. Because he believed that the basis of dreams are the wishes that are unacceptable to the conscious mind, it follows logically that Freud saw dreams as an attempt to conceal rather than reveal. This, as we shall see, indicates a major difference between Freud and Jung, a difference that has enormous implications for the understanding of our dreams. For Freud, the symbols conceal the true, or latent — as compared to manifest — level of a dream. So we find, in Freud, consistent with his repressed sexuality theory, that almost any long, pointed object in a dream can be a symbol, or substitute, for a penis. Objects such as bayonets, guns, umbrellas, spears, posts, etc., were seen by Freud as phallic symbols. Female genitals, by contrast, were symbolised by container-like objects; for example, cavities, boxes, vessels, caves, rooms, etc. But it would be a mistake to imagine that Freud would have simply taken these symbols and given the patient an explanation. On the contrary, he used a process to work with the dreams called 'free association', whereby the patient said whatever came into his or her mind in relation to the object of the dream.

Having said that, it is also true to say that Freud and contemporary Freudians listen, or hear, the dream in the theoretical context of repressed sexual and other desires, and would assume that the dream, as reported, or as recalled, is really a cover-up of the true or latent meaning. Therefore, by associating to each and every symbol in the dream, the analyst will decode the dream and discover its true or latent meaning, which inevitably will be about repressed instinctual urges and thoughts emanating from early childhood experiences. So, symbolic language for Freud, unlike Jung, is not a language that is the best possible expression of something we have not yet fully understood, but rather symbolic language symbols are expressions of certain unacceptable, specific, primitive, and instinctual desires. In Freud's view, based on his analysis of his patients, these desires are generally of a sexual nature, although aggressive feelings are certainly not excluded.

It is difficult nowadays, some eighty-five years after Freud wrote his classic work on dreams, to adhere unswervingly to his theory of dreams. Despite the obvious validity of Freud's thought, one is struck by the limitations of his theories when compared with Jung's. Fundamentally, these limitations derive from Freud's view that dreams are expressions of the irrational forces within us, desires, needs, etc., that have their origin in our childhood years, particularly the first five years, and which have been repressed because of the external demands of society. By necessity, then, this assumption leads Freud into seeing the interpretation of dreams as leading back to early childhood experiences through his technique of free association. Technically, this is seen as a reductive approach, but it is not only reductive in terms of going back to childhood, it is also reductive in so far as it reduces the symbol to a sign for something else. In this sense, it shrinks the symbol rather than expanding it. So a knife becomes a penis, instead of allowing an expansion on the actual symbol of a knife for the dreamer and exploring the symbolic meaning of the knife for that particular individual. Jung called the latter approach amplification in order to distinguish it from free association.

This reductive approach also leads one into a one-way street when approaching a dream, whereas Jung would argue that while a dream might well be about issues in the past, it is also about where we are trying to move, and in this sense it is prospective as well as retrospective, forward-looking as well as backward-looking. Holding this somewhat rigid view of dreams, Freud is caught in his own theoretical edifice, since the reductive approach is part and parcel of his wish-fulfilment theory, as we wish for the satisfaction of unmet desires from the past. Another major limitation of Freud's view is his insistence that the manifest dream, the one recalled and reported, is not the 'true' dream. The 'true' dream he designated the latent dream: that is, that level of the dream where the disguise has been lifted. Thus Freud saw dreams as trying to conceal meaning, where Jung categorically saw them as trying to reveal meaning. In Jung's own words:

> Since I have no reason to believe that the unconscious has any intention of concealing things, I must be careful not to project such a device on its activity. It is characteristic of dreams to prefer pictorial and picturesque language to colourless and merely rational statements. This is certainly not an intentional concealment; it simply emphasizes our inability to understand the emotionally charged picture-language of dreams.

One of the very practical, everyday consequences of this perception of dreams as concealing or revealing is that it alters an individual's attitude towards dreams. If dreams are singularly and singlemindedly seen as concealing nasty, unpleasant truths from our childhood, then most people will avoid listening and paying attention to their dreams. But if, on the other hand, we see them not only as concealing, but also as revealing, not just all good, but negative as well, then one's attitude will change from fear and avoidance to potentially one of co-operation. In this shift in our attitude towards the actual dream we are at the same time shifting in our attitude towards the unconscious mind itself. This is a shift that can only be of benefit to us in our journey towards wholeness, since, according to Jung, our dreams facilitate the movement towards wholeness by using images that tell us about parts of ourselves that we are ignoring, suppressing, or simply not using. In this way the unconscious mind is a partner, not an adversary, not an opposing thought threatening to undo us. This comment takes us back to Homer's gates of Horn and Ivory, the gates of truth and the gates of delusion. One is left wondering whether Freud contributed to the decline of the recognition of the validity of dreams by his rigid insistence on the theory that the 'real' dream is not the one remembered. No doubt such a position has added to the mystification of dreams and provided fodder for the objections of the rationalists in our society, who are ever ready to point out that dreams are meaningless, irrational rubbish. This distinction between the manifest and the latent dream has also inherent in it the risk of not taking the dream for what it actually is: that is, a metaphorical statement from the dreamer to himself or herself. The distinction creates too great an opportunity for the professional therapist to ignore the meaning of the dream as such and to impose a theoretical interpretation onto the dream. The 'disguise' theory seems to me to do two things; firstly, it convinces the dreamer that she or he really does not know what the dream is about, and, secondly, that it requires an 'expert' to interpret it, and such an interpretation is more often than not purely theoretical. Ullman and Zimmerman, in an excellent book on dreams, state:

> Jung swept away most of the categorical restrictions inherent in the Freudian view. In so doing he took a giant step toward making dreams potentially accessible to the non professional.

Having said this provides us with a ready point of transition to Jung's theory of dreams and dreaming. Although, also in having said that, Jung would immediately contradict me, since he stated:

> I have no theory about dreams, I do not know how dreams arise. And I am not at all sure that my way of handling dreams even deserves the name of a 'method'.

and

> I leave theory aside as much as possible when analysing dreams — not entirely, of course, for we

always need some theory to make things intelligible. It is on the basis of theory, for instance, that I expect dreams to have a meaning . . . but I have to make such an hypothesis in order to find courage to deal with dreams at all.

In these seemingly vague and contradictory statements one nevertheless gets a sense of Jung's flexibility in approaching dreams, in contrast to Freud's seemingly rigid approach. Indirectly, in discussing Freud, I have also been discussing Jung, but mainly up until now by way of contrast. This could easily create the impression, which some people appear determined to perpetuate, that Jung was a pupil of Freud. Nothing could be farther from the truth. They had independent careers, Jung's specifically in a mental hospital, where he developed his own individual views about the psyche. It is, nevertheless, true that Freud and Jung collaborated for a number of years in the early part of this century; but Jung could not accept Freud's insistence on the central role of sexuality. Jung's clinical experience in the Burghölzli Mental Hospital convinced him of an additional state of mind, which Freud had not discovered. Jung came to call this additional state of mind the collective unconscious mind.

I have written of the collective unconscious elsewhere, and thus will not explore it in any depth here other than to assert that this notion of the collective unconscious is a major factor in differentiating Jung's approach to dreams from Freud's. The collective unconscious refers to that level of our psyche that is the repository of inherited qualities and potentialities, and we come into life with it as part of belonging to the human species. As with our bodies, so it is with our minds: we carry around within us archaic modes of thinking and behaving, which belong to the species rather than to any of us as an individual. Jung referred to these patterns of instinctual ways of behaving as archetypal patterns and to the images that occurred in the psyche, representing these patterns, as archetypal images. The simplest way of grasping archetypes is perhaps by turning one's attention to mythology, for constantly appearing in myths are archetypal images, such as the hero, the earth mother, the deliverer or saviour, the seducer, the law-maker or king — all representatives of deep-seated archetypal patterns within each of us. The important implication for dreams at this level of mind, which do not come from our personal life or history, is that when such images appear in dreams, they cannot be explained by the Freudian reductive notions, since they do not arise from our individual history in the first place. These images, then, point to dreams as being composed of far more than just irrational urges, as Freud would have us believe.

Because this collective unconscious level of mind contains ancient, universal, and deep patterns of mankind, it is to this level that we are often forced to resort in order to deal with major transitions in our lives. It is as though we are digging deep, back into our human history, to discover approaches for dealing with some of life's major transitional crisis. Thus, at these times, we have what ancients or primitives would call 'big dreams', or, in the context of the previous chapter, we receive 'messages from the gods', since the 'gods' can be seen as personifications of the archetypal level of mind. These 'big dreams' are usually experienced by the dreamer as literally a 'message from the gods' in so far as they have a numinous quality. The word numinous comes from the Latin word *numen*, which means presiding spirit or deity. Apart from this feeling of numinosity, one can usually identify an archetypal dream because it has an enormous amount of energy about it, and that energy keeps us engaged with the dream in such a way that it becomes one of those dreams that people describe as: 'Oh, it is a dream I could never forget.'

The 'never forget' quality is often due to the very unusual symbolism in the dream, unusual settings, characters, scenes, which we simply could not have derived from our personal history. Dreams that include the ordinary aspects or objects of life, such as cars, houses, work, colleagues, etc., are clearly derived from everyday life, which does not render them any less valuable, it simply locates their source in a different place within the psyche. Indeed, one of the inherent dangers in people exploring their dreams within a Jungian framework is that they are for ever seeking the 'big' or archetypal dream and, as a result, undervalue the ordinary dream, which can be full of very pertinent observations about ourselves. Because archetypal dreams usually involve symbols that are unfamiliar to the dreamer, the work in understanding such a dream often requires some familiarity with fairy-tales, religious symbols, and mythology, since in these fields one can recognise the recurring symbols. As Karl Abraham, a contemporary of Sigmund Freud, said in the early part of this century:

Myth is the dream of a people and a dream is the myth of the individual.

Thus familiarity with these worlds can aid us in amplifying the symbols, although it is by no means a requirement. Perhaps the following example from my own professional experience will serve to reinforce this point and also to convey the quality of an archetypal dream. The dreamer was a thirty-eight-year-old woman, a highly intuitive feeling person, who is a regular member of a weekly dream analysis group that I conduct. This is not a theraputic group in the sense that problems are discussed and analysed, it is a group that meets strictly and solely for the purpose of exploring dreams. Here then, is the dream, which she herself has entitled:

ANCIENT BURIAL CITY DREAM

I live in an ancient city, which is set in a valley, but is completely surrounded by high hills—ringed by them.

These hills have well-worn paths which spiral upwards leading to burial chambers—where not only

*those who die in this city are buried, but others from
our culture from other cities are brought here to be
buried.*

*After the dead body is prepared, and after the flesh
has been taken off the limbs, not the head, it is taken
by an old wooden cart drawn by a man to the burial
chamber. The arms of the skeleton are always reaching out with open palms in a welcoming gesture. The
hands are very noticeable as the fingers are also
outstretched.*

*As you walk around our city, you can look
upward and invariably see a body lying on a cart
in this gesture being wheeled around the mountain
side to be buried.*

*My dress in this dream is a tunic type attire, tied
at the waist with a cord—and leather sandals with
criss cross footing and an ankle strap.*

*I look up one day as I walk around our city and
see on one of the burial carts what appears to be the
body of my father. He has his glasses on—I stare,
knowing this is out of context, as we, in this culture,
don't wear glasses. I also recognise his hands—with
their once long elegant fingers. I feel more curious
than shocked—as I realise—sense—this is not my
present father but the father of my future.*

The dreamer in her personal history had no connection to any such burial rituals, but it is important to
note that she had this dream some six to eight weeks
after the actual death of her father. Psychologically
one knows that the peak time of a crisis is a six-to-eight-
week period after the event. So, in the very basic sense,
this dream is a comment from the unconscious mind
upon her inner experience of her father's death. In other
words, it has come at a major life-crisis time and, as
such, it is a dream drawn from that level of mind where
we have ancestoral modes of coping, the collective
unconscious mind.

Without discussing the dream in detail, one is
immediately struck by the setting: old, ancient, not

48

of our contemporary period of history. There is also the theme of repetition, an obvious one in the dream story, the endless burial cart going around and around the mountain track. When this is put in the context of the dreamer's everyday life, it is as if the age and repetition of the dream is a symbolic expression to her from the depths of her own psyche, to see her father's death not within an ego-conscious time-frame, but in that vastness of the collective psyche, where time and space do not exist. The dream can be seen to be 'reminding' the dreamer of the fact that life and death are ever-repeating cycles — the wheel of life. The manner in which the bodies are prepared for burial is an interesting, specific detail in the dream. Firstly, all the flesh is stripped, which in alchemical terms could be seen as symbolising mortification of the flesh in order to release the spirit. (Interestingly enough, about a year after the person had the dream, an article appeared in a local daily newspaper concerning ancient Tibetan Buddist funeral rites — called 'sky burials' because they took place on a mountainside — in which the flesh was reportedly stripped and fed to vultures in order to insure the reincarnation of the deceased.) Secondly, as so often hapens in dreams, there is an amazing level of specific imagery, and in this dream we find that all the flesh is stripped, but 'not the head'. The head is where one would metaphorically locate the mind, spirit; and thus this image can be seen as conveying to the dreamer the fact that consciousness, or the spirit, transcends physical death. Finally, we have a further reminder of the endless cycle of life and death in the last line of the dream: 'This is not my present father but the father of my future'. The entire dream can be seen as providing the dreamer with wisdom from within herself, from the archetypal or collective unconscious level, as to how to respond to the physical death of her father.

While one could interpret this dream in a Freudian sense, perhaps as a death wish towards the father, it does seem to do a violence to the richness of the dream and, in my opinion, the outstanding healing qualities that are inherent in it at the manifest level. A dream, far from being irrational, is both constructive and purposeful, in so far as it points to the way to deal with grief, thereby allowing the dreamer to continue with life and her own journey. With this sort of inner wisdom available to us, it is little wonder that the ancients saw their archetypal dreams as 'messages from the gods'. Such dreams are to be found not only at times of death, but at other major transitions or events of our lives, such as birth, separation, divorce, adolescence, marriage, and mid-life. These events characterise man's existence throughout time, to which the archetypes and archetypal images are representations of our historical ways of dealing with them. When we discuss the mid-life transition, which inevitably involves the archetypes that Jung designated anima and animus, I shall share a dream that captures these archetypal images at the crisis time of mid-life.

While the dream just recorded may appear interesting and confirming of the archetypal level of dreams, the question that still remains to be answered concerns what Jung believed to be the purpose of dreams. If dreams are not wish-fulfilling, as Freud maintains, then what are they? What is their purpose? In a word, Jung's answer to this question is that dreams are compensatory. According to Jung, the function of dreams is one of balancing or compensating the conscious ideas, feelings, etc., with the opposite in the unconscious, hence the old saying 'dreams go by opposites'. Perhaps an analogy would clarify this law of compensation. I often think of it as being a bit like riding on a see-saw, the higher you are at one end, the lower is the other end, and the art of integration is probably trying to straddle the central point of the see-saw. Get too far up one end, and down you come, only to work your way back up the other. Sailing a yacht and maintaining the balance between the wind and angle and the boat's travel would be another analogy. In Jung's own words:

The psyche is a self-regulating system that maintains its equilibrium just as the body does. Every process that goes too far immediately and inevitably calls forth compensations, and without these there would be neither a normal metabolism nor a normal psyche. In this sense we can take the theory of compensation as a basic law of psychic behaviour. Too little on one side results in too much on the other.

In another place he simply states:

There is no rule, let alone a law, of dream interpretation, although it does look as if the general purpose of dreams is *compensation*.

The word compensate is derived from the Latin word *compensare*, which means 'to equalise', and this derivation captures the essential quality of the underlying mechanism of dreaming as Jung perceived it. The 'equalising', as already indicated, is the equalising of a certain conscious viewpoint with its opposite. So, for example, a very depressed and dejected young woman dreamed of a joyous party-going situation in which she was dressed in a bright, seductive, low-cut, yellow dress and was the life of the party. Likewise, the successful man-about-town, decisive, purposeful, direct, will have dreams that contradict these qualities. For example, a very successful forty-three-year-old businessman, characterised in the outer world by his directness, his goal-orientated behaviour, became depressed in mid-life and produced the following brief dream:

My car wouldn't steer and I tried to go through an old brick tunnel over a road and got stuck against the edge because of no steering. Also couldn't see ahead as I was on top of the hill.

Apart from being a crystal-clear diagnosis of himself in mid-life, his loss of direction, the dream

51

compensates his consciously held position of himself in the world as a successful businessman, and indeed shows him how he really feels about himself unconsciously. That is, that he is stuck with no steering.

One could legitimately ask, why do we need to compensate in our dreams? Why do we need to equalise? The answer in the simplest possible terms is because we are destined to try and move towards completing ourselves, trying to move towards wholeness, a destiny that Jung called individuation: Thus compensation provides the mechanism for healing the rift within ourselves, between our conscious view and our unconscious view of ourselves, thereby enhancing our sense of equilibrium or balance. This wholeness that one is drawn towards involves, in Jung's view, the recognition of opposites within ourselves, that we are composed of these opposite forces, and the farther we develop one side of our personality, equally strong will be its opposite in the unconscious mind. Like Freud, Jung believed that just because material was in the unconscious mind, it did not mean that it did not exert an influence on our lives. The particular problem with thoughts and feelings in the unconscious mind is that we are unaware of the influence except at night when we dream. By becoming aware of our opposite and suppressed or repressed aspects, we become more rounded and integrated as individuals, and we increase the element of choice as to how we wish to be in the world, rather than being driven by blind, unconscious forces. As we shall discuss shortly, these opposite aspects, which are brought into the dream via the compensatory mechanism, form shadow figures in our psyche, and from this shady spot they exert considerable influence on our everyday behaviour in terms of conflicts and moods. Very often, repeated conflict with a particular person is motivated by the shadow aspects of our personality. This repeated conflict will continue unless we look at our dreams and find the opposite figure lurking in the shadows, so to speak. Perhaps a short dream of a woman in her late sixties will help to clarify the role of this compensatory mechanism in alerting us to our opposite, shadow qualities, which interfere with our attempts to struggle towards wholeness. This woman had explored numerous growth experiences, and yet she remains stuck and disorientated. Seeking group after group, course after course, has seemingly not produced the results she hoped for. Here then is the dream:

I walk about in a big building full of people all very busy, shops and offices. I go into a male friend's office which is much smaller than the one he has in real life. My brother who doesn't know my friend is also sitting in this small office. I have something on my mind and want to talk about it. I start to talk and realise that no one is listening. My friend gets up from his desk and goes to a bookshelf. I say 'No one is listening to me', so then I decide to leave.

Although this dream has two or three separate issues in it, the main point for the purpose of the present discussion is the fact that the dreamer complains that no one is listening to her. Given her history of a constant search for help and for growth-producing experiences, all to no avail, it seems highly probable that the dream is alerting her to the fact that part of her simply does not listen, and that she perhaps often prevents herself from listening by her constant busyness and activity, as shown in the opening scene. Another small item of compensation in the dream is worthy of note because it is so common, and that is the dreamer's image of the office in the dream being much smaller than her friend's actual office in outer life. From discussions with the dreamer it became clear that she overestimated, perhaps even idealised, this friend in her outer life, and her dream puts him in the opposite position by giving him a smaller office and thus diminishing him somewhat. It is also of some interest to note how she deals in the dream with the fact that no one is listening to her. She simply leaves. This points to her unconscious side being unwilling to look at why nobody is listening, or indeed why she doesn't listen, as she simply walks away from situations. Presumably this strategy had a lot to do with the reason why she floated from one course to another without achieving the substantial benefits that she had hoped for. As dreams can do, it also provides her with an additional insight: that is, idealising the friend, she could not see that he was not listening to her needs in the relationship. On the contrary, he is too busy pursuing his own bookish interests to pay attention to her.

As discussion opened up with this woman, it became very obvious that the dream was an accurate perception of the relationship with her friend. In outer life she had simply refused to accept this perception, so intent was she on seeing the relationship and the person as being ideal. The truth was that he was often too busy to discuss the things on her mind. So, we can catch a glimpse from this dream not only of how compensation operates, but also how a dream can have several layers of meanings. Broadly speaking, Jung would divide dreams into two categories: the objective dream (that is, objective in so far as the dream really is about people in our outer lives) and the subjective dream (where the people we dream of are personifications or images of those aspects of ourselves). In this case, as in many dreams, the meaning can be located in both an objective and subjective sense. The dream alerts the woman in both ways to take certain actions in her life to enable her to have her needs more adequately met. Thus, we can see that the cornerstone of Jung's theory of dream interpretation is his hypothesis that all dreams are compensatory. And, within this context, the interpretation of a dream, with some exceptions, is really an attempt to answer the question: what is the *'actual situation in the unconscious'* that equalises or compensates the dreamer's conscious situation?

Jung's concept of compensation can, I believe, be seen as broadening Freud's concept of wish-fulfilment, and indeed the differences between the two theories on this point may well be more illusory than real. Compensation provides, from the unconscious mind, what is need for wholeness, or at least a continuing movement towards wholeness. But it seems plausible to see Freud's idea of wish-fulfilment in this light too, if — and only if — we modify his use of the term *wish-fulfilment*. What do we know of this word 'wish'? It may be defined as 'a desire, to want, long for', and in one dictionary there existed a slight elaboration on this definition in so far as a wish was defined as a 'distinct mental inclination towards the doing, obtaining, attaining, etc. of some thing, a desire felt or expressed'. So a wish in this sense acts as an incentive to action, it keeps before our minds what we want and gives direction and purpose to our actions.

In this sense, then, one could reinterpret Freud's use of the term from wishful thinking to the more correct sense of wish-fulfilment. Are, then, the irrational contents of dreams that Freud focused on representative of material, thoughts, needs, and feelings that need to come into consciousness? Is their reappearance in dreams in order for us to face them and integrate these aspects of ourselves into consciousness in exactly the same way that Jung talks of compensation? If this is so, then Freud's view of dreams as wish-fulfilment could be seen as the wish to fulfil ourselves, to complete ourselves, to move towards individuation in Jung's terms. Perhaps Freud's mistake was to focus too specifically on the nature of the dream content and to miss the broader and more pervasive wish that lay behind the dream. For the patients that Freud saw in the early 1900s, people who were dominated by Victorian prudism, it may well have been sexual and aggressive images that needed

to come into consciousness in order to fulfil themselves. If one can accept that both Freud and Jung
were really talking about the instinctual wish to fulfil
ourselves, then their only difference is that they
focused on different aspects to be integrated, a fact
that could be directly attributed to their respective
clinical experiences. If this is so, then what is behind
this wish? Who or what is behind the urge to fulfil
ourselves? And how does it relate to dreams and
dreaming?

4
IMAGE, SOUL, AND DREAMING

Despite the variety of explanations, views, opinions, etc. on dreams throughout time, what emerges as an utterly consistent and immovable fact is that dreams are composed of images. Whether it is a disembodied soul, messages from the gods, a Platonic lawlessness, or Aristotelian image produced by the subtle movements of the body, a Freudian irrational urge, or a Jungian compensation — it is *always* in the form of an image. About this there seems to have been no quarrel throughout time. So one can unhesitatingly assert that dreams are images and that dreaming is an imaginal, not a logical language. But, having said this, are we any farther on? Do we know what it means when one says 'dreaming is an imaginal language'? And why has man been so occupied by dreams throughout time if it is simply imagination?

Here, we have to turn to Jung, who very simply and succinctly states: 'Image is psyche'. Again, one might be left with a feeling of 'so what?' But, personally, I think that in this simple definition lies the key to understanding the phenomenon of dreams beyond Freud and Jung, and yet, paradoxically, it includes both and goes even farther back, to the pre-literate societies and their disembodied soul theory of dreams. The essential quality of this pre-literate theory was that these people knew dreams were images, but they believed them to be real, a reality more substantial to them than outer reality. For example, the Senoi, we found, would apologise for damaging someone in the outer world if they had dreamed of damaging him or her in their dreams. So, what does Jung mean when he says 'Image is psyche'? And how could this extend our understanding of dreams? The next step one needs to take is to ask the question, 'If image is psyche, then what is psyche?' The answer is that *psyche* is a Greek word meaning 'soul'—not mind, but soul. So psychology, then, is the logic of the soul, the speech or story of the soul. A far cry indeed from what passes for psychology today! But this ancient meaning is critical to a contemporary understanding of dreams, because if one accepts that psyche is soul, then a new and broader perspective of the purpose of the dreaming is opened up.

Soul, of course, is a term that nowadays, if used at all, we associate with organised religious belief. Or, as James Hillman once quipped, 'Soul is the last four letter word left that is unmentionable among the in.' In Jungian psychology, the terms psyche and soul are used interchangeably, although it is true to say that the preference is for the seemingly more objective and rational word, psyche. However, the outstanding Jungian analyst James Hillman has been instrumental in restoring soul into the life of psychology. Of his many writings referring to soul, he consistently asserts that one cannot define soul, since it is not a concept, it is a symbol; that is, it is the best possible expression of something we do not yet understand. He says that soul is deliberately and necessarily an ambiguous term, because it resists 'definition in the same manner as do all ultimate symbols'. Even if we cannot define soul because it is an ultimate symbol—

for example, as we cannot define God — we nevertheless can point to other words and phrases that amplify the symbol, in much the same manner as one would attempt to amplify the symbols of a dream.

Perhaps the clearest and simplest place to begin an amplification of soul is to consider the anthropologists' description of the so-called primitive who suffers from 'loss of soul'. You may recall that Landtman, in discussing the Kiwai of Papua New Guinea, observed that they believed that if a sorcerer managed to catch the soul of someone while he or she was dreaming, then that person would never wake up. So 'loss of soul' is a serious disease to afflict a tribesman, he is usually described as not there, disconnected, dead, both to himself and to others. In short, he cannot find a connection within himself or between himself and others. Such a description is also very applicable to people, particularly males, undergoing a mid-life transition, which I have written about elsewhere. The most consistent and persistent phrases that such men use when seeking help through psychotherapy are 'I feel like I am dead' and 'There is no point to life'. The description that such men give of their personal lives and family life is identical to the one given by tribesmen whose souls have been stolen by the sorcerer. The contemporary mid-life man describes a situation of non-involvement in family life, loss of friendship, non-participation in social activities: in short, a massive withdrawal. Tribesmen who have lost their souls are described as being unable to participate or take part in rituals and traditions, and until they regain their souls they are regarded as 'not there'. Many a spouse of a mid-life crisis male will know the experience in living with someone who is 'not there'. The sorcerer — or worse, the devil — has got his soul; and where does the devil or Satan takes one's soul? To Hades, the underworld of Greek mythology and the symbolic representation of our own underworld, the unconscious mind. Such tribesmen, whether ancient or modern, have lost their souls into their unconscious minds. That is, they are no longer aware of their psyche; and if psyche is imagination, they are no longer being imaginative. They, like the Kiwai Papuans, 'never wake up', are permanently asleep, as a result of losing their imaginative capacity or soul. So people say to these men in the sloth of their despair, 'Wake up to yourself.' Speaking of the loss of soul, James Hillman says: 'So when I asked "where is my soul; how do I meet it; what does it want now?" the answer is: "turn to your images".'

Souls are not only said to be lost, for we also say such things as 'that person is a troubled soul', or 'this person is my soul mate', 'this is my soul food or music', 'I am searching for my soul', 'it is soul-destroying', 'bless my soul', and a person puts her or his heart and soul into something. Eyes are said to be the windows of the soul, places have been described as soul-less, and, finally, one can sell one's soul to either the devil or, in the twentieth century, to the multinational company. One could probably add many more phrases from our language that refer to soul, but the main one for our purposes is the loss of one's soul.

James Hillman recalls an interesting experience of a female patient in the Burghölzli psychiatric hospital in Zürich. The lady was sitting in a wheelchair because she was elderly and feeble. She told the attending psychiatrist that she was dead because she had lost her heart. The psychiatrist, according to Hillman, asked her to place her hand over her breast to feel her heart beating; presumably he reasoned that it must still be there if she could feel its beat. 'That', she said, 'is not my real heart!' Hillman concludes the story by saying:

> There is nothing more to say. Like the primitive who had lost his soul, she had lost the loving courageous connection to life — and that is the real heart, not the ticker which can as well pulsate isolated in a glass bottle.

But if her 'real heart' was not there, and if the mid-life-crisis man is not there, and the primitive who has lost his soul is not there, then presumably soul, whatever it is the symbol of, has a lot to do with simply being there. And if it is not there, where is it? Where does it reside?

To return briefly to the Greek sources, one discovers that the soul was presumed to be located mainly in or around the brain. Plato, for instance, held that the vital principle (soul) was in the brain. Hippocrates also placed the soul in the brain. Galen, the great forerunner of modern medicine, argued that the soul was located in the fourth ventricle of the brain, whereas St Augustine regarded the middle ventricle as the home of the soul. Roger Bacon, the thirteenth-century English philosopher, thought that the centre of the brain was where one could find the soul. One could go on and on with location after location, but what would characterise them all would be the attempt to locate the soul in a physical space, to make it tangible, touchable, knowable, literal, when we know it is the opposite of all these attributes, since soul is a root metaphor, a symbol. If we stick closely to its metaphorical meaning, then, when we ask where is the soul, the reply metaphor is inevitably one that implies depth, descent, a going down; whereas the reply to the metaphorical question where is spirit is equally inevitable in the opposite direction — up, beyond, and above. So if we are to find soul, we must descend, not ascend into heaven, and the only place we can descend to, within the metaphor, is to Hades, the underworld, the unconscious mind. The unconscious, then, is the door through which we must pass in order to find our soul, a journey into our own depth.

What we already know from Freud is that the world of dreams is the *via regia*, the royal road to the unconscious. So also must dreams be the royal road to the soul if it is lost or located in the unconscious mind. Hillman says: Through experiencing the unconscious I gain soul.' What could this mean? 'Through experiencing the unconscious I gain soul.' What would it mean to gain soul? To answer these questions, we have to enter the symbol of soul a little farther in order to return to the point that dreams, by deduction, must be the *via regia* to the soul.

Hillman again provides us with direction at this point when he says of soul:

> We take it to refer to that unknown human factor which makes meaning possible, which turns events into experiences, and which is communicated in love.

This 'unknown factor', if we briefly refer back to the philosophical attempts to locate it, and we re-work this literalisation at metaphors, then presumably, soul has something to do with an inner experience central within man. Since what is clear from the various philosophers' attempts literally to locate soul is that each of them metaphorically located it inside the person and not outside. Thus, soul means something inside and depth. So an inner connection to an event, and what transforms it from a mere event to an experience, this inner connection, then, can be seen as an act of imagination, an image. Thus when we casually say that something was a 'non-event', we usually do not mean literally that it did not happen; what we mean is that it did not happen for us; there was, in other words, no connection, no link between inner and outer, no imagination stirred, no soul in it. Hence, as Hillman says: 'Our life in soul is a life in imagination.'

For events to become experiences, we must feel connected to them, and images seem to be a mechanism that enables this connection to occur. Further, what we know from Jung is that psyche is image, so psyche or soul is a way in which we connect to events, turn them into experiences, and thus construct a sense of meaning. Otherwise the events remain as a simple literal event; no meaning. If it had meaning, then, in the language of today's younger culture, it would be 'an unreal experience', something that was more than an event, because if we experience a connection to it, it touches, or was touched by ourselves. It then seems to follow logically that if we can increase our capacity to *experience* events, then our need to maniacally pursue event after event in the outer world would diminish, since, paradoxically, one would have more experiences and fewer events. Such a change could be seen as a growth of soul.

The act, then, of soul making must be related to imagination; and not to be making soul, to have lost this capacity, must be tantamount to having lost the capacity to imagine. Hillman again speaks incisively about this issue:

> The act of soul making is imagining, since images are the psyche, its stuff, and its perspective. Crafting images is thus an equivalent of soul making.

If, then, dreams are composed of images and involve imagination, then dreams are not only the *via regia* to soul, but to dream is to make soul every night — dreaming is soul making. Hence, to dream of a thing or an event is to turn that thing or event, that literal level of existence, into an experience. Dreaming then becomes a means by which we can transcend literality and reconstruct meaning in our lives, since the transforming of events in the outer world into experiences is that act of giving them meaning and the overcoming of meaninglessness. Loss of soul then, to return to the earlier theme, is not only loss of imagination, it is also loss of meaning to which the characteristic and indeed appropriate response is depressive feelings. But in our society it is unacceptable to feel depressed, one *must* be happy and, if not, then the depressive feeling must be exorcised away through jogging or aerobics, etc., or medicated away or, in some instances, both exercised and medicated.

63

Our society does not encourage us to enter the depression, to go down into the mine of depression, to experience the leaden feeling, in order to extract some silver: a reflective quality that is so characteristic of soul. Hillman argues:

> . . . through depression we enter depths and in depths find soul. . . . The true revolution (in behalf of soul) begins in the individual who can be true to his or her depression . . .

Hence we say things like: 'Oh. He or she is in the depths of despair.' We instinctively or unconsciously know about depth and depression, but have chosen to avoid the depth and pursued the surface analgesic instead. By being 'true' to our own depression, I would take this to mean to stick with the images that arise from the depths of our depressive feeling, to let them exist and speak, and in this way heal ourselves from the loss of soul. Nowhere is this healing more readily available than in the natural process of dreaming, a process that is most likely to be interfered with by the use of medication. As Jung said, 'Image is psyche', and, according to Hillman, 'We stick to the image because psyche itself sticks there.'

Until now we have been caught in a sort of circular process, which is probably inevitable while trying to discuss soul, because, unlike spirit, it is not directional, linear, and upward. Inevitably, soul is circular and meandering. However, even within this circularity, this idea of images would seem to benefit from some further discussion and amplification. Edward Casey, in a scholarly and illuminating article, argues that imagining is 'a way of knowing'. Hillman, in discussing Casey's ideas, states that: 'An image is not what one sees, but the way in which one sees.' Hence, imagining is an inner way of seeing, of seeing through the literality of the world, to its symbolic meaning, a way of seeing that is reflective and sees more than just what is there, but also sees meaning in what is there. In this sense, an image, or to imagine, is to be like the medieval alchemist who transformed events (physical matter) into experiences (psychical). Indeed, Paracelsus, perhaps the best-known alchemist, warned against confusing daydreaming (madman's cornerstone, said Paracelsus) and creative imagination (*imaginationes*). According to Jung:

The *imaginatio*, as the alchemists understand it, is in truth a key that opens the door to the secret of the *opus*.

The 'key' is the 'way of seeing' and, for the alchemist, this would have meant seeing through matter to spirit. *Aurum nostram non est aurum vulgi* was their motto — 'our gold is not the common gold'. By seeing imaginatively, they would have distinguished themselves as the adepts or mystical alchemists, rather than the puffers, or literal alchemists. So, an image, being how one sees, is a way of speaking about being open to the inner, esoteric experience and not being condemned to an exoteric life of literality, to know that 'our gold is not the common gold'. To see in this way is a way of healing oneself from the dis-ease of literality.

Other writers, such as Henry Corbin, argue strongly against the common tendency to equate imaginary with 'unreal'. He emphasises that in the Islamic tradition the world of images is a primordial phenomenon, seen as being situated as an intermediary between the world of senses and the intelligible world. Roberts Avens, in a very similar vein, states: 'In the psyche [soul], idea and thing come together and are held in balance.' Here, we could take idea to be the equivalent of the Islamic 'intelligible world' (*esse in intellectu*), and thing as the world of senses (*esse in re*), worlds that are held together by images or soul (*esse in anima*).

Jung also speaks of images in the same manner as the Islamic tradition, concerning them being primordial or first phenomenon. In speaking of fantasy figures, he says that these images 'are as real as you

—as a psychic entity—are real'. In another place, speaking of images, Jung states that 'An image is a homogeneous product with a meaning of its own'. And, in yet another reference to image, he describes it as: 'An expression of the unconscious as well as the conscious situation of the moment.' Because an image is seen by Jung as the simultaneous expression of an unconscious as well as a conscious moment, this adds further to our understanding as to why images transform events into experience; simply because the inner and the outer moments are experienced coincidentally.

Finally, Hillman, in speaking of images and imagination, has this to say:

'To live psychologically means to imagine things.' To which we can add Jung's observation: 'The psyche consists essentially of images . . . a "picturing" of vital activities . . .' and finally: 'The psyche creates reality every day.'

From this we can conclude that whatever else man is, he is clearly seen as an image-maker, as experiencing existence through his capacity to imagine and to have soul, to perhaps have a soul mate, to be connected to our inner world of images. By contrast, to have lost soul, to be soul-less, to have a troubled soul, to be searching for soul, etc., all point to a loss of imagination and often to an attachment to the literal, outer world as if it were the only reality.

We have now explored soul in some depth, but, no doubt, questions are left unanswered concerning where the soul fits in with orthodox religion. Has soul not been the province of religion? Is not soul a sacred, holy thing, associated with God? These questions reflect the common confusion between spirit and soul, a confusion that James Hillman claims had its origins in the medieval period, personified in the Roman Catholic Church's Council of Nicaea (787) and again a hundred years later in Byzantium, in the City of Constantinople (869). When discussing the history of dreams the point was made that the church of the medieval period was preoccupied with its own authority and power, its self-appointed role as 'messenger of God' and thus imagination and, by implication, dreams were frowned upon and seen as coming from the devil. Hillman's psychological account of what happened at Nicaea in 787 is that images were deprived of their authenticity by a subtle differentiation between the adoration of images and the veneration of images. The veneration was sanctioned because it allowed the church to control which images were to be venerated, and further, more subtly, but more importantly, the images to be venerated were seen as those that represented some doctrinal idea. In other words, spontaneous images erupting from the psyche were seen as spurious, demonic, pagan, and heathen. In this way the church turned imagination and images into simply representation of abstract doctrinal ideas, and thereby turned soul (imagination or psyche) over to mind (*spiritus* or *mens*). So Hillman would argue that each time we treat an image as representing something else, as Freud declares (for example, knife equals penis), we are damaging the image, destroying it, in favour of the idea behind it: we have connected to the idea (mind) not the image (soul). So, if you dream of a cat, saying that it means your anima, or feminine spirit, we have venerated the image, used it to impose an idea, often a psychoanalytically doctrinal idea, upon soul.

In earlier traditions the world was a tripartite one, consisting of body, mind, and soul. By identifying or confusing soul (psyche) with spirit (mind), we have produced a dualism today, of mind and body. Thus we can witness in our materialistic world, obsessed with literality and tangibility, an absolute plethora of mind theories, including spiritual and metaphysical knowledge, on the one hand, and an equal plethora of information and focus on bodies, on the other. The latter is exemplified in the jogging mania and the body beautiful syndrome, and the amazing proliferation of tactile therapies. Each, no doubt, is of some benefit in its own right, just as spiritual and metaphysical knowledge is, but the problem is that we have lost soul in this activity. We have no end of gurus telling us about karma and reincarnation, matched by an equally large number of gurus informing us of the various gains and losses to the biorhythms if you eat this or that, but no one talks of soul except by collapsing it into spirit or body.

Regrettably, the spiritual point of view always posits itself as superior, perhaps because the spirit is inevitably concerned with ascendance, with higher and higher spirals of knowledge, of which mind is but one level. Spirit chooses the path of making all one, encourages us to look up and beyond, gain distance, be above things, a way of being superior. Soul, by contrast, as we have already seen, is concerned with what Hillman would call 'the valley of life, not the peaks'. So we have sayings like 'vale of tears', 'valley of the shadow of death'. Valleys are depressed places, low places, flat places, they refer to sad things, vulnerable states, troubles, lowly, earthy. In short, valleys are dominated and characterised by Yin qualities, whereas spirit seeks the sky, and is characterised by the Yang qualities. In a letter to Peter Goullart, the fourteenth Dalai Lama of Tibet draws out the distinction between soul and spirit, a distinction that we have lost in our subsuming soul under spirit:

> I call the high and light aspects of my being *spirit* and the dark heavy aspect *soul* . . . But the creative soul craves spirit. . . . no spirit broods over lofty desolation; for desolation is of the depths, as is brooding. At these heights, spirit leaves soul far behind.

Finally, from the same letter, a line that captures the sense of separating soul and spirit:

> People need to climb the mountain not simply because it is there *but* because the soulful divinity needs to be mated with the spirit.

The 'soulful divinity needs to be mated with the spirit'; that is, imagination needs mind, yet also does mind need imagination. Otherwise we finish with dry, boring, parched, desert-like thoughts that have no meaning, no feeling, no moisture. Or, alternatively, we finish up with endless water, but no harnessing of it, no form to it.

The ancient alchemist knew of this tripartite arrangement and, under the cover of their chemical terms, they call it sulphur (mind), mercury (soul), and salt (body). The role of soul was as mediator between mind and body. The alchemist realised that all three were required, and when established in harmonious relationships with each other the result was transcendence. Regrettably, in blatant violation of the alchemist dictum, without soul the body and spirit have separated today and we are oppressed by the dualism that lacks or even denigrates imagination. Psyche, or soul, is symbolised by the alchemists as mercury, *aqua permanens*, the permanent water. When one reflects on this, it is the most exquisitely accurate symbol for soul or imagination, since mercury seems on the surface, so to speak, solid, but try and pick it up and it is elusively liquid. It would be hard to imagine a more satisfactory symbol of imagination itself.

Not to have soul or imagination, in the alchemical metaphor, would lead to an excess of sulphur (mind) or salt (body). To extend the metaphorical language of alchemy, one could say, then, that those individuals or systems of thought that have an excess of 'sulphur' would be powder-dry, acidic, burning, and indeed, in the contemporary parlance, they run the risk of being 'burnt out'. Academics provide an excellent caricature of over-sulphurised people. In fact, we often speak of their lectures and discussions as 'dry': dry and acidic or cynical, because they lack the water, the fluid quality of mercury or soul. In short, they lack imagination and a sense of connection to their spirit — it is disconnected. On the other hand, those individuals of whom we would say 'salt' is in excess will be earth-bound people, heavy, literal, concrete, pedantic, boring, and lacking in imagination. But the alchemists, in their wisdom, did not say that we need only mercury. No, they simply state that mercury acts as a mediator between body and mind. So those individuals in whom 'mercury' is in excess lack either sulphur, salt, or both; in short, they will be lacking in direction and purpose, and suffering within their souls will not make any sense. They will literally feel 'all at sea' and have a quality of not being able to stick at anything, or achieve any coherence in their lives: they become the classic daydreamers. As the Dalai Lama of Tibet said, 'soulful divinity needs to be mated with the spirit'.

The real risk today is not an excess of mercury, however, but an overpowering excess of sulphur and sulphuric compulsion to know and produce more and more information for mind to absorb in the false hope that such information will generate meaning. Indeed, all it finally achieves is a form of learned literality. Excesses of salt come a close second to those of sulphur, as we witness the ever-growing obsession with health, on the one hand, and facts, on the other, since facts can be seen as a 'body' of information. So computerisation of life is almost the complete personification of an unholy alliance between sulphur and salt, between mind and fact. Computers do not have souls, our last redeeming quality as human beings. In fact, computers are so soul-less that you cannot relate to them, hold them responsible or accountable, even when they go on spewing out incorrect information about you, or send you the same account three or four times over. This computer age could be seen as an archetypal symbol of this soul-less age.

The role of dreams as the royal road to the unconscious and to our lost souls becomes vital as we try to overcome the excess of sulphur and salt in our psychological beings, and we discover some of our mercurial qualities and then allow these to find expression and inform mind and body. The loss of the tripartite view, culminating in the collapsing of soul under spirit, has left us devoid of meaning. We need to return to the valley and spend less time pursuing the peaks. We need to spend more time attending to our inner world and its vulnerabilities and less time in the manic pursuit of the proverbial high, whether that be physical or metaphysical.

From this alchemical talk of sulphur, mercury, and salt, I would now like to return to the commencement of the modern era of dream theory to Sigmund Freud and the same issue, that of soul. In a recent book the esteemed American psychoanalyst Bruno Bettelheim asserts that Freud has been consistently mistranslated, and whenever he is translated as saying mind, he actually wrote soul (*seele*). Bettelheim argues that if Freud had meant mind, he would have used the exact German equivalent (*geistig*), but throughout his psychoanalytical writing, he uses the German word *seele*. If we wish to understand Freud, says Bettelheim, then we need to grasp this fundamental flaw in translation of the word *seele* to mean mind instead of soul. And, secondly, says Bettelheim, we need to remember that Freud used metaphors a great deal. In the context of metaphors, the poet H.D. (Hilda Doolittle), speaking of her experience with Freud during her analysis, said: 'He is midwife to the soul.' As Freud's atheism is well known, it is abundantly clear that when he speaks of soul (*seele*), he is talking not about a religious phenomenon, but about a psychological phenomenon, for which soul is a metaphor. Bettelheim states that by soul or psyche 'Freud means that which is most valuable in man when he is alive'. He continues:

Freud was a passionate man. For him, the soul is the seat both of the mind and of the passions, and we remain largely unconscious of soul.

Nowhere, according to Bettelheim, an astute and learned student of Freud, does the latter give any precise definition of soul, which in fact confirms the contemporary views of Hillman regarding it being beyond definition. Bettelheim, like Hillman and Jung, suggests that Freud probably does not define it because 'its ambiguity speaks for the ambiguity of psyche itself'. He contends that the only reason that Freud's original meaning of soul was corrupted was a wish on the part of the American Psychoanalytic Movement to render psychoanalysis a medical specialty; and 'mind' and disorders of mind suited this purpose far better than diseases of the soul. However, Bettelheim asserts that in Freud's Vienna (where, incidentally, Bettelheim himself was born in 1903), the word *seele* meant man's essence, 'that which is the most spiritual and worthy in man'. *Seele*, he asserts, ought to have been translated in this particular and quite specific sense. So, when we take another look at *The Interpretation of Dreams*, where Freud is discussing the origin of dreams, Bettelheim states that *Dass der Traum ein Ergebnis unserer eigenen Seelen-tätigkeit ist* means not that the dream is a result of the activiy of our mind, *but* that the dream is a result of the activity of our own soul. This immediately places Freud along the same line of thinking as Jung and Hillman, for whom soul is the essence of dreams. Also, according to Bettelheim, Freud believed that the study and understanding of dreams would make possible the comprehension of that unrecognised inner space of soul. Bettelheim also points out the strength of Freud's conviction that psychoanalysis should not exist solely within a medical framework, and this can be gauged from a letter that Freud wrote to his friend Oskar Pfister in 1928, in which he refers to two of his recent books, *The Question of Lay Analysis* and *The Future of an Illusion*. Freud says in his letter:

I do not know whether you have guessed the hidden link between *Lay Analysis* and *Illusion*. In the former I want to protect analysis from physicians, and in the latter from priests. I want to entrust it to a profession that doesn't yet exist, a profession of secular ministers of souls, who don't have to be physicians and must not be priests.

In this sense, Freud was stating that psychoanalysis, which we now understand to mean analysis of the soul, was to be neither a medical discipline nor a creed. In other words, it was to be saved from becoming body (medical) or spirit (creed), and this so poignantly establishes that Freud saw analysis as being concerned with that middle kingdom, that intermediatory phenomenon called soul.

If we now return to the basic Freudian notion of dreams having the sole purpose of wish-fulfilment, then it becomes possible to say that what Freud may have meant was that the wish to fulfil oneself was achieved by experiencing soul. This would be entirely consistent with the idea that Freud saw dreams as the activity of the soul. By systematically mistranslating the German word *seele* to mean mind, psychoanalysis has tended to become an analysis of mind, what we think, *not* what we imagine. It has in many ways lost the calling of its vocation, which was to attend psychopathology — the suffering of the soul. By being too closely aligned with medicine, it has tended to become what Freud would term 'a mere housemaid of psychiatry'. Thus we have developed a whole approach to soul, which betrays it by turning it into disorders of the mind requiring treatment.

Furthermore, the entire field of counselling and psychotherapy has been heavily influenced by this gross mistranslation that Bettelheim alerts us to, so we have a tremendous growth-industry in mind therapies, but where do we take the soul to have its psychopathology healed? The answer lies, at least in part, in turning back the clock to the Asclepian temples, where we can and where we do heal soul in our dreams. Hence the dream groups that I conduct are, as already mentioned, not about problems that belong to mind, but exclusively about dreams, which belong to soul. The groups provide a unique opportunity for soul conversation and soul making. But we can all participate in this process in a less formal way, each night when we throw down the drawbridge between consciousness and unconsciousness. Then, we think in Freudian or whatever terms, soul making can occur.

5
MEETING THE DREAM

Aristotle claimed that 'the most skilled interpreter of dreams is he who has the faculty of observing resemblances'. This statement is still valid today, since 'resemblances' lead us to think in 'as if' terms; that is, in metaphorical terms. As Jung said: 'Every interpretation necessarily remains an "as if"', simply because psychic images are not necessarily images in the ordinary sense of the word, rather are psychic images, images as metaphors, resemblances. The dictionary says that metaphors transfer meaning, so the image, as metaphor, transfers meaning from the outer world to the inner world. Thus, if we for a moment return to the idea of image as not what one sees, but a way of seeing, then to see imaginatively, which is what a dream does, is to see resemblances, to see things, people, or events as 'as if' rather than 'is'. Therefore, images and imagination, the stuff of dreams, are not unreal, as Corbin reminded us, but, on the contrary, they are another reality, an 'as if' reality. So, if we are to follow Hillman's dictum, repeated several times already in this book, to 'stick to the image', then in practical terms it means that we must stick to an 'as if' way of dealing with images and dreams and avoid literalising them. We could easily and readily detect signs of literalisation in such phrases and words as 'is', 'it's only natural', 'surely you would agree', or 'if this, then that'. All these phrases, in particular the word 'is', point outwards to the literal world of events, the world of salt, to use the alchemical metaphor, a concrete view of the world. This mode of viewing, the concrete, is the most dangerous way to approach an image or a dream, because it pulls, pushes, and badgers the dream out of the world of metaphor, out of resemblences, out of 'as if', to 'IS'. As the dream does not exist there in the literal world, it can be denigrated and scoffed at only when it tries to be there. Thus the literalists can once again reinforce their concrete view of the world as the one and only view of it, and another round of 'seeing the world as flat' is commenced. The literalists or pragmatists among us, sometimes referred to as the people having 'lots of common sense' (the emphasis ought to be on the common), will collude with the intellectual (mind) and demand that we provide proof for the dream, or that we demonstrate evidence, cause, and effect. Again, the dream, like poetry, does not exist in the realm of positivism, but in the realm of metaphor — soul is a metaphor and dreams are the language of the soul.

Repeatedly I find that when the imagery in a dream makes a person anxious, the more anxious they become, the greater the tendency is to literalise the dreams. 'Oh. I know why I dreamed of John B. last night, it was because I was speaking to him only yesterday' or 'I know why I dreamed that, it was because of my poor relationship with my mother.' Here we see the intellectual literalist (mind or sulphur) at work, telling the dream what it means, in order, I contend, to contain his or her anxiety about what the dream may actually mean. So long as we can tell *it*, then we can maintain the illusion that we are in control: all is well and in order. Yet Jung reminds us that 'The mystery of dreams [is] that one does not *dream*, one is dreamt'.

Another way in which we damage the images of dreams is to approach them with rational interpretations, mind interpretations, instead of soul: 'Oh. That is my shadow' or 'That is my animus.' Having identified it by a nice Jungian term, we can then sit back and feel safe, safe from having been touched by the dream. When we lose our contact with the metaphorical quality of a dream, its imagery, then we lose contact with soul and tend to call into operation either body, in the form of a body of fact, or mind, in terms of theories and concepts. One classical way of losing touch with the metaphor is through using the body of facts we call personal history. By reducing the meaning of a dream back to our personal history, back to a specific event in our childhood, we are literalising it by facts, and have lost contact with the metaphor. Hence the limitations of the Freudian reductive approach back to childhood. Alternatively, theories and concepts are the other flight away from the metaphorical perspective. Flight into rational thinking takes the very specific form of asking 'Why?', inevitably a rational question, which is based on the assumption of something causing something else to happen. Then we can build an intellectual (mind or spirit) edifice and burn the dream images up with sulphuric reasoning, which leaves them parched and discoloured, but, to our conscious relief, the threat of the dream's meaning revealing itself has at least temporarily been halted. Causality (and the intellectual seeking of causes) in relation to dreams is perhaps one of the major ways in which we incorrectly and destructively approach a dream. 'Why?' is fundamentally motivated by curiosity, and curiosity turns the focus of attention into an object to be looked at, but not participated in and with. So the mind question 'Why?' to a dream distances us from the dream, antisepticises us from the dream, but in destroying the bugs it kills the dream. Curiosity, the motivating force behind the question 'Why?', also tends to lead us into interrogating the dream for its meaning, chasing after it in such a way that the dream has no choice but to elude us. Curiosity is a destructive way to approach a dream, because it usually springs from feelings of doubt and uncertainty, and therefore, instead of listening to the dream, we tend to want to make it conform with what we already know consciously in order to alleviate our anxiety. Curiosity and asking 'Why?' tend to rush the dream, want to move it on along too quickly, not allowing time in the unconscious mind, where soul resides or hides. To St Bernard of Clairvaux, whose *Nosce Te ipsum* describes the spiritual discipline of self-knowledge, the primary step off the path of self-knowledge was not pride, was not sloth, not lust — but curiosity! He speaks mainly of its destructiveness in terms of the harm the curious mind can cause the peace of soul and spiritual enlightenment.

I have observed again and again this flight into mind via the question 'Why?', and yet it is so destructive a way to approach a dream. Some people have already asked the 'Why?' before I see them and then produce a *fait accompli* interpretation of the dream, primarily to keep me and them away from it. But, as a rule of thumb, one can safely assume that if one knows what the dream is about, then one would not have had it! James Hall, a Jungian analyst who has contributed substantially to our knowledge of dreams, says: 'If you already know what the dream seems to be saying, then you have missed its meaning.' Others simply begin the work on a dream — the work always being composed of a dialogue between dreamer and listener — by asking: 'Why would I have this dream?' 'Why would I dream of my aunt Joan?' The question is usually followed by 'Oh. That's a stupid thing to have dreamed of' or 'How silly of me to have dreamed of that'.

In these simple statements one can see the denigration caused by the anxiety of the dream, and the need to dismiss it that lies just behind the 'Why?' When the 'Why?' does not work as a way of avoiding meeting the dream, then denigration seems inevitably to come next. Intellectuals — or, in Jungian terms, thinking types — tend to denigrate the deams more subtly by answering or attempting to answer the 'Why?' question. These are the people who find it most difficult to meet their dreams, because they want to meet it on their own ego-conscious terms, they want to tell the dream what *it* means and forget the fact that they and their intellects were asleep when they had the dreams. As Jung said: 'It dreamt them.'

Resorting to the body of facts or soaring up to the lofty heights of the intellect are two ways, two very common ways, in which we avoid a true meeting with our dream. This is simply because both these extremes do a violence to the 'as if' quality of a dream. In other words, they de-soul the dream, remove its psychic quality. This is not to suggest that the psyche does not need both thinking (spirit) and concrete reality (facts), rather is it to make the point that both mind and facts are destructive when they assume a priority over the image and, as a consequence, take things at face value only, robbing them of their metaphorical value; that is, their soul significance. What we established in the previous chapter was that the transformation of an event into an experience was achieved through images, through psyche or soul. To rob the event of its metaphorical value, of its resemblance, of its 'as if' quality, is to sever the inner connection to the event, leaving it merely as an event with no meaning. The literalist is finally a destroyer of meaning, since she or he does not want events to be any more than they are and she or he is obsessed with *is* and detests the 'as if'. Thus, for the literalist, it is either 'is' or 'is not', an attitude that is totally contradictory to the world of dreams, since the meaning of a dream is never exhausted, even if it seems completely understood.

Having discussed some of the ways in which we ought not to approach a dream or meet the dream, the task remains to outline some positive or useful techniques for approaching a dream. To do this, we must first briefly return to the nature of images as they appear in dreams, since this will establish the world we are approaching. Having established it, then one can discuss what sort of conscious attitude to adopt towards the dream. By now it has become clear that dreams are composed of images, but what one also knows is that these images in a dream are not linked together in a linear, straight line, cause-and-effect manner, they are linked together by connections, almost like a painting or a piece of sculpture. The parts form coherences, because no part or image has priority over the other. Patricia Berry has called this connective form the 'full democracy of the image'. That is, all parts have a equal right to be heard, and there exists no privileged positions such as we would have in an ordinary cause-and-effect model. The images also in part depend on each other for meaning, so we cannot take one bit of a dream and interpret it in isolation without doing some violence to the complexity of the dream itself. Calvin Hall confirms this viewpoint when he asserts:

A dream is an organic whole; one part of a dream should not be lifted out of context and interpreted for itself alone. The dream should be interpreted as a whole, because it reflects an interconnected network of ideas in the mind of the dreamer.

Another way of speaking about this is to say that images in a dream seem to appear simultaneously; that is, no part precedes or causes another part of the dream. So, in a way, it does not matter which part comes first, since as in a painting all is given at once. It is only when we need to narrate the dream that we impose order upon it. Yet, even then, one can find oneself saying: 'While this or that was going on, so was this and that.' The word 'while' points to the simultaneous nature of the dream images. So often, then, a dream can feel and appear incoherent, because when we try to relate it verbally, we need to speak or write in terms of something coming before something else. Narrative demands a sense of sequence, whereas a dream is reversible, with no fixed order or sequence. In this sense it is interesting to note that the Greek word for dream, *oneiros*, actually means 'image', not story, so trying to put a story to an image is hard work, as anyone who has tried to relate or write a dream down well knows. It is, as T. S. Eliot declared:

Words strain,
Crack and sometimes break, under the burden,
Under the tension, slip, slide, perish,
Decay with imprecision, will not stay in place,
Will not stay still.

Because of this simultaneity of the image, one can see how contradictory it is to seek causes in a dream, even more so *the* cause. What we need to do is to approach the dream seeking the interconnections within the dream, which are often signified by a change of scene. Furthermore, because the dream is an image, it is its own meaning, we can elaborate upon it by working on the dream, but the meaning is already in the dream, it is complete. As James Hillman says: 'An image is not an image *of* an object. It images itself.'

Jung, in a similar mode, is often quoted as attributing to the Talmud the saying that 'The dream is its own interpretation'. Presumably, he regarded this as identical to his own thoughts, where he expresses the opinion that the dream is not a disguise, as Freud held, but rather it 'expresses exactly what it means'. Although most people experience the opposite (that is, the dream meaning is rarely apparent), this is primarily because of its metaphorical nature. Take, for example, this abbreviated dream, which was

81

related to me. The dreamer was a forty-year-old man in an acute state of uncertainty about whether to leave his wife and live with his mistress, or not. In the dream he found his wife touching him, and this was unpleasant to him, so he went to brush her way, and in so doing he brushed her leg with his hand and her leg fell off. The dream 'expresses exactly what it means'. The dream is its own meaning: if he leaves his wife his fear and guilt is that he will leave her without a leg to stand on! Here, the metaphor is clear. To have gone any farther in terms of his wife being the feminine part of himself, and hence him 'cutting it off at the knees', while probably accurate and valid would have gone beyond where the dreamer was and the situation that the dream was metaphorically commenting on.

In passing, it is worth noting at this point that a golden rule of thumb in dream work is to be very familiar with the context of the dream in the dreamer's life, what is currently happening to him or her, what he or she is thinking about before going to bed, or on that particular day. The context (the facts) provide us with a backdrop against which we can hear and listen to the dream. If the dream is, as many dreams are, governed by the law of compensation, balancing up our conscious viewpoint or attitude, then knowing what the attitude is is absolutely vital in facilitating understanding. Perhaps you will recall that this was one of the pieces of advice concerning dream interpretation that Artemidorus prescribed.

If the image is its own meaning, then Hillman's dictum of sticking to the image becomes an important ingredient in approaching the dream, since it directs us to stay in the dream, inside the metaphor, and not take flight into thinking or fact. Jung states very unequivocally:

> If someone dreams of a lion, the correct interpretation can only lie in the direction of the lion; in other words, it will be essentially an *amplification*

of this image. Anything else would be an inadequate and incorrect interpretation, since the image 'lion' is a quite unmistakable and sufficiently positive presentation.

In other words, one sticks to the image, not only because psyche sticks there, but also because meaning does. Take the following brief dream of a forty-two-year-old man in the midst of a mid-life crisis.

I dreamt that the construction of a freeway in a Melbourne suburb is nearing completion. There is a vast expanse of asphalt but no median strips, painted arrows or traffic lights.

He was a man who found it very difficult to let his imagination run, since he had long lost his soul. With such people I find it sometimes helpful to get them to expand upon the image of the dream in a form of active imagination. We did this, and I asked him 'What would happen on this newly completed freeway if there was no median strip, etc.?' He replied: 'That there will be chaos, because the traffic would have no way of indicating which direction or side of the road it should be on.' As it happened, he was able to associate the freeway as being located in a Melbourne suburb that seemed very specific. This freeway, in his dreams, was being constructed in a suburb right near where he lived during his adolescent years. Thus, by sticking to the image, one can see that this dream is about not having direction, and that this loss of direction was related to his adolescence, since he in the dream has located the freeway near his family home — a home, incidentally, to which he moved during his adolescent years, with his earlier years being spent elsewhere, in an area not referred to in the dream. So the dream is quite specific as to the locality of the freeway, a construction for moving vast amounts of traffic.

When I asked him what he would do if he was responsible for this freeway without median strips, he replied that it certainly would be 'too expensive to dig it all up and start again'. So instead he thought he would arrange for some temporary-cum-semi-permanent concrete blocks to be set in the freeway in lieu of the median strip. Was he also telling me, or his dream image, that he did not want to 'dig up his past' — it would be too expensive?!! What he wanted, indeed, was some aid in his loss of direction. He was a classic mid-life-crisis man, who had lost all direction and was feeling chaotic, a situation that I believe the dream accurately portrayed. But it is even more specific in that it locates the source of this loss in adolescence, perhaps in choices that he made or did not make at this point in his life. It is characteristic of the mid-life transition that people find themselves having dreams using physical locations that indicate that the psychological space they need to attend is back to adolescence. Often we have to return to adolescence to rework issues, choices, identities, relationships, in order to facilitate our moving through the mid-life period. This simple dream was already pregnant with this meaning, but the delivery was a little more complicated!

In other words, a cardinal rule for understanding dreams is to remind oneself constantly that the dream is the creation of the dreamer. Not to have 'stuck to the image', and to have interpreted freeways in any other way would have been incorrect, because this freeway in this dream was about loss of direction as the dreamer saw it. This focus was on the absence of median strips. The dream expressed exactly what it meant.

Perhaps another example of the importance of sticking to an image may be helpful, and the following dream is another example of the image being its own meaning. This is the dream of a forty-year-old man, an academic, experiencing profound periods of depression, but also an obsessive concern about his wife's infidelity. Briefly, his history was that his family had migrated from Europe to Australia when he was nine years of age, an event that he had never considered to be very important. This is the dream he brought me, early in our therapeutic sessions. He called the dream

THE BROKEN BACKED EEL

On a walk up a mountain we (my son and I) encounter on a stump, on the right hand side of the road, the eel. I think at first it's dead, but can see that its back is broken or badly wounded and it is stiffened into the posture it displays, which is odd, rearing laterally outward from the flat stump top, with only a bit of its tail on the stump. My son touches it, a small flake-like piece comes off its mouth, and it speaks and moves. 'How are you' I say, somewhat put off, still unbelieving. Its mouth is wide open, it has no fangs, I can see by that that it is an eel and not a snake. 'Well, I haven't been fed for days have I?' it says, in a most civilised voice. I ask whether it wants vegetables. 'No'. 'I suppose you want worms?' Answer is 'Yes'. I feel slightly disgusted by this. I wake up.

The dreamer, being a very intelligent man and widely read, quickly asserted that he thought the eel was a symbol of his own unconscious mind. Here he was quickly trying to get into his head, safe and familiar territory for him as an academic, and out of the dream. Although this dream has a great deal in it and is a very rich dream, the central point for this current discussion is the image of the eel. I confessed that I knew absolutely nothing about eels and inquired whether he did, focusing on sticking to the image of the eel and not the intellectual interpretation about eels. I wanted to know about this eel, not what this eel represented. After some time he volunteered the piece of information that he thought eels migrated across land from pond to pond and sometimes got stuck or lost in between. Here, then, as he said it, was the meaning of the eel; he, his 'eel', had got damaged in migrating from Europe to Australia and it required his son (now approximately the same age as the dreamer was when he actually migrated) to touch the eel to find out if it was still alive. He thought it was dead at first, *but* (an important word in dreams is but) 'the son' part of him established it was alive and what is more it actually speaks to him and tells him what to feed it if it is going to be restored to health. Interestingly, it wants worms, creatures that live underground, are associated with earth. So presumably he needs to feed this damaged eel part of himself some earthiness. How appropriate and accurate this was, since as an academic he was in short supply of earth and grounding. The dream, then, was very precise in its images, and to have interpreted the eel rigidly as a sexual symbol would have violated the meaning. That is not to say that sensuality may not have been part of the earthiness that needed development, but· the meaning of *this* eel was about its migration and the fact that the man's migration as a small boy had 'broken his back'; in other words, broken his soul. If he had not gone walking with his son in the dream, he would never had discovered the damaged eel. Again, the dream is its own interpretation: if he had not made contact with his son within himself, with his own nine-year-old feelings, his eel would probably have died, and his depression would have continued.

As a metaphor, the eel is also very illuminating, since it lives below the surface, so whatever got damaged during migration for this man also lived below the surface. The dream shows its capacity for specificity when it also indicates that this is clearly an eel not a snake, since it has no fangs. Finally, there is the very specific request from the eel in the dream in terms of what it wants to eat. As I have already mentioned, the eating of worms could mean that this part of himself, living below the surface, requires feeding with some earthiness, but even more specifically, worms (about which, incidentally, he feels slightly disgusted in the dream) are associated with both putrefaction (rotting matter) and bodies, and also with rejuvenation and fertilisation of the soil. So, wanting a feed of worms is perhaps a metaphor for that part of himself that, if it is to be restored in health, needs a good feed, taking into consciousness both rotten and good feelings, thereby re-fertilising his psyche. His own association to the vegetables that the worm rejected was that he had become a vegetarian after attending a conference on Eastern philosophy in Europe. His attendance at this conference followed on immediately after a nostalgic return visit, as an adult, to the European village of his youth. What is of interest is the timing of the occasion of becoming a vegetarian, which followed directly after having made some contact with his earth. This could be seen as him unconsciously turning his back on his own earthiness and pursuing the higher path, but the 'higher path', the path of the spirit, was in his case the development of his intellect, or his thinking function, in Jung's terms, at the expense of his earthy feelings. Perhaps the final comment one could make about this dream, and one that might be easily overlooked, is that in the dream he actually speaks to the eel and inquires about its well-being. For me, as a therapist, this was a very positive indication of this man's willingness to face and relate to the eel within. Also from my point of view as a therapist, the value of the dream in understanding what troubled this person may not have been fully appreciated if I had been an 'expert' in the orthodox sense and not confessed my ignorance about eels. The statement of 'not knowing' can, I think, help to create an environment in which the dream or the soul might come to us, rather than us going after it. Jung says something very similar to this when discussing dreams. He says:

So difficult is it to understand a dream that for a long time I have made it a rule, when someone tells me a dream and asks for my opinion, to say first of all to myself: 'I have no idea what this dream means'. After that I can begin to examine the dream.

Another quality of images, or psychic facts, as we could call them, has been briefly referred to in the eel dream, when speaking of it being an eel and not a snake. I have been constantly amazed at how specific and precise an image can be, and in this specificity is another major clue to the meaning of the dream, since one can do a contrasting technique and ask of the image why it is this and not that. For example, if one dreams of being on a train, why a train and not a bus, a tram, or a car? The specific quality of the image is carefully chosen, unconsciously, and a great deal of attention should be paid to this quality. A further rule of thumb in approaching a dream is the one we have already mentioned, called 'the full democracy of the image' by Patricia Berry. In other words, each and every detail of the dream images needs to be considered, and often considered in the contrasting mode I have just mentioned. It is worth remembering that nothing appears by chance in a dream and, furthermore, it is all put there by the dreamer; thus each image has a meaning.

Having covered some of the characteristics of images as they function in dreams, the remaining section of this chapter will be concerned with the critical question of the attitude to adopt towards dreams. How do we not chase the dream away with intellectual inquiry? How do we manage to remind ourselves that this is metaphor, an 'as if' mode of seeing? How do we hold the organic wholeness of the image and not dismember it with curiosity? The two people on whom we have drawn heavily in this book to date, Jung and Hillman, provide a framework for the attitude we might adopt towards a dream in order to facilitate our understanding of it. Jung, in advising a dreamer how to approach a dream, says as follows:

. . . the best way to deal with a dream is to think of yourself as a sort of ignorant child or ignorant youth, and to come to a two million year old man or to the old mother of days and ask, 'Now what do you think of me?'.

Hillman, on the other hand, adopts a more democratic view, perhaps a more contemporary view, partly created by the rich and scholarly work that Jung had already done on dreams. Hillman's attitude is one he has borrowed from existential analysis, and that is to *befriend* the dream.

To participate in it, to enter into its imagery and mood, to want to know more about it, to understand, play with, carry, and become familiar with — as one would do with a friend.

In another place Jung, discussing how to relate to a dream, what attitude to adopt towards it, says:

One would do well, therefore, to treat every dream as though it were a totally unknown object. Look at it from all sides, take it in your hand, carry it about with you, let your imagination play round it, and talk about it with other people . . . Treated in this way, the dream suggests all manner of ideas and associations which lead us closer to its meaning.

What each of these quotations reflects is two attitudes; the first is one of *humility* in the face of the dream, and the second is to allow plenty of *time* to just be with the dream. When the ego-conscious, rational mind grabs hold of the dream, it negates both these attitudes, because part of us wants to impose meaning and cannot abide letting the dream reveal its own meaning, which takes time. To extend James Hillman's idea of befriending the dream, then to assert superiority over a person with whom you wish to form a friendship is likely to chase the person away (if he knows what's good for him!). Likewise with the dream, and further, one would — at least should — not commence a friendship by insisting on a collection of whys. What we say more often than not is a 'What then?' to expand our inquiry and to let the process of befriending continue via storytelling about ourselves or the other person. 'Why?' is inevitably associated with accusation and would force the beginning friend into a defensive posture to defend or justify himself or herself. So also is it with dreams: 'What then?' is a far more productive way of approaching a dream than 'Why?'. 'What then?' keeps us in the image and facilitates our sense of the interconnections within the dream, saving it from intellectual dismemberment or factual interference.

The issues of humility and time also return us to the incubation rites of the Asclepian temples, where we saw that preparing to receive a dream was considered vital, indeed an essential part of receiving the healing message. One way in which we can discipline ourselves to maintain humility in the face of a dream is to remember that we are asleep when it dreams us. For anyone helping others to work on dreams, whether she or he be friend, neighbour, or therapist, the reminder to be humble in the face of a dream can come from the clear and unequivocal recognition that the dream belongs to the dreamer. Somewhere, the dreamer must know what it means. Being respectful of who actually had the dream, or who was dreamed by the dream, serves to remind us of appropriate boundaries, a factor important in building any friendship. We can then take our time and not be intrusive or rush in where angels or devils fear to tread. If we do not approach the dream with humility and patience, then it will resist understanding and, as a consequence, we will seek to gain information from the dream in an avaricious manner, exploiting it for the sake of the ego and/or power. Friendship or befriending, on the other hand, wants to keep things flowing, to keep the connection open long enough to get a sense of each other.

With respect to time, I think it vital that we contain our anxiety, arising from the sense of inadequacy one feels in facing a dream for the first time. This anxiety, emanating from the sense of inadequacy, can drive us into manic flights, upwards, in search of an instant (well almost instant!) understanding of the dream. But this pursuit upwards is a defence against the anxiety that one often feels in the face of a dream, the flighty conclusions of such flights are usually little or nothing to do with the meaning of dreams. In other words, to return to one of Hillman's metaphors, we need to meet our new friend and commence the befriending process in the valley and not shoot straight for the peaks. We know that the soul lives in the valley, so if we are to befriend it, then we must walk in the vale of one's uncertainty, anxiety, bewilderment, humility, envying the peaks; and with a commitment that the friendship is worth it. That is, a respect for the friendship with soul.

T. S. Eliot, in one of his *Four Quartets*, 'East Coker', captures this waiting and patience aspect beautifully when he says:

I said to my soul, be still, and wait without hope
For hope would be hope for the wrong thing; wait without love
For love would be love of the wrong thing: there is yet faith
But the faith and the love and the hope are all in the waiting.
Wait without thought, for you are not yet ready for thought:
So the darkness shall be the light, and the stillness the dancing.

'Wait without thought' is perhaps Eliot reminding us that to think alters the pace, pushes it on too quickly; we must learn to see the 'darkness as the light', the darkness and moist of the valley, not the dry and bright light of the peaks. Hillman picks up a familiar note regarding darkness, when discussing dreams and images. He says that by getting images to speak, we are seeing them as 'soul-mines'. But he adds: 'mining doesn't require modern technical tools . . . what does help mining is an eye attuned to the dark'. One of the ways we know that helps to 'attune our eyes to the dark' is to stay in the dark long enough for our eyes to adjust and become familiar with it. Staying with our dreams allows our eye, our metaphorical way of seeing, enough time to adjust to seeing in the dark. The waiting is an attitude that does not require any special knowledge of dreams, it opens up the possibility to anyone who is prepared to spend some time wandering and meandering in the valley. While meandering, we can speak to the dream, and let it speak to us — a process technically called *active imagination*. By speaking to the images we allow and encourage the dream to go on telling its tale and, by doing this, we are deepening our relationship to the dream. Often it is helpful simply to ask some character in your dream, 'Why are you there?', 'Why now?', 'What do you want?' Here we see shades of the Senoi, who treated the images 'as if' they were real and related to them.

When waiting, walking, or speaking with a dream, we will notice that the story, or stories, usually have a beginning, a middle, and an end. If we listen to where the dream begins, take notice of where we are and who we are with, then we shall also have taken note of what the concern of the dream might be, just as a theatre programme sets out the *dramatis personae*, time and place. By listening in this non-interpretive way, we can get close to the myths that may be operating in the dream, and recall the words of Karl Abraham:

Myth is the dream of a people and a dream is the myth of the individual.

Hillman states that in encouraging a dream to tell its own tale, we are becoming our own mythologists: 'tellers of tales'. Also, we can do this for others, not just ourselves. It has become increasingly difficult in this expert-ridden society to believe that one can do very much at all — other than the handyman or do-it-yourself hobbies. But with dreams, simply by listening to one another's dreams, with an attitude of humility and patience, we can affirm and recognise the products of the soul.

Beyond simply listening, there remain a few more points to make that might assist and inform the listening to a dream. One would be the general rule that Hillman provides: 'A wrong path into the dream occurs when we take one path only.' One of the ways to avoid taking 'one path only' is to be mindful of the quotation from Aristotle that we commenced this chapter with: 'The most skilled interpreter of dreams is he who has the faculty of observing resemblances.' We can observe resemblances by asking the simple question of a dream image: 'What is it like?'. That is, we can use *analogy* and seek, not literal likeness, but likeness in function. Analogies keep us in the images, so we can ask of a scene: 'What is this scene like?' Or, if it is a fear, 'What is the fear like?' By seeking analogies we can deepen the image, get closer to soul, which lies in depth. The analogies, like the psyche, are endless. I have found that analogies are particularly useful if people are experiencing difficulty in amplifying a particular image. It seems easier at times to speak of an image being 'like' something, than directly to amplify it. I find this particularly useful when a dream starts with a vague, seemingly nondescript scene, by asking the dreamer 'What is the scene like?' it tends to add specific depth to the image, which very often proves critical in understanding the dream. Not infrequently, the answer is 'Well, it's a bit like', which very often tends to lead to an earlier memory, and this memory often holds the key to the likeness in function between what the dreamer is struggling with now and what she or he was struggling with at that point in her or his past history. Analogies, then, allow us to alter time-frames in a manner that can assist the psychic location of the scene; that is, what part of this person's life this dream is wanting to focus on.

93

Hillman suggests several other techniques that one can use with dreams and images in order to deepen our understanding of them. Each of these techniques essentially involves semantic manipulation to open the dream image up. The first he calls *eternalisation*, which simply means taking the word-sequence when/then from a dream and changing it into 'whenever'. The word 'whenever', Hillman claims, has the effect of making one feel the connection in the dream is necessary, thereby adding strength to it. So, if we take the simple example of a dream in which a person says, 'When I turned the corner then the car got out of control', it would read, 'Whenever I turn the corner the car gets out of control.' It provides thereby a compelling quality to the image, which brings it to life and yet stays within the image. Another strategy, called *contrasting*, we have already discussed. In contrasting one brings out the particularity of the image and feelings associated with it. It also helps to overcome any feelings of boredom or disconnection from the image due to familiarity. For example, instead of simply being 'my old house', it becomes 'Why this old house and not another?' Usually this question opens up a range of amplifications and thoughts about 'the old house', which otherwise may well have lain dormant in the boredom and familiarity of the image.

Singularising is a further technique suggested by Hillman, in which one uses the word 'only'. For example, looking at a dream, one may say, 'I notice that you do that *only* when your mother comes into the room.' The use of 'only' specifies the action and helps us, once again, to take the image deeper. It also has the same effect of other techniques in facilitating our ability to stick to the actual image.

Speaking of *sticking to the image* introduces another technique, which has the aim of keeping images around that otherwise would have escaped into thin air. Usually, they are the complex and difficult images, which we prefer to skip over in a dream, because their presence makes us very anxious or interferes with our well-worked-out interpretations. But, remembering Patricia Berry's dictum concerning the 'full democracy of the image', if we leave complex ones out, if we skip over them, we run the certain risk of an incorrect understanding of the dream, one dominated by our thinking about the dream, rather than the dream itself. So James Hillman urges us to keep the difficult images around somewhere, to wait and see whether they become clearer in the light of the other images. I find one of the distinct advantages of a dream group as such is that there are enough people for images to be held by one or more members, while the others work with the dream. Then someone will say, 'But we haven't discussed the black dog yet.' Invariably, what we have not discussed, what we have not kept around, proves to be vital to the understanding of the dream. Hillman, in a poetic mode, describes this process for keeping images:

> I can keep the image (and tell the patient to keep it) around for a while, like standing a bottle of wine upright on the table in plain sight in the middle of my living space, letting it warm to room temperature. And sure enough, a sedimentation occurs; it begins to clear; it loses opacity; its specific quality lightens through the glass. It's ready to be appreciated, its subtleties disclosing themselves without heavy work.

Here, Hillman provides us with an excellent and enticing metaphorical description for keeping images around. The theme underlying it is once again the theme of waiting, of patience, of letting time elapse, but, in this instance, of keeping one's eye on the image.

Robert Grinnell noticed that there is often a moment in a dream when a hiatus or break occurs. I have often been struck by the turning-point quality of these breaks in a dream, when one can see that, as a result of the break, the dream takes a different course of action, like a watershed moment in a story. The following is the beginning part of a very much longer dream by a forty-three-year-old woman.

I am taking my 16 year old daughter to school. I am riding a bicycle and she is walking. She is wearing my school uniform. Suddenly the bike wheel starts to become square and buckles. I can't go on! The bicycle becomes impossible to move but I try to turn it around to go home.

Here one can see that the hiatus moment is conveyed by the word 'suddenly'. If this had not occurred in the dream, then presumably she would have continued on taking the daughter to school. As it happened, the turning around in the dream led her to an amazing series of dream adventures. In passing, and once again to highlight the image as metaphor quality, the understanding that emerged from this beginning scene was that the dreamer, when sixteen years of age (here, her daughter denotes this), was attending a Catholic boarding school and 'buckling under' the strict teachings of the church. Now, at mid-life, she had to return to that particular spot in her psyche when she buckled under, in order to rework and renew issues from this particular time.

However, to return to the point of this section, the hiatus in a dream usually reveals a nodal point, and James Hillman claims that the exploration of this nodal point can be very rich. He concludes by stating: 'For I suspect that in the little hiatus absconding Mercurius hides.'

Throughout this chapter the insistence has been on 'sticking with the image'. This is because the primary metaphor of psychology must be soul, and that soul is to be found in the images of our dreams. To deviate from the images is to suffer the loss of our own soul! However, it is probably the task of psychology to find a logos for the soul, to find a way of providing an account of psyche, and this task involves

96

theory and concepts. Theory is vital for practice, since otherwise we remain unaware of what we are doing. The ancient alchemists provide an example *par excellence* of the need to combine theory and practice: beside, usually adjoining, their laboratories, they had another room specifically set aside for prayer, meditation, and thinking about their experiments. Soul seeks spirit, just as spirit seeks soul, and both need to be connected to the material world. The next chapter is aimed at providing some form, some logos, for psyche; a logos that derives its being and inspiration from the psychological theories of Carl Jung.

6

A MAP FOR THE JOURNEY

A map for moving from the valleys to the peaks and
returning is essentially theory, since theory is a set
of concepts, ideas, systematically connected in a way
that makes logical sense and order of our experien-
tial or inner world. But it is important to remember
that they are maps, and as the adage reminds us: 'We
must not mistake the map for the territory.' This
mistake in technical terms is called reification, a
process of converting or regarding the concept as a
concrete, tangible thing. Within the terms of this
book, it would be an act of excessive salt! And the
dis-ease of literality would have once again taken
hold.

So, in providing this map, the inherent risk is that
terms such as shadow, anima, animus, etc., will be
reified into things, objects, and we shall find ourselves
literally believing in *the* anima, perhaps imagining that
it is located just to the left of our hypothalamus! We
must see theory as a map. And looking at a map
for the journey from Sydney to Melbourne, or from
Melbourne to Los Angeles, is a vastly different order
of reality than actually experiencing the journey. We
could have taken any number of maps for plotting

this walk around the psyche, around the valley of the psyche. However, I am firmly of the opinion that Jung's theory is both the most comprehensive and most accurate map for this land of the psyche that we inhabit.

In saying this, I think it is also important to draw attention to the fact that theories are not 'true' or 'untrue', but more or less comprehensive, and in this sense I do not regard Jung's theory as a 'true theory', but a comprehensive one.

In discussing such matters as theory and theoretical concepts, we are entering the reality of mental activity, which I see as a basic level of the spiritual phenomenon or that of spirit. It is essentially spirit, because, at the level of mind, spirit seeks knowledge and the ascending path to higher and higher levels of knowledge. But this seeking ought not to be separated from soul, which is constantly seeking to be known by the spirit. On the other hand, we also live in the world of outer reality, the world of objects, and the soul or psyche is also yearning for expression in this world, yearning to animate the world; that is, to put soul into it. The word 'animation' is derived from the Latin word *anima*, which means soul. So, between these two realities of mental activity and objects lies the third reality, one that James Hillman describes as a:

> . . . a realm mainly of 'meaningness'. In these states of soul we can feel connection to nature and to ourselves . . . an inner life come to life.

This third reality lies between mind and matter, and perhaps governs both, perhaps is the starting-point for ideas and objects. Roberts Avens sees 'Imagination is Reality' (which is also the title of his book) and Patricia Berry states that:

> Image is prior not in time, not because we need take it up first when considering a dream; but image is prior in the sense of most basic, that to which we return again and again, and that which is the primary ground and spring of our imaginal awareness.

Thus if this third reality is prior to the mental and object realities, the realities of mind and matter, then thinking, and its product theories, must be retrospective, or at least ought to be. By this I simply mean that rational thinking comes after we have grasped something. It has always felt to me to be a form of *post facto* justification and ordering of something that we have already understood. In being this, it allows us to objectify, make consciously known to ourselves, what we have already grasped, and thus this knowledge becomes available to use again when we meet the same phenomenon. The danger is that in reifying theory, in rendering it concrete, we let the theory determine what we can know; that is, we give it priority. In this case we can know things only mentally, intellectually, but not from within ourselves. These are the sort of people that one says of them, 'Oh, he or she is all in their head' — usually a very accurate diagnosis. Others use theory as a way of communicating what they know in their soul, imagination, or inner world, and in so doing facilitate, stimulate, and elaborate this knowing in other's souls. The difference lies in asking the question, 'Where did the knowledge start?' — in the valley of the soul or in the dizzy heights of the peaks of the intellect? It is interesting to notice, by way of an aside, that tertiary education often refers to such degrees as 'higher degrees'.

One of Jung's great achievements must surely be that he so plumbed the depths of his own being, his own soul, that his knowledge is applicable and relevant to very many other people today. At the individual depth he explored, he discovered universal truths about human beings; the depth was so profound that he found mankind, not just Carl Gustav Jung. Thus we read his theory of self, animus, and types, and feel a sense of connection, an 'ah ha' experience, because the content, the knowledge, finds its origins in the soul; the mind has merely provided the mechanism for organisation.

One can readily see this in Jung's personal life by recalling that following his break with Sigmund Freud in 1913, when Jung would have been thirty-eight years of age, he commenced the recording of his images and imaginal world in what has come to be known as the 'Red Book'. But at this stage, and indeed for many years he had no real conception of what the imaginal material that he had recorded in his 'Red Book' meant. He had simply dedicated himself to entering in it his imaginal life. Theory was not what he recorded in his book, and in fact it was not until some fifteen years later, in 1928, that he was to get the first glimpse of the theoretical sense, and this came through his attention being drawn to the ancient Chinese alchemical meditative text *The Secret of the Golden Flower*. Richard Wilhelm had translated the text and sent it to Jung with the request that he write a commentary on it. Jung's response is recorded in his biography:

> I devoured the manuscript at once, for the text gave me undreamed of confirmation of my ideas about the mandala and the circumambulation of the centre. That was the first event that broke through my isolation. I became aware of an affinity; I could establish ties with something and someone.

Here we see Jung's clear admission of the lack of sense, lack of logos, which existed for him concerning his psyche until he was fifty-three years of age. We could not ask for a clearer picture of soul or images being prior to mental activity. In fact, Jung makes this priority explicit when he says:

> Psychic existence is the only category of existence of which we have *immediate* knowledge, since nothing can be known unless it first appears as a psychic image . . . To the extent that the world does not assume the form of a psychic image, it is virtually non-existent.

Having, hopefully, established the priority of soul, let us now turn to some maps for the journey. To recapitulate, we have spoken of meaning being derived by the connection between the inner and the outer worlds. When an event becomes an experience and we feel a link, a connection, at that moment it has some meaning for us. Presumably, in our present age, a great number of people merely go through a manic, rapid succession of events and are desperately short of experiences as such. Psyche or soul was seen as that realm that was the middle kingdom, and images were the mechanism for changing or transforming events into experiences. So time spent in one's soul is time spent in the realm of imagination, where we see events 'as if'. That is, imagining is a way of seeing through the literal event to its symbolic or inner meaning.

In Jung's terms the psyche is engaged in the process of individuation, best understood as an instinct to complete ourselves, to experience wholeness. This wholeness we can take to mean a reconciliation of the opposites within us, the fundamental and overall opposite, being the opposite of consciousness and unconsciousness. So 'wholeness', then, would be the experience of knowing self, since the self is an archetypal image of integration and wholeness. In speaking of self, which is the goal of individuation, Jung describes it as follows:

[It] is not only the centre but also the whole circumference which embraces both consciousness and unconsciousness; it is the centre of this totality, just as the ego is the centre of the conscious mind.

Marie-Louise von Franz speaks of it in the following terms:

The goal of individuation, as pictured in unconscious images, represents a kind of mid-point or centre in which the supreme value and the greatest life-intensity are concentrated.

If self embraces both consciousness and unconsciousness, then those moments when we transform or transmute an event into an experience, when we are connected, inner to outer, are moments when we experience Self. Thus these moments very often have the quality of energy that von Franz speaks of. We can sometimes hear ourselves or others saying: 'I really feel myself today' or 'I feel really connected to myself today' or 'I feel like my old self'. These are all metaphorical statements referring to a moment of wholeness.

Temporary as it may be, and as elusive as mercury itself, it nevertheless is a moment when meaning prevails against the despair of meaninglessness. Presumably the theory suggests that the more able we are at staying in touch with soul, the more able we are to maintain the 'as if' or symbolic view of outer reality, then the greater sense of Self we will experience. This experience, according to von Franz:

> . . . brings a feeling of standing on solid ground inside oneself, on a patch of inner eternity which even physical death cannot touch.

Here we can see the link between soul and immortality, for if soul is the means by which we experience Self, then little wonder that we should think of soul as surviving physical death or being reincarnated. The imaginal realm could hardly experience physical death, just the manifestation of it, mind and matter experience death. The soul is for ever beckoning us to higher and higher knowledge of it, whether we see that as taking place in one lifetime, or many.

If we relate this process of individuation to Jung's law of compensation, which we previously discussed, then compensation could be seen as that law operating to remind us constantly of the opposites within and to address our conscious attention to the task of integrating them in order to move towards wholeness. Compensation, then, becomes a mechanism for individuation. In a broad sense we could see the law of compensation, the balancing of opposites, as the balancing of the fundamental opposites of the literal world and the imaginal world. If one takes this view, then we can look at the compensatory process in dreams as redressing the imbalance between our outer selves and our inner selves.

It seems to me that it does this through a variety of ways, but some of Jung's concepts allow us to more or less organise, theorise, about this 'variety of ways'. Otherwise we simply fall into the trap of simplistically saying 'dreams are the opposite to my conscious view' and leaving it at that. By using some of Jung's concepts, we can sharpen our understanding and hopefully take some action in order to recognise our inner figures and build a relationship with them. In this vein we can follow Jung's example, which he so eloquently records in his *Memories, Dreams and Reflections*, of actually taking our inner dream images 'as if' they were real, and befriending them in the interests of advancing our journey towards wholeness. In this sense of compensation — or the Freudian idea of wish-fulfilment, being the wish to fulfil oneself — the concepts of persona, shadow, anima, and animus, seem to me to refer to the most regularly recurring images in dreams and the ones of most value to us in the journey. We shall briefly discuss these now, and the theory of types, and then the remainder of this book will be dedicted to an exploration of these figures, their moods, their personalities, their behaviour, etc., as witnessed and observed in individual dreams. It is these figures in our dreams that direct us towards meaning and facilitate the symbolic view of life.

PERSONA AND SHADOW

The persona is, in Jung's view, an archetype, an inbuilt pattern to enable us to interact or be in the outer world. Persona literally means 'mask' and is derived from classical Greek plays, where an actor simply raised a mask over his face in order to play the role required. It is important to recognise that we need such masks, as personas, to adapt to the outer life;

the psyche needs to put on a face, so to speak, in order to connect to the outer world. In short, the persona is to do with the part in life we play, the front we put up. It is the archetypal pattern for relating to the collective conscious situation, analogous to the social psychological concept of roles.

If we could attribute a sense of geography to the psyche, then one would place the persona on the outermost region that adjoins the external reality. Hence it tends to show up in dreams usually in terms of clothes that people wear or the lack of them. So the type of clothing we wear in a dream — a uniform, for example — can be an unconscious symbol of our own persona. A common dream theme is the one of being naked or semi-naked, and yet usually no one else in the dream notices the nakedness, only the dreamer. Nakedness means we feel exposed, so presumably it points to our persona being inadequate, the mask we show to the world is slipping, and therefore we feel vulnerable. Sometimes personas show up in specific articles of missing clothing: pants, shirt, brassière. By and large the part of the body that the missing clothing should be covering tends to be symbolic of the aspect of our persona that is inadequate and the aspect of our psyche that we feel to be vulnerable. For example, dreaming of no pants might represent that our sexuality is showing and the mask we have used to cover it and show to the world has slipped. A woman's breasts being uncovered could represent that her mothering persona has been exposed, perhaps she is feeling vulnerable in her role, or the role she displays to the world as a mother. The persona, when personified by another person in a dream, almost without exception is of the same sex. This, as we shall shortly discuss, is also true of the shadow. Both these figures are represented as images of the same sex, whereas anima and animus are represented by images of the opposite sex. So, in essence, the persona functions to enable us to relate to the outer world. Problems arise when we identify with it, and believe that we are our mask; this has the effect of disconnecting us from the inner world and attaching us to the outer world. We need to look behind the mask if we are to journey towards wholeness, and dream images can often alert us to this very need.

The major problem with the persona, as already indicated, occurs when there is an insufficient sense of ego-identity in the individual that is separate from the social persona role. In this case, if the role, or persona, is threatened, then it is experienced as a major threat to the entire identity. The much-talked-of 'empty nest' syndrome can precipitate feelings of profound depression in a woman if too much of whom she sees herself as is tied to being a mother. Then, when her children leave home, she is left bereft of a sense of identity. The middle-class executive who totally identifies with his job and then gets retrenched is another example of how depression is precipitated by the loss of role, because the sense of 'me' is too closely tied to the persona. So the task of individuation with respect to the persona is to find a working arrangement with our mask or masks, so we can relate to the outer world without deriving too much of our identity from the role. If we get too far out into the world, then the law of compensation will provide us with an image regarding dress or clothes, which will call us back inside ourselves.

A dream that captures both persona and shadow aspects is of a woman whom I recall was involved in an extra-marital affair. She dreamed of herself in a clown suit; in other words, she unconsciously believed she was making a fool of herself. Here the clothing depicts the unconscious attitude towards her outer behaviour. We can also see in this dream the compensatory principle operating: the excitement, thrills, etc., that were occurring on the outside were balanced by the inner clown.

SHADOW

The shadow is, in a way, the reverse of the persona. Instead of those images that we wish to convey or project out into the world for all to see, the shadow represents the dark side of our nature, all those aspects of ourselves that are unacceptable to our conscious view and certainly utterly contradictory to the face we wish to convey to the outer world. In the process of developing our ego, certain innate tendencies in the individual will be accepted by our parents; and other attitudes, impulses, etc. will be negatively valued and thus rejected. However, these attributes, impulses, and tendencies, while rejected and considered unacceptable by the family one is reared in, are not simply lost. They are, on the contrary, banished to the unconscious, to the land of the lost soul, to Hades. There, these rejected and unacceptable tendencies cluster together to form figures, shadow figures, because they are shadows formed by the light of the other acceptable conscious qualities within our personalities. The shadow, broadly speaking, is made up of the negatives of the ego's positives. Because the shadow, like the persona, is potentially part of the ego, the conscious part of mind, it tends to have the same sexual identity in the image as the ego. Because the shadow also personifies unacceptable tendencies in ourselves, feelings of guilt are usually associated with it. By simply being out of sight it does not follow that the shadow is out of mind, and indeed the shadow — or more accurately, the shadow figures — go on exerting a powerful influence over our everyday life, often with us being totally unaware of this influence.

To return to a continuing theme in this book, we are driven to express images, like a moth to the light, so the shadow images will be operating, affecting our behaviour, only under the cover of darkness, so to speak. The shadow is most frequently personified in dream images by either one's brother or sister, or very

107

often by old school friends, particularly those from adolescent years. Sometimes the shadow will be in the image of a next door neighbour, a servant, a foreigner. Not uncommonly, we will say of a shadow figure in our dreams: 'Well. I couldn't really recognise her, she was sort of shadowy.' The dream, with its usual capacity for metaphor, has enlightened us as to the nature of this figure. The 'not recognising' is also a very familiar theme in dreams, and it means what it says, the dream is its own meaning; that is, we are simply not recognising the particular aspect of ourselves that is personified by the shadow image. Alternatively, the shadow will be dreamed of as either not having a face, or having its back turned away from the dreamer. Again the image is clear. We have not, or are not, facing some aspects of ourselves. Thus, watching what the shadow does in a dream and where we locate it in a dream are vital clues as to how it will affect and influence our everyday life. For if we do not come to recognise those qualities within ourselves, then we start recognising them in other people; that is, we project the shadow images onto others in the outer world of the same sex. Thus our *bête noire* is usually somebody onto whom we are projecting our shadows. If, for example, anger is an unacceptable tendency, then it will form in us as a shadow figure, and if we do not recognise him or her in our dreams, then we will find ourselves being very moralistic, or disapproving of people getting angry. Repeated conflict between two people of the same sex usually reflects shadow activity, shadow boxing if you like.

Not coming to grips with our shadows can result in constant conflict in our lives, but perhaps more seriously it means that we have left a substantial part of ourselves outside — outside conscious awareness. For many of us, the first time we get a glimpse of a shadow is when we project it onto others. We can then be either psychologically lazy and leave it there, seeing all the faults in the world in other people, or alternatively, we can engage in soul making and try and re-own this part of ourselves. It is part of us, part of our wholeness, and although it may be a part or parts that are not particularly admirable or worthy, they do belong to us and give us an awareness of our own shade as well as our light. Realising that our so-called worst adversary is actually part of ourselves is a tremendous step forward, since it facilitates a sense of community with others, rather than a sense of acrimony. Yet many people prefer the luxury of acrimony, or superiority, to the task of facing their own shadows, and so are driven farther and farther into the outer world, farther into persona, which they rigidly identify with. They consequently develop a plastic, soul-less quality. One is often left wondering where the real person has gone, or, if he is there, would he please stand up!

Facing the shadow figures is very much the beginning of the psychological opus; the alchemists called this phase the nigredo, the black phase. In itself it presents a task of considerable difficulty, for which there is no short answer except to say that I think it is a life's work, for new shadows seem to be for ever recurring in one's dreams. The false and childish hope is that we can eliminate the shadow, but that can never be done, so the task is to recognise it and see how it plays out in our lives. The recognition of shadow figures, although arduous and at times a thankless task, does give the person who is coming to grips with his or her shadow a sense of solidity, of perspective, the sort that comes from proper use of light and shade. As P. W. Martin so simply says: 'In the last analysis, the shadow is also one's substance.'

It has by now, no doubt, become apparent that the shadow is very similar to Freud's notion of what resides in the unconscious. That is, unacceptable urges and wishes that are prohibited from expression in our everyday lives. Indeed the two seem identical, hence we again see the link between wish-fulfilment and compensation. One can agree with Freud that the dream represents a wish-fulfilment, but it becomes clear that lying behind the images is the wish to fulfil oneself by bringing into our conscious awareness the unacceptable, ego-rejected contents. Likewise, if the law of compensation is balancing the opposites, then the shadow figures could be seen as the first layer of opposites, the recognition that it is 'as if' the person we hate passionately is part of ourselves. As the shadow figures are potentially part of the ego, therefore close to consciousness, it seems natural that the law of compensation will commence the integration of inner and outer at the level that is initially closest to conscious awareness. I would therefore hold that we can see compensation operating in all dreams, only at different stages of depth, or different levels of soul, the first stage or phase being related to shadows. Thus these images are the ones most likely to be reclaimed and hence contribute to soul making. The alchemists tell us that if we survive and progress through the nigredo, the next phase is the albedo or white phase, which is to do with the marrying of opposite principles, masculine and feminine, or Yin and Yang.

PSYCHOLOGICAL TYPES
However, before we move on to anima and animus, or images of the opposite principle in each of us, it is necessary first to make a brief excursion into Jung's theory of psychological types. Again this is not the place to explore them in any depth, for I have done this elsewhere, but merely to introduce them as road signs, part of the map, so to speak. The notion of types is derived from what Jung termed the four functions, or four different means of orientating ourselves in the conscious world. Respectively, these are thinking, sensation, intuition, and feeling. Two of these are regarded as rational functions: that is, thinking

and feeling; and two as non-rational: sensation and intuition. In broad terms one could see sensation as the function that tells you something is — only that: it does not tell you what it is. Sensation as a function is tied to the five physical senses of taste, touch, sight, hearing, and smell, and it is through these senses that we take the raw information in, through them we have outer perception. Hence it is regarded as a non-rational function, simply because it does not make any order of the information or make any judgements about it. It simply establishes the presence of something. On the one hand, sensation can be a very important function in aesthetic appreciation, of tone, texture, colour, etc., along with a sensitive awareness and appreciation of one's own body. At the other extreme is what could only be called the *genus philistinus* quality, the concrete boots quality, whereby individuals use sensation to establish the point that the only reality that exists is the one that can be perceived with the senses. Such individuals will be ignorant of the aesthetic, or more inner and feminine side of the sensate function, these outer sensation people are the literalising magnates of society: 'proof of the pudding is in the eating' is their primary guideline in life — pragmatism elevated to the level of a divinity.

Intuition is posed as being in the opposite position to sensation, like the west point of a compass contrasted to the east. Instead of telling us that something is, intuition tends to tell us what may be. It is located in future time, rather than present time. It is the proverbial hunch that anticipates the occurrence of an event. This sort of perception, termed inner as opposed to outer perception, comes straight from the unconscious mind, and therefore is primarily composed of images. Intuition is a way of seeing, a way of seeing through things, events, or people, which allows us to then have the proverbial hunch. 'It is as if he saw right through me' is the sort of comment one hears if a correctly intuitive observation has been made. The 'seeing right through me' quality is the imagination, or the imaginal way of seeing life as if it were a metaphor.

However, intuition, like its opposite, sensation, is a non-rational function, since it simply is unconscious perception, perception that needs organising and weighing up. Both sensation and intuition require one or other of the functions of thinking and/or feeling. These latter functions, like intuition and sensation, are theoretically seen as opposites, so to continue the analogy of the compass one would see thinking as the north pole and feeling as the south pole.

Thinking in its simplest definition is seen as telling us what a thing is. Thinking is concept formation, it is naming things, differentiating between things, putting things into logical categories and organising events along logical causal lines of 'if this, then that'. In short, it is our rational mind at work. Without thinking, life and its events would lack order; but likewise if there is too much thinking then life lacks spontaneity and imagination. Feeling is the theoretical opposite of thinking within the Jungian framework or map, and it, like thinking, is seen as a rational function. This, of course, immediately presents a problem to most people, since we erroneously equate feeling with emotion and assume, therefore, that feeling is irrational. If thinking tells us what a thing is, then feeling tells us what it is worth to us. Feeling is about values, a valuation function. While intuitives might imagine a beautiful house, sensate types build it meticulously, and thinking types reason its location, structure, layout, etc., feeling types will tell us its value, whether it is a house or a home. Feeling discriminates as a function on the basis of values, not concepts, on the basis of good, bad, etc., and ought not be confused, as it so often is, with a capacity for ardour and warmth. Feeling is a rational judgement, so feeling people can equally well be cold or warm, tell us straight out that they dislike us, or alternatively that they like us or value us. We have, for all sorts of cultural and social reasons, equated feeling with either emotion or sentiment. Emotion, if we return it to its Latin root, where so often one can find the precise and correct meaning of a word, comes from the Latin word *emotio*, derived in turn from *emotus*, which means 'moved out' or 'to be moved'. Thus emotions 'move us', we 'don't know what got into us', 'he is beside himself'. So emotion is something that happens to us and moves us out of ourselves. Often, we are emotional when we do not know what we feel; that is, when we are uncertain or unable to work out our values or the value of an experience or event for us. When the feeling function is well developed in a person, or in technical terms differentiated, then this type of person, contrary to the emotional, will know exactly what he or she wants. Sentiment is also confused with feeling, whereas I would consider sentiment as a version of underdeveloped feeling, a heightened sensitivity to emotion, but it is skin deep and not anchored or rooted in the psyche. Sentiment, more often than not, finds its home much closer to the persona, and hence sentimental people often lack a sense of solidity, a lack that comes with too close an identification with the persona.

Brief as the foregoing discussion of the four functions is, it is obvious that people tend to be more accurately described by one or two than by the others. It is the 'more accurately described' that decides what type of personality one is. Our early family experience and natural disposition systematically shape our personalities, and this results in some functions being more adequately rewarded, and thereby reinforced, than others. The particular function that finishes up in adult life as being the one we use with the greatest ease and efficiency, Jung would term our superior function. So if, for example, an individual grows up in a family where the use of rational thought, words, concepts, etc. is highly regarded, then the chances are

113

that she or he will develop as her or his superior function, thinking, leaving its opposite, the south pole, feeling, in the least developed state, hence called the inferior function. The inferior function being the least developed function is also the one that is most closely and intimately connected to the unconscious mind, wherein the superior function is the one most connected to the conscious mind.

Hence, to return to the persona, this mask is almost without exception identical with the typical attitude associated with the superior function. So if sensation is the superior function, then the persona would be a matter-of-fact, down-to-earth, no-nonsense, let's-get-on-with-the-job-at-hand type of mask or face to the world. In a person with sensation in the superior position, the opposite would be intuition, so the higher sensate no-nonsense, attention-to-detail person will have a very inadequately developed imaginative and intuitive sense. In short, an inadequate relationship to her or his own unconscious, inner world. Yet such are the people that society holds up as outstanding achievers, models of how we all ought to be.

Magazines and newspapers regale us with stories of the woman who is a full-time research scientist, high-powered, publishing learned paper after learned paper, also the mother of three children, and at the same time we are told of the many committees of which she is a member. 'How does she find the time?' 'She is such a capable person.' She usually finds the time and the capability at the expense of her inner world of feelings and imagination. In a society that is increasingly dedicated to the concrete, the tangible, the measurable, how could one expect any other model to be offered? But the dreams of such a woman will very often contain scenes of cars getting out of control, falling scenes, lifts not stopping, and aeroplanes crashing. All these dreams symbolically point to the opposite theme within her psyche, that of loss of control. Since in having an inadequate relationship

114

to the inner world it simply is as if it is out of control. The workaholic male, of course, is no different. But instead of raising the three children as well as his job, he joins many more organisations and committees. And his dreams will indicate exactly the same themes of loss of control and sometimes the theme of neglect and dereliction of various dream characters.

The same sort of comment could be made regarding intuition and feeling, when either of these is the superior function. Here, for example, if intuition is the superior function, then the person will sometimes lack a strong development in the sensation qualities, the earth qualities, and hence will tend to be full of fantasy, images, and wonderful ideas. The only problem is that very few of these get transformed into action. This is the person who is the proverbial daydreamer. Likewise, if feeling is the superior function, then this is the type of individual who, while knowing exactly what she or he wants and what she or he values, will very often find it difficult to articulate these needs, since thinking, concept formation, is usually in the inferior position. The central point of these somewhat overdrawn examples of types is to make the point that the predominant function determines what psychological type we are.

The inferior function is the individual's Achilles' heel! That is, the spot from which one's anxieties and difficulties in life will emanate. This is simply because, as has already been indicated, the inferior function is the one that is closest to the unconscious mind, and therefore very often we are unaware of its effects on our behaviour, which is mostly in the direction of compensating for the superior function. For example, the very rational, thinking man will suddenly find himself having inexplicable fits of irrational anger or depression, a sure sign that feeling, as an inferior function, is at work. But if he had found time to pay attention to his dreams he would have been alerted to this quality within himself, since in the dream world the functions are generally imagined as personifications. Either the dreamer uses his own image, or those of others who personify the function that the dream is concerned with. As we shall see when we discuss anima and animus, I think there is an intrinsic relationship between the inferior function and the anima or animus images in our dreams.

It is interesting to briefly reflect upon Achilles and why one might see the inferior function as an Achilles' heel of the psyche. The Greek myth tells us that, as an infant, Achilles was plunged into the river Styx by his mother and thus rendered invulnerable, except in that spot by which she held him, which was his heel. Eventually he was shot in the heel by Paris, or some say by Apollo, and Odysseus then saw Achilles in Hades. Two points in this myth are of considerable relevance in understanding the inferior function. Firstly, the vulnerable spot is caused by the mother holding him there. Metaphorically, it is as if our inferior function is related to the hold that our mothers have over us, perhaps the hold of wanting our mother's approval and fearing disapproval. This may mean that we have or have not developed particular functions, because they would have not met with one's mother's approval. Secondly, after Achilles is killed, Odysseus sees him in Hades; that is, symbolically the inferior function finishes up in the unconscious mind. From there, the task is to try to bring it back into conscious awareness, where one can see its effects on our everyday lives, thereby moving us towards wholeness. The full implication of this discussion on superior functions is to make the point that whichever is our strong function, no matter how efficient it is, it can only give us one-quarter of the truth of any phenomenon. We need to develop the other three to arrive at a complete understanding, and that task of developing all the functions is very much the task of individuation. A task, we shall see, in which anima and animus, the male and female images in our psyche, play a vital part.

However, before we move on to the discussion of anima and animus, it is important to clarify that it would be a rare person indeed who has developed only one function. Usually what one finds is that the superior function is flanked by an adjacent function. So, to return briefly to the compass analogy, it is that if the north pole of thinking is the superior function, then either the psyche's direction will be north-west, that is, thinking with intuition as the shared or auxiliary function, or alternatively, north-east, with sensation as the auxiliary or shared function. Many people have a third function reasonaby well developed also. However, a reliable observation is that everyone has the Achilles' heel of an inferior function.

In summary, it is useful to have some knowledge of what one's superior function is, because we can reasonably assume that the opposite function will be the inferior one. This knowledge can be of considerable value in making sense of many of our dreams, since, according to the law of compensation, the opposite will appear in our dreams, particularly around mid-life, in order to balance the consciously developed superior function. But it is not always easy to pick our superior functions, short of doing a Jungian typology test. However, there are some rules of thumb based on the notion of the paired opposites of thinking-feeling and sensation-intuition. As thinking and feeling are alternative methods for making judgements and weighing up particular situations, one can observe how we, or others, carry out this process. A thinking type will normally be challenged and respond to a problem because thinking is related to problem-solving through the process of analytical thinking. On the other hand, feeling types tend not to focus on the problem or behave in a specific problem-solving way; rather, they will focus on the human element in the problem, the owner of the problem, rather than the problem *per se*. So the feeling type explores the personal meaning of the problem for the individual, what value he or she attaches to it, what values are threatened by the problem. The thinking type, on the other hand, will analyse the problem and work out appropriate, logical, and reasonable solutions.

The paired opposites of intuition and sensation are alternative ways or methods of perceiving, and this also can be observed in operation. The sensation type will focus on foreground and details and really physically look at the object, whereas the intuitive type's perception tends to look beyond and around the object, through it, rather than at it, and as a result will miss much of the detail. It is a case of the old saying of one not seeing the forest for the trees and the other not seeing the trees for the forest.

Another rule of thumb involves identifying the inferior function, then, by implication, its paired opposite will be the superior. Generally speaking, the guideline that the inferior function is operating is that it escapes conscious control and we experience an increase in anxiety when having to use it. Thus the inferior function will have an emotional quality about it, and I have observed that people actually feel young when required to use their inferior function. The prevailing fantasy is that we are the same age throughout our entire psyche, and we assume that age to be the same as our chronological or biological age. In reality, it seems to me we are many ages, even many ages in one day, and the inferior function tends to be a great deal younger than the superior one. So when this inferior function is called into operation, it will be visible or identifiable in those situations where, contrary to our normal operating level of competence, we are aware of feeling very incompetent and sometimes very young and awkward. For example, women returning to tertiary studies as part of the mid-life transition at around thirty to thirty-five years of age, often having suspended their formal education in their late teenage years, will frequently feel (and indeed in some cases behave) like a teenager. They will feel young and inadequate when doing essays and will be intimidated by their lecturers, whom they still perceive in a schoolteacher mould rather than colleague mould. Mostly, when in this situation, people will be aware of their inappropriate feelings, thoughts, and images, and will even say things like: 'I don't know what makes me do it, I just behave so childishly.' The 'I don't know' is the confirmation that the inferior function is operating, and proof that it is operating unconsciously; that is, out of the range of conscious awareness. We can also identify the inferior function because it will not feel natural, and we will be very laboured and painstakingly slow in whatever it is that requires us to use it. The anxiety that comes with using it and the sense of awkwardness can very often drive people into acting out inappropriately and thereby unduly complicating their lives. An awareness of one's inferior function increases the opportunity for true psychological choice about our ways of being in the world. In contrast to the inferior function, when we use the superior function we are aware of a sense of ease, and it is as if it comes naturally, almost without conscious effort, and we feel our own age and sometimes older than our biological age.

Thirdly, we can generally spot our inferior function by what we find ourselves disliking intensely in others, or inappropriately admiring in others. Through the mechanism of projection, we project our discomfort and dislike or unfamiliarity with our own inferior function onto individuals in the outer world whom we perceive as having well-developed versions of our own inferior function. Undue denigration or idealisation both provide a sure sign of an inferior function in operation. So, to return to the example of a thirty-five-year-old woman beginning tertiary studies, one can sometimes observe in her an undue valuing of the academic ability. This reflects a rejection of their own repressed or inferior thinking function. But the importance of dreams in this context is that personification of our inferior function will occur, giving us a chance to recognise these qualities within ourselves and at least temporarily making it that bit more difficult to project onto others and thereby also making it that more difficult to act out. Since, so long as we leave the inferior function firmly planted on someone else, very often our partners, then we are condemning ourselves to being only half there. Obviously the inferior function and its repression would seem to be similar to the shadow, and indeed it can be joined up with the shadow. However, I think reclaiming our repressed or inferior function, our opposite quality, is a far more complex and arduous task than shadow material, which tends to be much closer to consciousness. Hence this task of recognising and integrating into consciousness the inferior function can be seen as the second level or stage of compensation, the task of developing our 'other half', and it is in this connection that we now turn to anima and animus.

ANIMA AND ANIMUS
Of all of Jung's theoretical ideas, the notions of anima, the feminine image in males, and animus, the masculine image in a woman's psyche, are the most difficult to comprehend. They represent a deeper and more complex level of the psyche, and they refer to the collective unconscious mind; they are, as a consequence, archetypal. This level of mind will always, by its very nature, defy adequate, logical definition, since in some respects the anima or animus can be seen as the archetype of the psyche itself. One could sooner catch a rainbow in a jar than verbally or logically describe the psyche. It is primarily because of the location of the anima/animus within the psyche

that a second level of difficulty arises, and this is the individual's ego's need to assert control and order over the psyche. With respect to the anima and animus, they potentially, like so many unconscious factors, threaten an invasion of consciousness and assimilation of the ego by the archetype.

As an aside, it ought to be stated that Jung asserted time and time again the danger of consciousness being overwhelmed by the power of the unconscious mind, resulting, on the one hand, in disintegration or psychotic states, and, on the other, in ego-inflation, whereby the self becomes assimilated to the ego. There is a tendency among some people involved in psychological work and education, particularly where the emphasis is on so-called 'growth', to perceive the ego as an enemy to growth. But very often the 'growth' is actually a regression back to earlier and more primitive states of mind, where the unconscious and a sense of 'I' become fused, often resulting in a temporary sense of euphoric well-being, but, regrettably, often followed by a profound sense of loss and despair. This regressive, highly pressurised process of returning to earlier psychological patterns, unrestrained by the demands of consciousness, is often at the expense on conscious awareness and, as a consequence, achieves the very opposite of its espoused aim. Any psychological technique that accentuates or encourages a rapid and speedy descent into the unconscious mind is more than likely to achieve this at the expense of conscious awareness and is therefore encouraging regression, which is definitely not in the interest of ego-consciousness.

One is reminded of the timeless wisdom of the ancient Greeks in the mythological story of Theseus and Pirithous, when the latter decided to enlist the help of Theseus to abduct Persephone from the underworld. It is told that they made the descent to the underworld successfully, but Hades chained them to a rock as they tried to ascend, and they thus found

121

themselves unable to get out of the underworld until freed by Herakles. Psychologically speaking, the myth reveals that it is a lot easier to enter the unconscious than it is to come out, particularly when one is intending to abduct a figure that resides there.

Unless unconscious material is integrated into the ego, then no permanent expansion of consciousness itself is achieved. As already stated, the euphoria of instant growth — whether this be by rebirthing, regression therapy, hallucinogenic drugs, or whatever — tends to assume that the ego is a barrier to growth, when in fact these practitioners are really referring to the persona. The ego can be seen as the eye of the needle through which consciousness must pass, hence the Freudian adage: where id is, ego shall be. Jung asserted the importance of ego-responsibility when he said:

It must be reckoned a psychic catastrophe when the *ego is assimilated by the self*. The image of wholeness then remains in the unconscious . . . If, therefore, the ego falls for any length of time under the control of an unconscious factor, its adaptation is disturbed and the way opened for all sorts of possible accidents. Hence it is of the greatest importance that the ego should be anchored in the world of consciousness and that consciousness should be reinforced by a very precise adaptation.

Whitmont, in relation to the importance of the ego to the process of awareness and individuation, is even more precise when he states:

Only when the ego can preserve its own identity and separateness from the Self and not be burned in the fire of cosmic dissolution — only then can individuation take place.

He goes on to warn that a very fine line exists between individuation as a conscious process and disruption of the personality in the form of a breakdown or psychosis, which is always the outcome when the unconscious forces in us gain the upper hand. The

122

ego is the part of the psychic system that is the centre of the conscious personality and thereby the source of conscious choice and personal identity. It must, on the one hand, remain separate from the unconscious, and yet, on the other, be open enough to allow a relationship with the deeper unconscious aspects of the psychic system. The risk it constantly faces is disruption either by losing its separateness and being taken over by the unconscious, or by assimilating the unconscious mind to its own level. The latter risk results in a sense of megalomania, where one loses sight of one's personal and human limitations; and an example of this would be the person believing he or she is Christ or some other charismatic leader.

It seems very natural that the ego would be alert to a takeover bid from the unconscious, and this, I believe, has been behind a further source of difficulty in discussing and understanding anima and animus. Remembering that both these aspects of the psyche are archetypal and therefore potentially capable of destroying consciousness, the ego has, I suspect, in a defensive way attempted to ward off this threat by personalising these archetypes and claiming them for itself by calling them 'my anima' and 'my animus'. The implicit hope of the ego-conscious mind here is that, by personalising the anima/animus they will be de-potentiated and brought under ego control. A partial result of this is a loss of contact with the deeper source of these figures and a severing of contact with the unconscious mind. One hears individuals saying again and again: 'Oh! That's my anima speaking' or 'My animus behaving that way'. Indeed Jung reminds us that '. . . it often seems advisable to speak less of my anima or my animus and more of the anima and the animus'. In this way we are reminded of the objective and separate force within ourselves, which has two faces: an archetypal one and a personal one. But in neither instance is it appropriate to defend ourselves against its influence by personalisation and claiming it at a personal level. Rather, one is obligated to attempt to build a relationship to this fundamental aspect of the psyche and, in so doing, to engage in an ever-deepening awareness of our own complexity. In the final analysis, anima and animus are, I believe, the archetypal images of Yin and Yang, the opposing principles within us that the ancient Chinese believe are the essence of all life. The personalising phenomenon has also resulted in a sort of genderisation of these archetypes by equating Yang with men and Yin with women, but at the level of the collective unconscious they are far more encompassing than this. In Chinese philosophy the Yang principle is associated with energy, activity, the sun, the sky, heat, stimulation, and spirit. It is concerned with separation, but is also restrictive and related to individualisation. Yin, on the other hand, is receptive, inward-going, passive as opposed to active, symbolised by the earth and moon and characterised by darkness, moisture, and the world of nature, not spirit. Yin is the feminine principle and Yang the masculine. Yang finds its scope in the expression of discernment, spirit, order, abstraction, and is represented by such images as father, hero, and wise old man. Yin, on the other hand, finds its expression in the experience of receptiveness, yielding, containing, and in the flow of inner images and intuition. Linda Fierz-David describes Yin as

> The mother-womb of the soul, conceiving and giving birth. Whatsoever falls therein is born, ripens and is ejected, regardless.

It is represented by such images as Demeter and Persephone, on the one hand, and Aphrodite, on the other.

These two powers reside in all human beings, and the relationship between them is best described by the sinologist Richard Wilhelm, who was so important to Jung in his scholarly work on alchemy. In his comments on the I Ching, Wilhelm says:

> The receptive primal power of yin . . . is the perfect

complement of the Creative — the complement, not the opposite, for the Receptive does not combat the Creative but completes it.

These thoughts are perhaps rendered a little clearer if one considers Yin in terms of negative energy, not in a value judgement sense, but in terms of energy, which is receptive and passive. This is the complement to Yang, as positive energy, which is assertive, outgoing, and initiative-taking. Thus the task, so to speak, psychologically, is to come to an awareness of these forces within us, a task that constellates the reconciliation of opposites in Jungian terms, the task of individuation.

The second stage of this task, after integration of the shadow figures, is the exploration and familiarisation when the opposite-sex images within us, those images referred to as anima and animus. Anima, then, represents the archetype of a man's Yin, and animus the archetype of a woman's Yang. The union of these opposites can be seen as equivalent to the ancient alchemists' chymical marriage, which is the stage that occurs before the production of the philosopher's stone. The alchemists regarded this stone as symbolic of the enduring and eternal Self. In pragmatic terms, coming to grips with the opposite-sex image, that image of the 'other' within ourselves, I see as a necessary courtship prior to the chymical marriage. This is a union that results in the full I-thou of Martin Buber, where love and aggression and creative understanding and emotional gestation all interact without one polarity existing at the expense of the other. Such a union would also bring about a working arrangement between separateness (Yang) and attachment or involvement (Yin), a polarity that modern man increasingly deals with by splitting them into the extremes of either attachment or separateness, a solution that negates the fructifying quality of the interactive dynamism between Yin and Yang.

The previous statement (that an understanding of the anima and animus in males and females is a

125

necessary courtship to the marriage of Yin and Yang) is also meant to convey the relationship between anima and animus and between Yin and Yang. Anima and animus have both a collective unconscious quality, an archetypal quality, and a personal unconscious aspect. If one could resort for a moment to a topographical metaphor, it is as if anima and animus reside or live on the border between the collective unconscious and the personal unconscious, with one foot or face towards the collective, hence Yin and Yang, and the other turned towards the personal unconscious and the various repressed opposite qualities that lie within this province, in particular the repressed or inferior function. It is this theme or face that the focus of the present book will be concerned with when discussing anima and animus. In this way the link or connection can be made between the second stage of compensation, beyond the shadow aspect, to that of the awareness of opposites, including the inferior function and the anima and animus images. The face that turns towards the collective unconscious, the more pervasive archetypal forces of Yin and Yang, which give rise to anima and animus, could within this context be seen as the third and final level of compensation, the philosopher's stone, that of balancing and integrating the primal opposites of consciousness and unconsciousness.

This so-called borderline location of anima/animus in the psyche contributes to its often referred-to role as a mediator or psychopomp: the hermetic quality that conveys messages between the unconscious and the conscious mind. These messages consist of making visible unconscious contents to consciousness, with anima/animus images acting as vehicles for the transmission. That is, at the personal level one tends to have either anima or animus images in the form of human figures, sometimes figures we recognise from outer life and at other times figures from fiction or films. The characteristic of the anima and animus at this level is that they are human, and not numinous, or godlike, which would characterise the archetypal face. One could reasonably expect at major transitions in life the appearance of an archetypal anima or animus image, but it is more likely to be in a form we are not familiar with (for example, a snake, eagle, the sea), images that transcend and convey the transcendence of ordinary human qualities and thereby point to the archetypal issues. In this role of mediator between consciousness and unconsciousness, the anima/animus image is conveying messages to consciousness from the collective unconscious. This is that level of mind that we tend to resort to when required to seek wisdom concerning major transitions in life. The following brief dream is a simple example of this archetypal feminine quality, or anima personification. It is the dream of a man in his early forties, a man who has severely repressed his Yin, receptive, intuitive qualities in the interest of an almost exclusive and obsessional development of his rational, logical aspect.

A dream in which three yellow snakes emerged from a hole in the middle of the kitchen floor, dancing a sort of ritualistic courtship dance which involved them coming in and out of the hole. I in the dream assumed my son (3 years old in the dream) had been bitten by the snakes and was anxious to take him to hospital. My wife was unconcerned, doing the dishes or some such activity and my daughter was also unconcerned. The snakes were very, very beautiful and I tried to grab one, it bit me on the wrist, I was aware of the bite but not worried.

It is not appropriate at this point to go into every detail in this dream. Suffice it to say that a strictly sexual interpretation would be far too obvious and blatant. On the contrary, one is struck by several questions: for example, Why are there three snakes? Why are they yellow? And why are they coming and going out of a hole in the kitchen floor? Why not the bedroom or lounge-room floor? The dreamer gets bitten only when he tries to grab the snake, perhaps a way of saying that one cannot grab or hold aspects of the collective unconscious. The snake can be seen as an anima image, and the yellow may in turn be seen as indicative of an intuitive quality. The triplicate is perhaps a way of emphasising the strength. The intuitive quality is the quality that I have already mentioned, which the dreamer had neglected in himself. We find that it bites him when he tries to grab it, which is perhaps a way of symbolising that he tries to grab every image and fantasy with his logical mind, instead of just simply observing it and letting it dance its beautiful dance. The courtship ritual could indicate a desire on the part of the anima at this primitive unconscious level to form a relationship with the dreamer, but not be controlled by him. The fact that the women, personal aspects of his anima, are not interested is further confirmation to my mind of the archetypal quality of the snakes. The son, three years of age in the dream, points to the dreamer perhaps having had a negative experience with these deeper feminine aspects of himself when about that age: 'Once bitten, twice shy!' The kitchen is a room normally associated with sustenance, nurturance, and particularly the transformation of raw materials into energy-giving food. It is, then, very interesting to notice that the snakes come from a hole in the centre of this room, thus perhaps locating themselves in the aspect of the psyche that is connected to transformation of energy. But to try and grab and control them, as already indicated, to rationalise or intellectualise the subtle aspects of psyche is likely to turn them into negative forces. One of the most common ways in which males grab and get bitten is by persistently seeking logical causes for their malaise, rather than reflecting and observing their feelings, observing the ritualistic comings and goings of the snakes within themselves. His own lack of energy and oppressive mood, in this context, reflected his persistent failure to embrace the feminine principle within himself, his Yin and source of creativity. As a by-product of therapy and his own attention to dreams, this man experienced an upsurge of creative energy, expressing itself in a renewed and strong interest in his own artistic work. When we come to discuss the anima and dreams in more detail, other dreams reflecting both the personal and archetypal aspects will be explored.

Whether it brings into consciousness material from the collective and/or personal unconscious, the role of both anima and animus is one of mediator between our conscious mind and the deeper aspects of the psyche, constantly urging us to continue the journey. As Emma Jung says:

The urge toward increased consciousness seemingly proceeds from the archetypes, as though, so to speak, there were an instinct tending toward this goal.

It is the mediation of this process that forms such a vital function of both anima and animus, and at the personal unconscious level is, in my opinion, related to the pushing into consciousness of the inferior function. Herein lies a further contemporary difficulty in understanding these archetypes—a difficulty that stems from these images having been frozen in a specific period of history. It was in the 1930s that both Emma and Carl Jung developed their ideas and understanding of the anima and animus images. This is fifty-five years ago, a period that has witnessed an amazing social revolution in what is perceived as male and female. In 1930s Europe, a male could normally have been expected to develop the thinking and sensation qualities, and a female the feeling and intuitive ones. Hence we have simplistically come to assume that two of these, thinking and sensation, constitute the animus, and feeling and intuition the anima. In short, we have genderised an archetypal image. Here we can witness the danger of reifying a theory and potentially rigidifying it into irrelevance. No doubt what Jung observed in the 1930s was an astute and correct observation for the time, a time when females were actively discouraged from developing thinking qualities, in particular; so thinking would of necessity have been the inferior function and in the unconscious mind of the females. Thus the animus, in its role as mediator, would have pushed a thinking type of male image into the dreams and fantasies of 1930s European women in order to draw their attention to what needed to be brought into consciousness. This pushing into the dreams and fantasies of women of the 1930s could also be seen as the beginnings of the women's movement that emerged in the 1960s. Likewise, for males, rationality and pragmatism would have been valued (indeed, little has changed!) and hence the feeling and intuitive qualities were underdeveloped or, in other words, have come to form the inferior function. But the impact of the women's movement has changed much of this, and if a woman's natural inclination is to develop her thinking function in the first half of her life, then this is increasingly as acceptable as developing her feeling side. Thus to associate thinking with males and feeling and intuition with females and see these as anima and animus respectively is to be inappropriately tied to the past, resulting in sexist and incorrect views of anima and animus. In referring to this historical fixation of anima (and we could indeed apply the same argument to animus) James Hillman says:

> We should therefore not identify a *description* of the anima in a rigidly patriachal, puritanically defensive, extravertedly wilful and unsoulful period of history with her *definition*.

The role of the dominance of cultural values of a particular historical period of time would equally well

130

apply to animus as anima. Hillman continues and makes a most important assertion concerning the contemporary task of understanding anima and, by implication, animus. He says:

The task now is to discover what descriptions suit her in this time and how is she mythologizing today.

Earlier in this book I quoted Karl Abraham as saying that myth is the dream of the people and the dream the myth of the individual. From this statement it follows directly that one of the ways in which we could take up James Hillman's challenge is via the world of dreams. It is here that we should be able to catch a glimpse of the contemporary mythologising of the anima and animus. When one looks, what I have found occurring regularly is that animus does not equivocally personify the traditional view of being concerned with thinking and sensation. Indeed, equally often, the animus image in a female's dream is associated with the so-called traditional feminine traits of feeling and intuition. That is, she will have a dream of a male whom she will associate with these particular qualities. While, by and large, in the male psyche, anima does still personify the feeling and intuitive functions, the traditional aspects of the feminine principle, there are signs, even here, of change. A clear-cut example of this will be the highly creative artist who has used feeling and intuition in the first half of his life, and then finds himself in mid-life besieged by pragmatic and outer demands. His refusal to attend to these can very often prove a destructive experience for him. What he has been asked to do is to pay attention to the thinking and sensate qualities that have so traditionally been associated with masculine values.

The past twenty-five years in particular have witnessed such a profound sociological revolution in our notions of masculine and feminine that we simply cannot afford to hold sexually stereotyped views of anima and animus at the personal level. This level, because it is closer to consciousness than the slow-moving and cthonic archetypal level, will of necessity experience and reflect those broader social changes. The role of anima and animus is to aid and mediate the process of individuation, and at the level of the personal unconscious this is to bring into conscious awareness the inferior function as a second stage of development. It is as if the personality of the personal anima or animus is in part determined by the inferior function or functions. In this way, by familiarising ourselves with the opposite-sex image within our dreams, we are at the same time familiarising ourselves with our inferior functions. By bringing it into conscious awareness we are strengthening the ego and reducing the risk of unconscious invasion from the archetypal level of Yin and Yang. As the four functions belong to the ego level of mind, leaving one or two of them embedded in the unconscious, not being aware of our inferior function, is like leaving large gaps in the ego through which the powerful archetypal material can rush, creating disturbances and ego-inflation. So the man who is unaware of the fact that feeling may be his inferior function is vulnerable to the dis-ease of falling in love and dramatically altering the course of his life. All of this will be done in an unconscious, unreflective way as the powerful Yin forces simply invade consciousness unrestrained and unfiltered by ego awareness, because the inferior function of feeling has provided the gap. As Emma Jung says, confirming her husband's views:

It is essential in establishing a relation to the unconscious that the ego be strong and well-defined enough to resist danger, always present when one deals with the unconscious, of being overwhelmed and extinguished by it.

The implication is that an ego is not rendered strong when it tries to exercise control over the unconscious by endless resolutions or logical, rational thought.

Rather is the strength derived from understanding and awareness. It is absurd to think that the unconscious can be analysed away, or beaten in some heroic battle, slayed like the proverbial dragon. One is not 'cured' of the unconscious. On the contrary, the task is conscious confrontation, so we can take into account factors that otherwise we would be unaware of. This 'taking into account' is an act of recognising our own complexity and realising that the ego is necessary in this task and yet, at the same time, is not alone in the house of the psyche. Awareness is essential to any relationship and a working relationship with ourselves requires an awareness of as many facets as can be. Within this context, anima and animus are truly guides of the soul as we negotiate the journey from our own Olympus to the underworld and back again. Nowhere, as we shall discuss shortly, are they more active and vitally involved in these negotiations and mediations, than in the mid-life transition, when the task of developing true relatedness commences in earnest, when the ego-conscious 'I' confronts a 'Not I'. However, this reclamation task must first be preceded by the task of facing and confronting one's shadow, and it is to this aspect that we now turn.

7
SHADOWS IN THE NIGHT

The shadow was discussed in the previous chapter, but the task remains to identify and discuss it with more precision, particularly in reference to dreams. In setting out this task, I am acutely aware of what Jung once said about the shadow: 'To find out what the shadow really is, is sometimes quite a task.' He goes on to state in connection with the shadow and illusions about it:

> Here we are not speaking of such assumptions, but of the shadow as it ordinarily is in reality, namely, the unconscious part of the personality – and that is an exceedingly real thing.

As the theory has developed in relation to Jungian psychology, there has been a tendency sometimes to restrict the shadow to the same-sex image of other people in dreams or the same-sex person in the outer world onto whom we project the unacceptable qualities within ourselves. Either way the concept has increasingly come to be more or less specifically tied to a person or image separate from the dreamer. While it is correct to see the shadow as a personification of those elements, attitudes, or attributes that are unacceptable to our ego-conscious view of ourselves, I think it is not entirely satisfactory to fall into the trap of limiting it to the figures in our dreams of the same-sex person, for this has the effect of excluding the image of the dreamer himself or herself as a shadow.

Fundamentally, the shadow is an archetypal pattern, the archetypal experience of 'other' that is a necessary and indispensable aspect of normal ego-development. It is the necessary consequence of the clash between society and the individual, the product of the split that comes about through establishing a sense of identity at the ego-conscious level. The shadow, therefore, consists of complexes and personal drives, urges, behaviour patterns, which definitely belong to, or reside in, the metaphorical dark side of our personality and feel as if they are 'Not I'. In short, as has already been stated, the shadow is made up of the negatives of the ego's positive. If an attitude or feeling does not fit with our conscious view of ourselves, then it is repressed or removed to the unconscious mind, where it continues to live and thrive, very often providing food for other aspects of the psyche, such as a negative animus or anima image. In psychological terms, what this means is that if we are not aware of our shadow or shadows, they may lead a psychic life of their own and perhaps join up with the opposite-sex image, which Jung claims would result in either an anima or animus possession. In Jung's words:

. . . people who do not possess and are not aware of their inferior shadow side, may appear to be marvelously good people, one can discover no flaw in them, they are white as milk. They tell you themselves that nothing is wrong with them; everyone else is wrong, but never they. Yet, because they deny their shadow, such people are absolutely possessed by devils; the women are all eaten up by the animus. Strengthened by that excellent nourishment, he grows so strong that he is able to possess consciousness, to rule it.

135

Here Jung is highlighting the need to be aware of those qualities in ourselves that we regard as inferior and unacceptable, otherwise we run the risk of being dominated by deeper, unconscious forces within ourselves. Yet, to be aware of the shadow aspects of ourselves is in Jung's own words:

. . . a moral problem which challenges the whole ego personality; no one is able to realize the Shadow without a considerable expenditure of moral resolution. To confront it involves recognising the dark aspects of the personality as *actually present and morally binding*. Such confrontation is the essential condition of any kind of self-recognition.

The shadow, despite the difficulties of the task, often seems willing to be known, as can be seen in the regularly recurring dreams that individuals have of some unacceptable character knocking at a door, wanting to be let in. Yet so often, the dreamer, both within the dream and in outer life itself, refuses to let the shadow in. Regrettably, our egos and personas and a long-trained sense of 'goodness' and 'morality' work against letting the shadow in, let alone relating to it. Yet, so often, when let in, he or she turns out to be helpful, after all. It is part of us, our own substance, and cannot be eliminated or removed. The task is to struggle towards seeing ourselves as we really are, 'warts and all', instead of wishing or fantasising about being something or someone else. This struggle, as has often been mentioned, is the first step in the journey towards wholeness, the first staging-post on the journey to meet the Self. As the shadow represents those aspects of ourselves that are unacceptable to our conscious view of who we are, it can, perhaps somewhat paradoxically, be composed of positive attitudes, although the most common experience by far is of negative qualities. But if, for example, an individual has been reared in a household in which emotional deprivation and rejection were the characteristic features of the family life, then one would expect to find positive or hopeful facets of the individual in the unconscious mind, as shadow aspects. In this situation, to feel 'good' about oneself, would have been unacceptable, therefore repressed to the unconscious. The following simple dream of an individual who came to therapy for a wide range of difficulties, embracing a mixture of depression and anxiety, highlights the positive and helpful features of a shadow. This person was a thirty-four-year-old male, twice married and currently in a third relationship, whose mother had died unexpectedly when he was four years of age. This was a very traumatic experience for him, and I felt it was systematically related to his repeated pattern as an adult of totally severing any links with the past, as if it did not exist. So, for example, he had no contact with his wife or child of the first marriage, a decision he made for himself, and not one imposed upon him by an outside authority. Yet, despite this persistent conscious rejection of any connection to the past, a blatant attempt to turn his back on it, all perhaps indicative of not being able to face that moment of profound loss when his mother died, he had the following dream about mid-way in our therapeutic contact.

I dreamt I was driving our old Ford truck with wooden sides and on the back was a suitcase full of memorabilia. I was going to dump the whole lot, truck and all, but then suddenly just before I was about to dump it decided that I wouldn't, I would restore it instead.

Here, we can see the role of the shadow in the form of the dreamer, his alter-ego taking a dramatically opposed stance to his conscious position. It is a clear example of the potential helpfulness of the shadow, when admitted, and also demonstrates a positive shadow aspect, which in fact enabled the therapy to move on successfully and facilitated a reclamation of his psychological or inner memorabilia. The practical outcome of this inner shadow decision to 'restore' was that after a period of almost sixteen years he contacted his son from the first marriage. But the 'restoration' meant facing the profound pain of loss and the anxiety of risking being abandoned yet again.

This dream, apart from being a clear example of a shadow as a potentially positive aspect of the psyche, serves to raise another issue about the shadow that warrants clarification. It is the issues that I was alluding to in the beginning of this chapter regarding the limitation of the shadow to images of other people of the same sex and, by implication, excluding images of the dreamer himself or herself as a shadow. This image is often referred to as the 'dream-ego'. In a sense the restriction could be seen as a form of literalisation, acting as a defence against the anxiety of coming to grips with one's shadow. Restricting its meaning to the image of 'another' serves to contain the matter. However, quite obviously, the shadow — if it is, as Jung indicates, the personal unconscious — is going to indicate a wide range of attitudes and actions, which can best be seen as shadow activities, rather than simply *the* shadow image. Within this context we can view the dream behaviour of the dreamer himself as a shadow aspect, and not simply restricted to a dream image of a brother, sister, boss, etc.

In my view the two facets of the shadow probably reflect two different stages or phases of the location of the shadow aspect in relation to consciousness or a conscious awareness of them. My view is that when we dream of ourselves engaged in shadow activities of ourselves carrying out some action in a dream, then the particular action is probably fairly close to consciousness. This may mean, on the one hand, that it is close to acceptance or ready for acceptance. On the other, it may mean that it has just recently been disowned or rejected by our conscious view of ourselves and has not yet been adequately repressed. When we dream of 'others' as shadow images of

ourselves, for example, some authoritarian character from our lives, if we consciously see ourselves as
democratic, then I think this 'other' feature of the
image reflects a distancing from consciousness. In
short, it reflects that we are projecting onto others,
just as the dream image says, those unacceptable qualities within ourselves, and the dream indicates the
projection by imagining it as if it were somebody else.
When both the dream ego and other shadows exist
within the same dream, we can very often see the
interaction between various unconscious attributes of
ourselves, some of which are more repressed and
unknown than others.

The following dream of a forty-two-year-old male,
who was remarkably out of touch with his feelings and
feeling side, is a clear example of this point. He was
seeking help for his depression, which had been badly
affecting his body by a whole range of psychosomatic
symptoms. All organic causes for the physical
symptoms had been eliminated, thus establishing that
their origin was a psychological problem. This is the
initial dream that he brought to therapy:

*I was entering a house, going up some stairs, but
the stairs were not like a house, more like one
would find in a warehouse. I went up to the first
floor level where at the end of a dark corridor stood
three bikies, leather clad characters. While I
managed to talk to them somewhat fearfully, I
noticed shuffling up behind them was an old man
(a hobo type) and when the group noticed him they
calmly and coldly stuck a screwdriver into his back,
a yellow screwdriver, passed the body on to me,
no words spoken, and I simply let it fall down the
stairs. I then ran along the dark corridor out of the
building.*

In his outer life, this man's behaviour was characterised by seeming selflessness, of living entirely for
the other. He was always agreeable, always doing as
the other person requested, including his wife, who

was experiencing his 'goodness' as suffocating, smothering, and guilt-producing. In fact, he was 'too good to be true'. But what the dream reveals is agression, in the form of the negative shadow of the three murderous bikies. It further reveals his unwillingness to do anything about the aggression, since there is no indication in the dream of facing it. He disassociates himself from the murder by 'letting the body fall down the stairs' and then running away. As a result of discussing this dream he recalled that when he was fifteen years of age, he was involved with another boy at boarding school in a fight that got out of control, and he had hit the boy very hard. He remembered deciding, after this, that he would never be aggressive or let his temper get out of control again. This represents a strategy of the ego catching a glimpse of the shadow and reacting with an attempt to eliminate it by resolution rather than understanding. But, of course, all this strategy achieves is a repression of his own aggressive impulses, which had now turned in against himself and were contributing to his sense of depression and bodily symptoms. It is always a shock to discover that an exercise of will ('I won't be that way any more') does not eliminate the problem, it simply relocates it. This dream provided the man with an opportunity to come to grips with his shadow side, a very typical type of shadow, reflecting a personification of unacceptable feelings to his conscious mind in the form of the three bikies. The dream locates the 'bikies' on the first-floor level, perhaps indicating that the aggressive, negative feelings were not on the conscious level, but at least only one floor above or beyond consciousness. In this sense, these feelings are not buried deeply in an inaccessible cellar, but simply waiting in his pre-conscious mind for him to climb the stairs of awareness and face them.

Another brief dream that captures the more orthodox and straightforward view of the shadow figures can be seen in the following dream of a thirty-nine-year-old man experiencing a mid-life transition, which took the form of loss of direction and uncertainty about the future. He had built up a very successful business, which now threatened to devour him by its seemingly never-ending demands. A Jungian personality type test revealed that he was an introverted sensation-thinking type, which suggests that his conscious orientation to the world was practical, detailed, careful, and logical: an excellent problem-solver. However, this ego-conscious development of his practical and logical side had reached a point where it was out of balance. The following brief dream that he had is an apposite comment on this imbalance. He dreamed of himself on an island, being invaded and under attack from a group of Japanese emerging out of the sea. In the dream he realised that he had to stab them in order to protect himself.

His own thoughts concerning the image of the Japanese was that he regarded them as extremely task-orientated people, very efficient and businesslike. Here we find these very qualities attacking him as they emerge out of the sea of unconsciousness. In other words, the Japanese are symbols of foreign feelings in himself concerning the negative or dark face of his consciously developed, practical and efficient values. The dream further indicates, by its location of him as the dream ego, that his conscious development is isolated like an island in the vast sea of the unconscious, and that this probably represents the insularity of his attitudes and singleminded development of only one side of his personality. Presumably, deeper in the sea, below or behind the Japanese, reside anima images, sea serpents or mermaids perhaps, which lie in wait until the 'Japanese' have destroyed his defences and then invade his consciousness. Hence the critical importance of coming to grips with the dark side of his efficiency and pragmatism, the side that had insulated or isolated him from feelings and the feminine principle. Failure to do this would leave him wide open to what Jung referred to earlier as anima possession, which in this man's case took the form of moodiness and depressive feelings. The danger is that he may attempt to ward off these negative, anima-type feelings by a further, more vigorous pursuit of efficiency, rendering him more vulnerable to an attack from the shadow figures within. Thus the cycle would only continue; perhaps ending only in cardiac arrest. What was needed was some form of accommodation of the 'Japanese', by facing them and thereby reclaiming a bit more land back from the sea; that is, an increase in consciousness out of the unconsciousness. In many respects, increasing the size of the island, the metaphor of reclamation, is a very precise image for the journey of individuation. Freud himself used the same metaphor when discussing the goal of psychoanalysis as being akin to the draining of the Zuider Zee (now Ijsselmer), which literally involved the draining of a large inlet of the North Sea.

When one turns to the shadow figures in women's dreams, then I think a slightly different pattern can be detected. How widespread this pattern is and to what extent it is an artefact of the dreams I have had access to is impossible at this stage to say. However, over all, it does seem to me less common to find shadow images in a female's dreams that are not in some way involved with an animus image. One could speculate that a reason for this might be that the animus image in women is, as a consequence of the past twenty-five years of the women's movement, closer to consciousness than is the anima in males. This might mean that it is more frequently interacting with shadow aspects, which could serve as an explanation for the more militant version of feminism that regards males as a form of social disease. In this case a negative shadow aspect of aggression may well be unconsciously joined to an animus image, producing a form of righteous animosity. One therefore is left wondering whether the animus in women might have been awakened prematurely before shadow issues had been faced.

In saying this, I do not wish to imply that one never does come across dreams of females in which the shadow is not interacting with an animus image. The following dream is a clear example of such a shadow. The dreamer is a thirty-seven-year-old professional woman:

I'm in a train with other people whom I know in the dream but are not in my outside life. It is as if I am being held captive—I'm there against my will. There are conductors who are also acting as guards—dressed in buttercup yellow zipped up the front uniform type dresses, they remind me of the tramways uniform. All are women.

The train is moving through a cityscape which is familiar to me in my dream world though not in my outside reality. Building, bridges and a particular river scene. This train is like a genuine subway train—more like the Paris Metro rather than Vicrail—the train has mostly standing room and is quite austere. The city too might be Paris.

I decided I must move from the carriage I am in at the back of the train to the front of the train. One of the people I am with comes with me the others remain behind in this rear carriage. They stay behind because they do not want to take the risk of moving up to the front of the train.

I know that this move (to the front of the train) will make things somehow different for me but also that it is risky. I will be putting myself in a position of great vulnerability. I think it will also give me the opportunity for escape, to get off the train and away from the yellow conductresses. . . .

The dream continued with the dreamer finally passing the yellow conductresses and alighting from the train when it stops because of an obstacle on the track. However, the part of the dream recorded above reveals a good example of a shadow figure. It begins

143

in a very precise manner by alerting the dreamer to the fact that she knows the figures in the dream, but not 'in my outside life'. Thus the opening scene establishes that these shadow figures are not known by the dreamer in her ordinary, everyday, waking life. We further see that she is being held captive, so part of herself is imprisoned by the shadow figures, who appear in the dream as conductresses-cum-guards. The statement that they 'are all women' confirms the shadow quality of the figures. The figures of conductresses brings to mind the person who collects the fares, the toll due, so to speak, and hence authorises people to travel on the transport concerned. The figures seem to be blocking the dreamer's progress, holding her captive, perhaps waiting to be paid the appropriate fare, which will enable the dreamer to progress. The due fare, perhaps, is simply one of recognising the shadow aspects, confronting them, and then continuing the journey towards the front of the train. The dream provides a fine example of the sort of detail we are capable of while dreaming. Here we see that the conductresses' uniforms are very specific, they are 'buttercup yellow zipped up the front uniform type dresses'. Two features stand out in this description: one the colour and secondly that they are uniforms. At the simplest level, one could say of 'buttercup yellow' that it is bright, joyful, outgoing, and therefore extroverted. Within Jungian psychology, yellow is sometimes associated with the intuitive function, or, as Cirlot puts it:

Yellow, the colour of the far seeing sun, which appears bringing light out of an inscrutable darkness only to disappear again into the darkness.

In this definition we can readily associate intuition to being that 'flash of insight' that folklore so often refers to it as. So from this we can also deduce that these figures of the conductresses are some form of intuition, but negative, in so far as they behave as guards, blocking the dreamer's progress towards the front part of the train. Indeed, they hold her captive. As the dreamer is a very intuitive woman, the guards appear to represent the shadow side of her superior function, the unacceptable aspects associated with her consciously developed identity.

The symbol of 'uniforms' seems an apt metaphor for uniformity, all the same, conformity, stereotyped, and socially acceptable attitudes. Does this mean, then, that what is holding this dreamer up is an unconscious tendency to seek conformity and social approval? From the dream itself we have the symbol of a 'genuine subway'; that is, no pretending unconscious factor. On the contrary, the vehicle is genuinely underground, and what is more, she locates it in another country. She is also aware in the dream that a 'move to the front of the train will make things somehow different' and that she 'will be putting herself in a position of great vulnerability'. Nevertheless, she also knows that she must move from the back of the train to the front. Thus it could be inferred that moving from the rear of the train, where the guard is, towards the front is a move towards the driver of the train, that aspect of herself that controls and directs the vehicle in which she is travelling. In this sense the movement she feels she must make is towards consciousness, the need to bring into consciousness her own intuitive strengths, with the attendant psychological task of confronting her own shadow to conform, which in this sense could equally well be seen as a persona image. But she realises in the dream that, although it will make her vulnerable, this exposure also facilitates her escape from the guards. We can see, in this dream, the validity of Jung's words quoted earlier, regarding the courage required to confront the shadow. Indeed the dreamer is aware of this when she dreams that others — that is, other aspects of herself — remain behind because they do not want to take the risk of moving up to the front of the train. Perhaps it is inevitably more comfortable not to acknowledge one's shadow, since as Jung once said in relation to withdrawing shadow projection:

If you imagine someone who is brave enough to withdraw all these projections, then you get an individual who is conscious of a considerable shadow. Such a man [woman] has saddled himself [herself] with new problems and conflicts. He [she] has become a serious problem to himself [herself], as he [she] is now unable to say that *they* do this or that, *they* are wrong, and *they* must be fought against . . . such a man [woman] knows that, whatever is wrong, in the world is in himself [herself].

In this dreamer's case the temptation might be to complain about others being too conservative or stereotyped, and to project the blame for not developing her own creative potential onto others. As Jung said, when she realises it is herself, then she is faced with a new problem and a new responsibility. The dreamer seems acutely aware of this within the dream, when she speaks of the vulnerability of moving forward. But the 'moving forward' seems inevitable and, as Søren Kierkegaard was quoted as saying: 'To venture causes anxiety, but not to venture is to lose oneself.' The final part of this same dream demonstrates the dreamer's determination to venture.

I move up the train to the very front carriage, past the yellow conductresses one at the entry-exit to every carriage. I am determined and they do not try to bar my way.

This part of the dream points to the dreamer's willingness and determination to confront the conforming shadow, which functions as a guard and further indicates that, unconsciously, the appropriate time has probably arrived to carry out this confrontation.

As already mentioned, it seems increasingly common to find shadow and animus images together in female dreams, and the dream to be discussed next

146

is a good example of this phenomenon. The dreamer is a forty-five-year-old woman, recently divorced, whose inferior function was thinking, and hence she was constantly anxious about proving herself in her chosen profession of teaching. The previous marriage had, it seemed to me from her account, damaged her already frail sense of confidence and further pushed thinking into an inferior or repressed position. Hence the approval of male authority figures was, on the one hand, of considerable importance to her and, on the other, a source of constant annoyance and irritation. She was a daughter of a patriarch. Here, then, is her dream:

I was standing outside an old terrace house, a free standing one since either side had been demolished. I met John D. and he comments to me how good I am for working so hard and as a reward he offers to get me a new typewriter. Immediately he rings up a friend of his and does a deal and I know all along that I do not need a typewriter because I already have a new modern electronic printer. But I don't tell John and just say 'Oh. That would be nice'. The model he finally gets me is a traditional out of date one nowhere near as good as the one I already have and I have to pay for it!

The dreamer's own association to John D. was that he was a 'typical insurance salesman'. By this she meant in the dream that John D. represented a patriarchal sort of male, who regards females as an inferior species who provide him with the opportunity for being patronising. Yet it is to this man in the dream that she so weakly submits, and so finishes up with an outmoded typewriter she doesn't need and has to pay for. It is very difficult in this dream not to be struck by the theme of the dreamer's submissiveness to the male image. So despite her outward appearance, at times of confidence, unconsciously the dream indicates that the dreamer's shadow is powerfully submissive. A possible clue to this lies in the location of the dream, a freestanding terrace house. Now terrace houses as such belong in a terrace: a row of houses joined together. Yet, the dream image is that of a 'freestanding one', since either side has been demolished. Equally important is it to note that the action in the dream is reported as taking place within the freestanding terrace. As an image, it conveys the sense of being disconnected, separate, unattached, and inappropriately freestanding. This can be seen as a metaphorical way of seeing that this woman's tendency to be overly submissive to males takes place in a separate, disconnected part of her psyche, which has no side support. Perhaps the behaviour once belonged to a 'terrace', so to speak; a whole set of connected attitudes, but now it stands alone. This could reflect the effects on this woman's psyche of the women's movement, which has demolished the supporting beliefs that perpetuated her denigrated position as a woman, but still standing firm is an attitude of submission, a freestanding terrace of submission, so to speak. We can also see in this dream that simply agreeing with John D. results in her not valuing her own equipment — a modern electronic printer. It takes very little imagination to play with the symbol of a modern electronic printer. Immediately communication and words spring to mind, and this equipment is far superior in the dream to the one she so meekly accepts from John D. In other words, her own thinking capacity derived and generated from within her feminine self is more modern and superior to the thinking determined by outmoded patriarchal values. Yet the struggle for this woman is to reclaim her Yang qualities, to free herself from the tyranny of being a daughter of the patriarch. While this complex, fundamentally a father complex, resides in a 'freestanding terrace', it will, in all probability, go on acting autonomously. She needs to reintegrate it with the rest of her psyche, re-own her own thinking capacity and restore the terraces in which it is currently located. Therapy for this woman resulted in considerable progress in this area, slowly but surely moving her towards accepting the challenge to develop the inferior function of thinking from within herself and not simply have it as a persona that rendered her so vulnerable to seeking the approval of males in the outside world. In re-owning her Yang qualities, she was, at the same time, able to value herself better and thereby have fewer periods of despair and depression. But for many women the tendency to be submissive to males, particularly in the realm of thinking, remains an isolated and autonomous terrace within their own psyche. Often associated with the task of re-owning or restoring their thinking, their rational capacity, is a fear that in so doing, they will damage their femininity. This fear reflects the strength of the social conditioning that thinking and femininity do not belong together. The reverse situation is often true for men: the fear that if they re-own their feeling side, they will damage or diminish their masculinity. Society has exerted a powerful effect on us, dividing us within ourselves, a situation we need no help to do, resulting in a divided house, a harsh polarity between masculine and feminine, between Yin and Yang.

A final dream, which further demonstrates the interaction between a shadow image and the animus, is one of a fifty-year-old female, who is a health care professional. This dream is an initial dream, which she had the night before she saw me for the first time and which she brought to therapy. She was seeking assistance concerning much confusion and unhappiness regarding her marriage and underlying feelings of depression. The dream is as follows:

I am in a small office talking with P.O'C. There is a modern dark wooden desk (really a plank of wood) almost across the width of a room. I am behind the desk, P.O'C. the other side and there is a door behind him. We were talking in a friendly manner. Suddenly his secretary opens the door, doesn't address either of us and stretches across the desk and puts something down or takes something away. She is a tall, thin, blonde, wrinkled and middle aged and unfriendly (officious). When she leaves P.O'C. says to me we have to be careful of our clothes. She will report on wrong clothes. He moves around beside me to quietly tell me this so that his secretary won't hear.

Then there is a plate of scones on the table (desk) about three and a white plate with little geometric pieces of margarine covered in brightly coloured silver paper (squares and triangles). P.O'C. has a scone but no margarine and doesn't offer me any. While quietly telling me something I move near he says or indicates, 'Don't' as his secretary is there next door. The secretary is now sitting next door having lunch with a friend and the door between us is slightly ajar.

P.O'C.'s wife came into the dream. I can see her standing half turned away with her head down. She was slight and slim with straight reddish blonde hair. Did Peter or did I say we had to be proper because of his wife? Was she crying or did I want her to as I had known what it was like to cry? The tenor of the dream seemed that P.O'C. was rather scared of not doing the correct thing.

The first point to make concerning this dream is to state what has already been stated several times in connection to dreams: that is, they are a symbolic language, and thus the P.O'C. in this woman's dream must be seen as a symbolic expression of something she has not yet understood. To take it as a literal description of me is to miss the point entirely. Furthermore, this dream was immediately prior to her first consultation, so the P.O'C. of the dream has to be a projection, since at that time she had seen me only in passing, at a lecture. But, like most initial dreams brought to therapy, it contains a very rich and yet

150

practical picture of the problems to be focused upon. Of most interest, at this stage, is the role of the shadow figure, which is clearly seen in the dream image of the secretary, and the relationship between this image and that of the animus, personified by me.

The dreamer herself had, via a Jungian typology test, described herself as introverted, sensation, feeling type. Thus, in the inferior position, were the thinking and intuitive functions. Her conscious development of the sensation and feeling quality have been a major asset in her professional life and also the basis of a past satisfactory marriage relationship, in which purposefulness and the accomplishment of tasks were the main characteristics. Her own associations concerning the image of me in the dream were that she considered me intuitive and 'clever', the latter presumably referring to the thinking function. Regardless of whether I have either of these traits, the important point is that the P.O'C. image in the dream is this woman's animus image, and here we see it carrying the inferior function into consciousness, hence its 'personality' is one of an intuitive/thinking type.

The dream, then, concerns the relationship between the dreamer, her shadow, and the animus. The relationship initially seems to be going well, although the animus and the dreamer are on opposites sides of the desk. Then we find that hiatus word (which was discussed in chapter 5, on 'Meeting the Dream'), the word 'suddenly', appears in the dream. At this point, this watershed moment, the secretary opens the door, and from then on the relationship between the dreamer and the animus image becomes difficult and awkward. One is left wondering what might have happened if 'suddenly' the secretary hadn't opened the door. But for the purposes of the present dream she did, and we see in the dream that she is, above all else, a very officious lady, and she behaves in a powerful, threatening, and intimidatory manner. So, this woman has such a shadow aspect operating behind the scenes, which acts towards her in this way, an inner voice that constantly puts her down, behaves in an intimidatory way towards her conscious view of herself, and accuses her of being self-indulgent and full of self-pity. The dreamer was dimly aware of these thoughts within herself.

The setting of the dream focuses on therapy, and thereby points to the seeking of help from the intuitive thinking aspect of herself. It is interesting to note that she places the action 'in a small office', as if the dream is indicating her devaluing of this entire process. It is also as if she needs therapy or healing from these functions, with the ultimate aim of wholeness. Her professional and personal life had both enabled and resulted in an inner division between the outer world and inner world, with confidence being strong only in the outer space. But in the dream the situation is such that this very officious secretary literally comes between the animus image and herself. Thus we see that this must also be happening within her: the officiousness and efficient orderliness and downright bossiness is coming between her ego-conscious self and contact with her intuitive-thinking self; that is, this negative shadow is inhibiting her contact with the animus and thereby retarding the development of her intuitive capacity.

The nature of this interference, or barrier, between her ego-conscious self and the animus is clearly exemplified in the dream. Firstly, the P.O'C. or therapist image, the animus, warns her about clothes and the danger of the secretary reporting them for wearing the wrong clothes. Clothes are something we put on, cover our nakedness with, attempt to conform to. In short, clothes represent the persona or face we show to the outer world. Thus the officious secretary part of this woman, this negative shadow, is determining what attitudes this woman will display or exhibit to the world and is thereby curtailing the development of any alternative. In short, she is being ruled by an inner tyrant, who resides 'behind' the animus, so she is directing the psychic show from an unconscious, out-of-sight spot. The animus image is very threatened by her, since he speaks to the dreamer in such a manner as to prevent the secretary from hearing. The dreamer also notes at the end of the dream that the animus, personified by me, seems 'rather scared of not doing the correct thing'. Again this highlights the extent to which this woman's behaviour is dominated by a negative, bossy shadow, which operates and exercises power from behind and, further, always manages to keep the 'door ajar', just in case the dreamer should form a relationship with the animus.

She also seems uncertain about another dream image, and that is the image of the wife of P.O'C., who in the dream could be seen as another shadow figure, related to the animus, but a shadow that seems also to be intimidated since she is 'half turned away with her head down'. In this instance, it seems as if it is the dreamer herself, her ego-conscious attitude, that has something to do with the suppression of the wife of the animus. In the dream she asks whether she is behaving 'proper', because of this figure and, further, she wants her to cry because 'I had known what it was like to cry'. She seems anxious about this image, careful not to upset her any further, as it is related to the animus image, this figure may well represent the proverbial 'other half' of the intuitive aspect of this woman. The 'other half' of intuition is sometimes playfulness, spontaneity, joy, activities, and attitudes, behind which one finds the god Eros. In this sense one could say that the dreamer had suppressed her own sense of joy and spontaneity and this shadow had now got 'married' to the animus, with both of them living in the unconscious mind, intimidated by the secretary, who was acting as a sort of psychic landlady.

For this person, the dream indicated that the therapeutic work initially needed to focus on the 'secretary'. Her own elaboration of this shadow image led her to remember a nun who had been the 'mistress of discipline' in her Catholic boarding-school days. The dreamer had been in boarding-school from the age of twelve, and throughout the entire period of her adolescence she had been subjected to an authoritarian regime that had resulted in a severe repression of her spontaneity (hence the wife of the animus). This, in turn, had psychologically compounded her difficulties in making contact with the animus within herself and with the attributes of intuition and thinking. The 'mistress of discipline' was, in fact, the secretary, her negative shadow, which had taken shape in the boarding-school that she had attended as an adolescent. The shadow now, as an unconsious force, contributed to the dreamer's hopeless and depressed feelings about her future direction. Just as the 'secretary' disrupted the therapy in the dream, so also did she attempt to do it in outer life, by cultivating within the individual feelings of hopelessness about therapy itself. With the insight provided from the initial dream, the dreamer improved her chances of spotting the 'secretary' when she arrived in the room, so her power could be lessened. The long-term aim will be to build a relationship with the animus's wife of the dream, to built a relationship to the dreamer's own sense of joy, spontaneity, and Eros, as a necessary preliminary for bridging the gap between the animus and the ego-conscious self. Perhaps, then, the animus might even offer her a scone! Even if the door is ajar!

In situations such as this the therapist's role is very often one of initially providing an outer model for the animus and of challenging and confronting the inner secretary when she threatens to disrupt the therapeutic relationship. As the ancient alchemical dictum, reputedly from the Emerald Table of Hermes, states: 'What is below is like that which is above.' Similarly, what is outside is like that which is inside; hence recognising some of our own projections in the outer world is a major step in the journey towards wholeness. For this person, recognising that P.O'C. is not the intuitive-thinking person, but that she herself is, will be a large step forward in her psychological journey. However, the first task, an onerous one in itself, is to be aware of the secretary or mistress of discipline, the negative shadow within herself. It is only by finding the strength and courage to be aware of our shadow side that we can ever hope to make contact with the contrasexual images in ourselves, the anima and animus, to which we now turn.

8
THE MAN OF YOUR DREAMS –
ANIMUS

In chapter 6, on 'A Map for the Journey', the
animus was discussed, with specific reference to the
two faces of this image. Animus, the male image in
a female psyche, was seen to have both a personal
face and an archetypal one. These faces were related
to the personal unconscious and to the collective
unconscious, and the animus image was located as
living on the borderline of these two psychic territo-
ries. This present chapter will focus on the personal
face of the animus, as it is seen in the dreams of
women today. More specifically, the context within
which this face will be discussed is that of the mid-
life transition. There are several reasons for this
context, the simplest being that most of my professional experience has been with adults at or around
the mid-life transition. But, more profoundly, this is
the time when the soul calls the person back into
herself or himself, a calling to pursue the Kierkegaardian vocation to become oneself.

   Mid-life, that period between thirty-five and forty-
five, in my opinion, is that critical period in adult
development when we have an opportunity either to
continue to develop psychologically or to accept the

alternative of psychological death, of losing our soul. Dreams form a vital link to the living process, and provide the bridge, inspiration, and food for the continuance of the journey, the movement towards Self. For most adults, the commencement of mid-life is heralded in by the loss of meaning, which within the thesis of this book is the loss of a sense of connection between inner and outer worlds, a failure to convert or transmute events into experiences, a process that takes place through soul or imagination. The loss that individuals become aware of in mid-life very often appears first in connection with their work, whether that be inside or outside the home. This loss simply reflects the fact that the image or images of themselves that have provided a link to their work are no longer capable of doing so, since they have lost their relevance. The images of oneself become atrophised and, as imagination is a way of seeing, it is tantamount to saying that the way we see ourselves in the world becomes irrelevant and inappropriate. Primarily, mid-life ushers in a period of reckoning where one is compelled to face the psychological facts of ageing, change, death, and, above all else, the passing of time. This experience places a strain on the way of seeing that we have utilised and on the images that have moved and sustained us. This is simply because the images belong to the past. Our imaginal modes were determined initially and set in action by parents in childhood. Hence the common situation of the death of a parent coinciding with the mid-life period symbolically represents the potential ending of the parental images that have directed our lives. The struggle in the mid-life transition is essentially a struggle to re-create meaning by reworking old images or ways of seeing, re-assembling, re-constructing, and expanding soul. This work requires, in the first place, recognition of and reflection upon the extent to which our images are dominated by our early childhood experiences and unconscious memories of this. Since,

157

as Hillman reminds us, '. . . through experiencing the unconscious I gain soul'.

The following excerpt from the dream of a thirty-seven-year-old woman highlights the phenomenon of the past and its influence on our imaginal world or ways of seeing.

I enter a theatre. I am with two female friends and I am expecting to meet my mother. We find seats and sit down. I have a seat for my mother on my right and soon she comes and joins us.

I am carrying a navy blue handbag, reminiscent of the 1940s, onto which are tied, by a length of black cord, four pairs of spectacles. They all have black rims. I put on a pair, which turn out to be like spectacles within spectacles. The inner frames obscure my vision. I comment on this to my mother with some surprise. She points out to me that everyone in the theatre audience has on these similar black rimmed spectacles.

The play begins. The cast appears to be all female—they are dressed in an army uniform and have on hard helmets. They are manoeuvring a huge gun which has a nozzle 15 to 20 feet long. They are attempting to blow up a school which is at the back of the stage. However, there is much buffoonery in their attempt and instead of hitting the school, they shell a much closer building, near to which their leader is standing. She chides them and acclaims their gross incompetence. The scene has a quality of a melodrama.

There is much in this dream. However, for the present purposes, I shall simply focus on salient points. The initial setting of a dream is invariably critical. In this case it is set in a theatre. In its simplest terms this is a place where life is in the form of images, but it is also a public place; so it becomes a place where images are made public. Thus the dream 'locates' the issue in the dreamer's psyche as being about public images, shared images, collective images.

It is also important to note that the dreamer saves a seat for her mother, and when the mother joins the dreamer, the issue of the spectacles begins. The tying of the spectacles to a 1940s handbag is important, since it indicates that the way of seeing is tied to the 1940s values, since in handbags one carries valuables, those things that are valued. Thus the dream is indicating that the dreamer's images are tied to her mother's 1940s values, since in discussing the dream she associate the handbag with one of her mother's handbags. The effect of the spectacles through which she looks is to obscure her vision, but her mother — i.e. her mother's values — reassure her that everyone is wearing the same glasses, everyone is seeing things in the same way.

Further, the dream indicates that this 'same way' is to see women, dressed up as men, being clowning buffoons. The dreamer, being dominated by her mother's values and images, will tend to see the taking on of the masculine principle, the Yang-like quality, as a form of melodrama, as a move that is destined to highlight incompetence. Over all, the dream itself highlights the challenge for this dreamer, to take off the 1940s spectacles, her mother's values, and begin the task of re-imagining herself so as to include her Yang qualities as legitimate parts, a necessary drama, not a melodrama.

This dream captures the phenomenon of images determining what we see, not only in ourselves, but in others. If, then, we are to see more of ourselves, and as a consequence more of others, then attending to the restrictive and inappropriate images from the past becomes essential. It is as if the ways in which we see both ourselves and the world are through frozen images, frozen in time, which need to be thawed out and reformed. These frozen and fixed images are unable to transmute the changing events of life into experiences, and the inevitable consequence is one of strain, as events simply do not conform to the internal pictures. Some people adapt to this strain between images and events by simply denying that the strain exists at all. So the mid-life man denies his feelings of depression and loss, and says to himself that all he needs is more exercise, or another promotion. Or the woman whose youngest child has just gone to school, instead of facing the void created by the loss of full-time mothering, will fill the empty space with undue activity. The purpose of this constant movement is to protect her from facing the fact that the image of mother is now not enough to facilitate the next development in her soul.

What is required at this time of transition between images is a thawing of the old, frozen images, a process that can be achieved by bringing the underlying images into consciousness, whereby new choices can be made. The dreams of people in mid-life constantly present this opportunity in the form of anima and animus images. This thawing of old images also involves a return to earlier periods in life, when these images were first fixed and frozen. This fixing, in the main, occurs at two major periods, a period between five and six years of age, which Freud called the Oedipal period, and adolescence. These two periods stand out because they are critical times for the development of identity, times when we struggle with the question 'Who am I?' The Oedipal period involves the sexual identity and the alignment with the parent of the same sex, whereas adolescence involves the broader question of ego-identity and values. Mid-life is, following adolescence, the next major identity-crisis period, so it seems logical and natural that the psyche would return to earlier periods in order to check out what was left unresolved. The anima and animus images are very often guides in this journey back to the Oedipal period or adolescence, since they appear as images that draw our attention to choices that were made and losses that resulted from the choices. Prior to the influence to the women's liberation movement, many females, at thirteen and fourteen years of age, found themselves diverted from what were perceived to be masculine fields, such as sciences and mathematics. Many a very intelligent female found herself condemned to areas of learning that really were of no interest to her. Thus the mid-life period brings an opportunity to return, to explore the formation of these images, the choices that were made, and to re-form one's images in the light of current needs and aspirations. This return is personified in the animus image.

The following dream of a thirty-seven-year-old, recently divorced woman demonstrates this return to adolescence:

> *A train journey—I had the feeling that I was in the Blue Mountains in New South Wales, although there was no usual evidence for that in the dream. I was with a man—unclear, except that I think he was tall. He was carrying some luggage, perhaps a bag in one hand and something under his arm.*
>
> *I remember us going through several turnstyles as in the underground—it was fairly dark and gloomy, not like the one in Melbourne more like the London subways.*
>
> *I remember a dark downhill sloping passageway and looking at the subway map to see which line we had to go on—and it was right to the end of the Central Line.*
>
> *At one point as we were walking along he said that he didn't have any money—I remember feeling annoyed but said I would buy the tickets anyway.*
>
> *Changed then to me walking along a bright open platform with a red train at the station—a 'Red Rattler'. I remember looking in the windows—some of the carriages were 'dog boxes' and others were more open. I had been in that train before because I had had two rectangular manilla envelopes which I had left on the seat thinking 'I will be coming back*

so I will leave these here.' I was looking in the
window trying to find the envelopes but I couldn't see
them on the right seat—it was a central seat on the
left of the compartment as I looked in. There were
a lot of people on the train. In the end I had to get
in anyway, anywhere, without finding the right
place as the train was going to leave.

The opening scene of this dream immediately
introduces an animus image, and is located in the Blue
Mountains of New South Wales. I have often found
that the dream world establishes time by using place,
since place 'locates' the action in the context of our
individual history. For this woman, the association
with the Blue Mountains was that she had been there
some two or three years prior to this dream and had
met a man there, and this had signalled the beginning of the end of her marriage, although she had not
in fact become involved with this particular man. One
conclusion that could be drawn is that the dream indicates the task of building a relationship to the inner
man, and that this has something to do with ending
the projection onto her husband; as it turned out,
ending the marriage. Another way of expressing this
is to say that the 'real marriage' is to the opposite
within ourselves, what could be termed the vertical
as opposed to the horizontal or conscious marriage
to one's external spouse.

The dream indicates that this man is tall and carrying some luggage. The dream world, in compensating for our conscious attitudes, will sometimes
depict the dream images in the opposite manner
or form to our conscious view. So the 'tall' can be seen
as reflecting the fact that the woman had underesti-
mated the role of her masculine principle, or her
competence in the outer world. She was a very feeling, intuitive woman, and the thinking and sensation
qualities were relatively underdeveloped. Hence her
sense of confidence in her rational–practical self was
low. Two other factors stand out about the man in

the dream. Firstly, he does not have an identity: she does not and subsequently in discussion did not recognise him. This is a metaphorical way of saying that she does not recognise the masculine image and principle within herself. Secondly, he is carrying luggage, which, when taken imaginatively, refers to carrying psychological luggage, perhaps baggage from the past, a load from other aspects of the personality. The effect is that this image is probably carrying some rejected feelings from the past, and by bringing the image into consciousness these feelings will be recognised and unloaded and the animus will then be free to use his hands!

The dreamer then finds herself in a subway, and the specific reference is to a London subway, which relates to the fact that in her early years of marriage she lived in London. Not uncommonly, women lose contact with their animus when they marry, because they project it onto their husbands and 'forget' that it is part of themselves. The animus literally goes underground! Together with the man, she reads the map and discovers that 'the line we had to go on' was the Central Line. Immediately one is struck by the possible play on words, so that the 'line we had to go on' becomes the line to take, so to speak; and this, the dream indicates, is the central one. Again the 'Central Line' implies the middle way, the integrative part, the line of reconciliation of opposites. However, having discovered which line to take, she also discovers that he doesn't have any money and she somewhat irritably offers to purchase his ticket. It is as if, in discovering the way, she also discovers that the animus has been impoverished, no money, which is the dream's way of indicating that it has no value. She, in turn, is forced to give it value, to buy its ticket, so that she can have the animus accompany her on the journey. By not valuing her own thinking qualities, she cannot continue the journey with the animus, and thus would have perhaps gone on alone, with half of her left in the unconscious awaiting recognition and value. This would have left her open to invasion by the Yang qualities, and such women can then become very opinionated and animus possessed.

It is the agreeing to buy the ticket for the animus, agreeing to take it on board, so to speak, that seems to act as the change point in the dream, and suddenly the dreamer finds herself out in the open. A way of thinking about this is that in recognising the value of the animus, in paying the due fare, the dreamer gains a renewed sense of consciousness; that is, finds herself out in an open sunny spot, no longer in the dark underground. What then happens out in the open and sunny spot points to the quality of this renewal of awareness. Essentially, the action of the dream then concerns what the dreamer terms a 'Red Rattler' and the two lost manilla envelopes. Her association to the 'Red Rattlers' and 'dog boxes' is to a specific type of train, which ran in Melbourne when she grew up in the late 1950s and 1960s. During this time she was an adolescent and used to travel to secondary school on such trains. So this section of the dream seems to refer to her adolescent journey and, as the dream so clearly indicates, she left something behind. Perhaps the thing she left behind is indicated by the association of the dream to her secondary schooling; that is, she left behind a belief and value in her own intellectual ability. She nevertheless finds herself thinking in the dream 'I will be coming back so I will leave these here', and she now is searching for them. Symbolically, this clearly reflects the phenomenon of the mid-life transition, requiring a going-back to adolescence to see what we have left behind, what psychological business remains unfinished and needs to be completed. She did not have any specific associations to the manilla envelopes. However, one could imagine that these would have contained some form of communication, messages, perhaps even official messages, since government authorities often use such manilla envelopes. What she felt she had left behind in adolescence, was, as already mentioned, a confidence in her intellectual ability, a confidence she is now attempting to reclaim. In this sense she reflects the regularly recurring situation of so many young women of the 1960s, who were often discouraged from continuing their further education. Many of these women, under the internal pressure of the animus, find their way back to tertiary education at or around the mid-life period as an expression of the need to redress the imbalance occurring around adolescence.

The panic at the end of the dream, the dreamer felt, reflected the pressure she found herself under at the time of the dream, to get her life organised. She had left her husband and was being subjected to considerable pressure to 'sort herself out'. This pressure seems to be forcing her to undertake the journey before she is really ready. The risk at this time was that, once again, she would lose contact with the animus qualities, which potentially held for her a sense of competence in her problem-solving ability. As it turned out, this did not happen and she was able to withstand the pressure and give herself more time to work through these very complex issues.

The scene in this dream of the animus being impoverished and not being given value is a theme that frequently occurs in the dreams of women around mid-life. The themes of neglect, dereliction, and emaciation of either anima or animus images reflect the dreamer's lack of attention to the attributes contained within these images. The following dream of a forty-year-old married woman who had experienced a very orthodox and strict Christian upbringing provides a vivid example of the theme of neglect. In outer life she was a nursing sister, and she had developed considerable sensation and thinking abilities as her superior and auxiliary functions, qualities that have mistakenly, as mentioned before, been

165

associated exclusively with the animus image. In fact, for this woman, as for the woman who had the efficient secretary dream, the mid-life task is to build a relationship to her inferior function, which in this case was feeling. Hence one would expect the animus image to represent this function by being an image of a male with whom the dreamer associated feeling qualities. As it stands, the dream does not do this. However, the context of the dream, that ever-important quality, does throw some light on the issue. Her own recollection of the context was that she had this dream around the time that the Catholic missionary priest Father Brian Gore was being released from prison in the Philippines, after being found not guilty of murder, a false charge that was related to perceived dissident political activity. Her own thoughts about Father Gore were that he was a compassionate and warm man, observations confirmed by the priest's life and activities.

The dream world seized upon this outer event and used it to convey into consciousness the dreamer's repression of her own feeling function. It is interesting that she chose a priest, a figure that would be consistent with her own Christian ethos, and therefore enabled the integration of the image. Further, it is interesting to note the confirmation of the theory that the animus image is not exclusively tied to sensation and thinking, but that its role at the personal level is to convey into consciousness the inferior function. Here then is the dream:

I think I see horses and a carriage going along a street. Then I am at a jail. I hear that a well known dissident is going to be released. I hear that Channel 7 has got the rights to film his release. I go in the back, there are two big pens. I open the gate, or is it opened for me? I go to the man. He is cloaked and has a big hood. He turns, his face is a long way down. I recoil, because he is so emaciated. His arms are skin and bone. (I feel a mixture of revulsion and compassion.)

As I am standing there a horse and cart, or two horses and carts, back up to the gate where the prisoner will come out. He seems to be in the shafts of the cart, or have the shafts on him and I see that he intends to connect to the horse and cart with his shafts. He is so weak I wonder what will happen. Somehow, he is connected either by his shafts or by people helping him (who are on the horse and cart). Then I see him hauling himself into the cart and they drive off.

The link to the outer image of Father Brian Gore is obvious, and when we take into account the dreamer's own association to Father Gore, it becomes equally obvious that this is an animus image that is to do with feeling. More specifically, he is a 'dissident' in the dream, meaning he is one who dissents or disagrees with prevailing political values. Translated into this woman's life, one can see that given the strict and rigid quality of her Christian upbringing, to have had feelings would have been dissident. Hence, 'he' was jailed, imprisoned, locked away, and removed from the outer world of Christian behaviour. His appearance would have been entirely inconsistent with the persona. The unconscious choice of Father Gore as an image again establishes the amazing precision that the dream world is capable of. Not infrequently, people become defensive against this unconscious precision, this ability, as Jung would claim, of the dream to show

. . . the inner truth and reality of the patient as it really is: not as I conjecture it to be, and not as he would like it to be.

The defensiveness often takes the form of exclaiming that they know why they have dreamed of a particular person or event, because it occurred the previous day. This defensive strategy could be used against the precision of this particular dream, but the question still remains as to why, in the middle of the night, when she is asleep, does this woman choose such a particular and specific event from what had happened the previous day? If the only event that had occurred in the previous twenty-four hours for this woman was her awareness of Father Gore's release, then one could accept the view that the dream was totally determined by the outer event. But the reality is, of course, that many events occurred and the unconscious mind simply chose the one that can convey into consciousness an unfamiliar thought by using a familiar one. Hence the day residue is important, not in any literal sense, but rather as a vehicle for unconscious material about herself. This is because the dream and dreaming are not involved in adapting to environmental stress, as such, but are involved in psychological growth.

Various laboratory studies of dreaming and sleep confirm that external stimuli have no significant effect on the content of the dream. Hall, for example, found in studying the effects of a laboratory setting on dreams, when compared with dreams in the normal home setting, that no significant influence could be found regarding the laboratory environment. Indeed, in only 6.2 per cent of all dreams studied was there any indication of an incorporation of any aspects of a laboratory itself into the dream. The outer reality has to have some symbolic and unconscious links to material already existing in the psyche before it will be incorporated into the dream, not the other way round.

So the dreamer incorporated Father Gore because he was such an accurate symbol for her repressed feelings, which had been declared dissident by her fundamentalist upbringing. The action of the dream then reveals her entering the jail via the back. The back usually implies things like the back door of the mind: 'she sneaked in through the back door' is a saying that captures the fact that this is a secret, unexpected entrance, and therefore refers in her case to an unconscious awareness or meeting with the dissident. Interestingly, she is unsure, in the dream, whether the gate is opened for her, or whether she opens it herself, an indication that the material is ready to be accepted, as the gate can be seen to represent that transition between consciousness and unconsciousness. At first, when she meets him, the dream suggests his back is turned to her and it is only when he turns around that she notices his emaciation. Thus it is only when she faces the previously 'cloaked' animus that she observes the horror of his condition, and her reaction is a truly ambivalent one of revulsion and compassion: revulsion at what she, herself, has done to this part of herself, her feelings; and compassion for it because it is part of her that needs caring for. The entire theme is a poignant expression of the neglect that has ensued through her imprisonment of her own feelings.

The remainder of the dream captures the struggle of the animus image to literally 'connect up' to the vehicle that will transport him to freedom. The weak state of the prisoner raises doubts in the dreamer's mind as to whether he can attach his 'shafts' to the cart, but thankfully some other people, some other aspects of the dreamer, help him out. The seemingly odd reference to a television channel having the right to film the release may be seen as reflecting the dreamer's commitment to making this release of feelings public, to express her renewal of feelings in the outer world. Another way of looking at the involvement of the television channel is to see it as indicating a shift in the dreamer from having feelings solely in the fantasy world, to giving them expression in the outer world. As events transpired in her life, this proved to be the correct interpretation, as the dreamer became increasingly aware of and confident about her feelings, particularly the warm and affectionate side of herself. What she needed to do was to care for the dissident, feed him up by recognising him and restoring his viewpoint as a legitimate and not a dissident one. This meant, of course, a reworking and re-imagining of herself and the Christian context in which she had been reared; a reworking that would inevitably produce its own strains.

The dreamer's personal association with the horses in the dream are revealing in terms of frozen and fixed images. The image of the horses, in the dreamer, revived an old memory concerning them, which took place when she was around twelve years of age. She and her parents had been caravaning and, due to bad weather, had got caught between two mountain landslides. The ranger of the area had ridden out to see if they needed any help, and the dreamer recalled going up to the horse and touching its rear flank. Apparently this startled the horse, and it reared, resulting in the dreamer being most severely chastised by her parents. The evocation of this memory appears to confirm that she repressed her own instinctuality, her own sensuality and feelings, around the period of puberty. The memory serves not as a literal but as a symbolic statement of when, where, and how the image of herself as a feeling person became frozen, and hence the jailing and starvation of the dissident. Indeed, one could say that it literally hadn't been fed for something like twenty-eight years — little wonder that it looked emaciated. The dream again reveals that role of the animus in mid-life is to restore and rework adolescent material and images.

Both the topics of instinctuality and frozen images can be seen in the following dream of a forty-eight-year-old woman, a secretary, separated and awaiting divorce proceedings. The dream highlights the different attitudes and relationships a woman can have with her animus. The dreamer described herself on the Jungian type test as an introverted, intuitive-thinking type, with sensation as the inferior function, although the feeling function was also relatively underdeveloped. With sensation in the inferior position, along with feeling, one can theoretically expect that sensuality and the individual's relationship to his or her own body will be problematical. Often I have found that people with low or underdeveloped sensation qualities tend to have a distorted body image, and not uncommonly are uncomfortable with their body and bodily functions, which obviously includes sexuality. Hence the animus image in such a woman can be expected to have, among other qualities, an earthy, sensual one, since these are the qualities in the repressed position in these women's psyches. The animus image, therefore, needs to be recognised and renegotiated as a parallel to the woman reimagining and renegotiating her own sense of sexual identity and sensuality. Highly intuitive types have a remarkable capacity for having their best sexual life in fantasy, in daydreams, but not in their bodies! Developing the inferior function of sensation represents, at one level, a re-owning of their bodies and a reintegration of the physical with the fantasy world. Very often the reverse is true of high sensation-orientated individuals, where their sexual life runs the risk of being so physically bound that it lacks the imaginative, fantasy, or romantic quality that intuitive people are so strong on. Here, then, is the dream:

I am to have sex with a German army officer. I decide to, that is, without fight or resistance because I wanted to have sex anyway. He can't get his penis up and he has to masturbate to have an erection. Apparently we have sex (have no recall) and we are lying together, he still in me. I am on top of him. We are fully clothed and lying on the bare boards of the floor of a large empty room. A child comes past and talks to us and I to her. She is about 3 to 4 years of age. I think she will see my bare thigh but she is unperturbed about us being in this position. There is a woman

171

*somewhere in the background, a bit quizzical. He
is in his 50s with little, round, steel-rimmed
glasses, nothing vigorous or sexy about him,
unprepossessing, anaemic looking, but a big man
wearing black army uniform.*

*While we are lying there, we both have an
orgasm. He had become erect again within me,
stirred to have orgasm which set it off in me which
was beautiful for both of us. He tells me that his
name is Hanguin, pronounced with the gutteral
German 'ha' sound. He has a little difficulty in
pronouncing his name in a way that I will be able
to repeat it. I say I am Jennifer. We kiss in an act
of utmost love. No longer is he the enemy and
no longer is the meeting without life (mechanical
sex). We are both now filled with love. He can't
speak English and I can't speak German. He holds
me close and says 'Leibchin'. Dream ends there.*

This dream, like all dreams, has many possible
meanings at different levels. However, what is clear
from the dream structure itself is that it falls into
two halves. The first half in which the sexual
experience is mechanical and characterised by anon-
mity; and the second half, which is the opposite, the
sexual partner having a name and the sexual
experience itself being warm, loving, and involving.
Between these two halves lies a seemingly inconse-
quential event, albeit yet another example of a hiatus
or watershed moment in a dream. This is the
moment when the little girl walks into the room and
has a conversation with the dreamer, this scene in
the dream can be seen as dividing the dream in two,
or, alternatively, seen as residing between the two
parts of the dream.

The opening scene leaves little doubt regarding the
quality of the sexual experience. It has an unin-
volved, mechanistic tone, and the dreamer herself
has no recall as to whether she had intercourse or
not, the unconscious way of saying it was a total

non-event. For the German army officer it seems equally a boring scene, since he had to stimulate himself to achieve an erection. The overall feeling is one of a lack of involvement, lack of relationship, boring and functional. This lack of intimate feeling is further depicted in the dream by the fact that they are both fully clothed, and where they lie, where the relationship lies, is on the 'bare boards of the floor of a large empty room'. So the relationship between the dreamer and her animus, as personified by the sexual encounter with the German officer, is, to say the least, perfunctory. Seen as a metaphor of her inner world, one can see that the dreamer's relationship to her opposite functions of sensation and feeling is devoid of life, takes place on the bare boards of an empty room. In short, the dream depicts a barren relationship with her sensuous and feeling attributes. That she should choose a German officer, who in the first part of the dream has no name, reflects her non-recognition of her own animus qualities, her lack of differentiation of her feeling and sensation side'. Since an army implies a collective, a lack of individual identity, so one can assume that her sense of sensuality is lost in the collective, stereotyped, undifferentiated, and disowned aspects of herself. It has no recognisable, separate identity. Her own associations with the German officer were that she saw him as representing authority, order, organised behaviour, a lack of spontaneity, ritualistic, and institutionalised behaviour. The adjectives are an accurate description of the negative face of a sensation function, a senex-like quality, where the *modus operandi* is, above all else, order! No imagination, no *puer aeternus*, just rigidity, order, and the lack of individuality. One word probably sums up these associations, and that is 'routine'. So, at the unconscious level, the dream depicts that this woman's sensation and feeling qualities were routine, a description she confirmed applied to her marriage and hence the current divorce proceedings. Predictability had characterised her marriage, since it in turn was probably reflecting her inner relationship to the animus, a characterisation that fits many marriages when Eros has been banished to Hades.

The turning-point in the dream is the child walking into the room. Despite the dreamer's concern and anxiety, the child is actually unperturbed by the bare thigh. It is as if the child is at ease and natural regarding flesh, bodies, sex, and sexuality, and she simply carried on a conversation. The dream specifically depicts the child as three or four years of age, and in this context one could say that the last time that this woman felt at ease with her body and her feelings was around that age. Here we can see confirmation of the point made previously, that images are often frozen at two periods of life: Oedipal and adolescence. It could be said that the dreamer's acceptance of her own sensual and sexual side was arrested at this early age, around the Oedipal period, and it now has to come into the 'room' of her psyche before the dreamer's attitude towards and relationship with her animus can change. The child can also be seen as representing new growth, spontaneity, playfulness, fantasy, etc., Eros qualities that re-energise a sexual relationship. There is also another, unrecognised woman in the background, 'quizzical', perhaps another shadow figure looking on, unsure about this new development or reawakening of sexuality.

However, the appearance of the child seems to precede, perhaps even bring about the dramatic shift in the sexual relationship in the dream. Spontaneity enters the relationship, the perfunctory quality disappears, it simply 'happens' with them both experiencing orgasm. Interestingly enough, the second time the officer experiences sexual arousal while inside the dreamer; no need for masturbation to excite himself this time. It is as if the dreamer, by having the animus inside her, awakens his feelings and potency, states that he cannot feel or exhibit when condemned by projection to the anonymity of the German army! In other words, these are states that cannot be recognised when projected out onto the world.

This shared orgastic experience, the experience of fulfilling each other, results in him having a name, a separate identity. He reveals that his name is Hanguin, but, despite the German pronounciation that the dreamer insists upon, it seems highly unlikely that this is a German word. Yet, if we for the moment take cognisance of the fact that dreams very often involve clever puns, then one possible meaning of this symbol emerges. If the word is broken up and slowed down, what one gets is hang-u (you)-in, a possible reminder to the dreamer to hang in there until the feeling flows, until life or Eros flows back into her psyche. This seems precisely to be what the animus is doing in the dream, despite the abysmal quality of the first sexual encounter, he literally hangs in there, for which both are richly rewarded with a deeply satisfying experience. Does this mean in part, because of her early loss of contact with her sensation feeling qualities, that the dreamer simply aborts any real contact with the animus by being strictly mechanistic and not hanging in there? The answer is probably yes, and further that she regarded these qualities, carried by the animus, as the enemy. Now we find her saying, in the dream, 'No longer is he the enemy, and no longer is the meeting without life.' So, perceiving the animus as the enemy, by having a negative relationship to her own sensual and feeling side, the dreamer was depriving herself of 'life'; that is, Eros. It has been frozen since the age of three or four.

The thawing of Eros results in a close relationship between the dreamer and her animus, despite the fact that they do not speak each other's language, in itself an excellent pun! But perhaps the acceptance and closeness to her own physicality will transcend the difficulties of not speaking the same language. Thinking can often inhibit and interfere with one's acceptance of our instinctual urges and feelings, and intuition often provides the vehicle for these qualities to escape into the fantasy world. Thus, the closeness in the dream is more important than the language, the reality of actual physical contact transformed by the arrival of the 'child', the sense of spontaneity into the room of this dreamer's psyche.

What each of the dreams in this chapter has exemplified is the pressing urgency to make contact with the personal animus in order to bring into consciousness the repressed and underdeveloped function. In each of the dreams the loss of contact with the inferior function could be seen as occurring earlier in life, where it remained unchanged, frozen over in Hades, with no correction for the changed situation of the dreamer's life. Failure to face the animus, emaciated as he may be, is to turn one's back on individuation, a thwarting of the instinct to complete oneself, which can only result in psychological starvation and ultimately psychological death. The mid-life period is a critical turning-point in this process of restoring soul and thereby restoring energy and the imaginal way of seeing: a way of seeing that transforms mere events into experiences and heals the inner divisions within our psyche. As Jung so simply states:

   . . . healing comes from what leads the patient beyond himself and beyond his entanglements in the ego.

The recognition and building up of a relationship to the animus image lead oneself beyond ego-entanglements, by being aware that 'others' reside within the psyche other than the ego.

THE WOMAN OF YOUR DREAMS – ANIMA

What has been spoken of with respect to the animus image and its role in the psyche as a mediator between consciousness and unconsciousness is equally applicable to the anima image. Like the animus, the anima is composed of both a archetypal core and a personal associational level. At the archetypal level the anima, the female image in a male psyche, represents the deep, underlying, and unfathomable Yin element, the receptive, the darkness, the moon, and moist. Archetypally, the pattern is one of an instinct towards involvement, where Eros is the governing principle, the instinctual connectedness to other people. She can appear at the archetypal level in the guise of animals, mostly those animals that mythology assigns to certain feminine deities. So the archetypal anima quality can be represented by a cat, snake, dove, or owl, or, in the human form, as some goddess, perhaps a gypsy, a muse, saint, harlot, etc. The distinguishing feature of the archetypal level of the anima will be its numinous quality, its pointing to forces beyond the personal unconsciousness, the intrinsic pattern of the instinctual force of the eternally feminine spirit.

At the personal level the anima, like animus, seems to act as a vehicle for transmitting into consciousness the inferior function of men. As men have not as yet experienced the sexual revolution and liberation that females have, by and large the inferior function in men is related to the inner world, those aspects of the feminine principle that are concerned with feeling and intuition. A man's failure to build a relationship to his anima image most commonly manifests itself in inexplicable moodiness. If he is unable to recognise, express, and channel his feelings, then he inevitably falls prey to moodiness. As for females, mid-life for males is that critical period of adult development when they need to face the uncompleted psychological business from predominantly the period of adolescence. The anima image in a man's dream can very often provide him with both a diagnosis of his ills, his moodiness, and his irritable depression, and at the same time provide direction as to the necessary cure.

Males, more than females, seem condemned to live the first half of their lives, up until thirty-five or forty years of age, on the outside of themselves. Careers, ambition, acquisitions, prestige, power, etc., all seem to be the driving forces, attributes, and endeavours that belong to the heroic ego of their adolescence. But the pursuit of these outer goals, necessary as they may or may not be, are nevertheless at considerable cost. This cost is the loss of development of the inner world, the underdevelopment of their emotional, imaginative, and feeling life. So many men at the mid-life transition exhibit an alarming level of atrophy in their imaginative capacity. They are victims of literality experiencing a profound sense of loss, because the loss is loss of contact with their inner world. This renders them vulnerable to an excessive pursuit of outer events in the forlorn hope of transmuting some of them into experiences. However, with the imaginal world in a dormant or atrophised state, the mechanism for transforming the events into experiences simply does not exist. Finally, as the crisis of mid-life builds, they lose a sense of connection and purpose, and the inevitable result is depression.

It is at this point that the opus for the second half of life finds its most regular beginnings. As the wise old alchemists of the past knew so well, inside the lead lies silver, and inside the leaden feeling of depression lies the valuable silver of feelings. But so many men try and solve their inner malaise by exactly the same means that have brought it about in the first place. They increase their level of activity, become workaholics, buy a bigger and better car or house, take up with a mistress, increase their jogging, or combinations of all these, depending on the strength of the need to resist inner development! But as Jung reminds us in speaking of the mid-life period:

> . . . the problems that crop up at this age are no longer to be solved by the old recipes: the hand of this clock cannot be put back. What youth found and must find outside, the man of life's afternoon must find within himself . . . The transition from morning to afternoon means a revaluation of the earlier values.

An obvious place to look for the clues in this revaluation process is in one's dreams, since they reside in that very realm, that middle kingdom, between mind and body that so often needs to be recognised and incorporated as part and parcel of the revaluation itself. I have often found with men seeking therapy concerning their mid-life anxieties that when they actually commence to record and pay attention to their dreams, they have at the very same time taken the first major step towards healing themselves. Sometimes this moment occurs quickly, whereas in other cases it will take months of therapy before the bridge can be built back to the inner world that will allow the traffic of a dream. When such a man does pay attention to his dreams, invariably he finds a female image in various guises, positions, and states of well-being. The price of success in the outer world seems regularly to bring with it a neglect of the inner world, and the anima image in the following dream demonstrates this neglect. It is the dream of a forty-year-old professional man, the same man that had the three snakes dream discussed in chapter 6, in the section on anima and animus. In relation to the previous dream, I described the dreamer as a very rational man, who had literally turned his back on his feeling and intuitive side. This is his dream.

I am out for a walk—cross a bridge over water—on the right side funny shelter built out sideways—girl, pretty, dark haired, dark red dress—impulse to talk to her, pass on.

My hat blows off—walk on but then decide to retrieve it—turn back—old man with a small mob of cattle crossing bridge—car beside it—they pass, old man appreciative. I tell him I'm looking for my hat—he points it out to me, it's lying on the verge, near the bridge, under some trees—there's a dead horse there too lying on its side, looks as though swept down by a flood, among flood debris—I find not only hat, but also a canvas rucksack, somewhat muddied. I say to old man 'You've helped me find not only my hat, but also my bag, which I lost last week'. He smiles, is pleased.

I decide to go back, pass over the bridge again, walk back to the girl (I saw her when looking for my hat, her upper torso emerging as before, pretty as before) when I get near she ducks inside—I say 'Hello, may I talk to you'—I get the impression that she thinks I am only after a screw (which may well be at the back of my mind).

I duck down, look inside, she suddenly looks ghastly, is lying on her back, hands on her hips (I think for a moment she is masturbating, but no, she is sort of dragging herself backwards)—looks terribly emaciated, ugly—her nose has grown very long, moves like a cripple.

I'm seized by horror—walk rapidly away, looking back, frightened she might follow. I see a look of immense regret—'Oh. No'—across her face as I leave (she's sorry that she terrified me).

Looking back from a long way I see she's emerged from her shelter very ghostlike in her movements—she is looking after me, but not following—I get the impression she's a spirit—could easily catch up with me if she wanted—terrified— wake up.

Immediately one is struck by the similarity of the themes of neglect and emaciation that so characterised the Father Gore animus dream in the previous chapter. So here again is the dream world's picture of the dreamer's neglect of part of himself. It is a complex dream, and some of the dreamer's own personal associations are necessary in order to elucidate many of the meanings. His association with the bridge that he crosses in the opening scene was to a period in his life, around twelve, and a particular bridge in his life around this time. He also distinctly associated the girl in the red dress as being reminiscent of his very first girlfriend in early teenage years. We find in the dream that he comes across this girl unexpectedly, and the specific colour of her dress, dark red, suggests warmth, passion, and feeling: qualities that the dreamer had trouble knowing about and integrating into his conscious view of himself as a very rational and reasonable man. From this we could conclude that, as with so much of the mid-life material, this man's last viable contact with the anima image was in early adolescence, when he crossed the bridge into adulthood. This crossing over probably cost him contact with his feminine self, his anima. His impulse is to talk to her, but he passes on, probably a reference to his decision to pursue the rational, logical aspects of himself.

But then we find his 'hat blows off', and this event becomes a critical one in what then unfolds, since it seems from later in the dream that he once again glimpses the girl when he was looking for the hat. A hat, perhaps, can be best understood by referring to what it covers, one's head, and therefore can be seen as referring to one's thinking function or thoughts. Jung, in discussing a dream in which a hat had occurred, said of this symbol:

> The hat, as a covering for the head, had the general sense of something that epitomizes the head. Just as in summing up we bring ideas 'under one head' . . . so the hat, as a sort of leading idea, covers the whole personality and imparts its own significance to it.

In another place, Jung added to this exposition of the hat symbol, when he described the hat in the following terms:

> In a man's dream it usually means that he is especially concerned with his street appearance or with publicity. It represents a man's particular prejudice or grievance.

When one puts these two views of Jung's together with the hat in this dream, then one can hypothesise that the hat is a symbol of his rational, logical self, which 'covers the whole personality', and further, the image he conveys to the outer world, his 'street appearance'. When it blows off, his initial instinct is to walk on, but then he decides to retrieve it. The image of a hat blowing off is precise, and conjures up further images, of 'the winds of change', for example, or in slang terms 'he blows his lid or top'. All metaphors for saying that he temporarily lost his secure way of being in the world, it no longer covered him. Where he loses it is pointed out by an old man passing him with a mob of cattle. He had no personal associations to the old man, but one could theoretically see him as representing the wise old man within the dreamer, the dreamer's inner wisdom that knew

182

where he had lost his hat. On the surface this may not seem significant, but what is significant is that he not only finds his hat where the old man indicates, but also a dead horse. So where he loses his thinking, loses his thoughts, his rational self, he comes across his dead, or lost, instinctual self, symbolised by the horse. Interestingly, it has been washed down in a flood, perhaps referring to the loss of his own instinctual feelings in a flood of emotion, maybe an early traumatic experience that literally swamped him and his instincts, resulting in his choice of an exclusively rational path. He also finds there 'a canvas ruck sack'. The dreamer's own association to the ruck sack was that it was the one he used to carry when going on hunting trips with his father as a young teenager. These trips were vitally important to the dreamer and involved him in a close and intimate relationship with both nature and his father, who instructed him about nature. So the ruck sack could be seen as confirming the fact that he lost contact with his instinctual, feeling, and sensate self around early adolescence. Although one notices that in the dream he says he lost the bag 'last week', this may be a reference to how close the memory of the loss of contact with nature was for him.

It is in finding these objects that he decides to go back over the bridge again, presumably with the intent of seeing the girl, as he explains in the dream that he had already seen her while looking for his hat. So the loss of his hat, the loss of his usual mode of behaving, his intellectual mode, involves him in a number of events. This turning back and deciding to go over the bridge again could be seen as the return to adolescence that is so characteristic of a mid-life transition, since here, in the dream, he is deciding to go back over the bridge he initially crossed in the opening scene, a bridge that he himself so clearly associated with adolescence. Wanting to see the girl is further confirmation of this return to an adolescent period within his psyche.

However, his attempts to relate to her are not successful, since the girl seems to fear that all the dreamer really wants is sex, a thought that he himself confirms. This scene is typical of many males whose only contact with their feminine aspects, both within themselves and as consequences with women in the outer world, is sexual. Here, in this dream, we can see that the anima is not willing to be related to sexually, an unconscious portrayal to the dreamer that the previous mode of relating to his feeling side was strictly sexual and is now in need of change. Sex is very often the only culturally acceptable way males can express tender feelings, other expressions are feared, as they conjure up images of not being masculine. In addition, sex is a safe, predictable way for a man to express feelings, as it provides both a very common and very workable defence against intimacy. But, as this dream indicates, contact with the anima requires more than sex, in fact it demands feelings and a relationship.

It is the girl's withdrawal from the dreamer, her ducking inside her shelter, that leads the man into looking inside. So, by not being able to approach his feminine self, his anima, by sex alone, he is forced to look inside himself, and what he finds, to his horror, is an ugly, emaciated, crippled girl. A perfect and powerful image of his inner world of feelings. Even then, he initially mistakes her crippled state for sexuality in so far as his immediate thought is that she is masturbating.

His response to her state is interesting. He walks away rapidly, he is unable to face the neglect of his inner world, the inner emaciation. She, on the other hand, displays immense regret; after all, he has turned his back on part of himself. He simply looks back from a distance, fearful that, as a spirit, she could easily catch up with him. Symbolically, this could be seen as his unconscious fear that she will invade his fantasy world, 'ghost-like in her movement', and produce paranoid and destructive thoughts, which in reality is precisely what was happening to him. What is needed is to give some tangible form to the 'spirit', to face her again and the shame of neglect, and to begin the process of healing her instead of running away. But to do this he may once again have to lose his hat in order to find her and other lost objects.

While this dream highlights the theme of neglect and a turning away from the anima, the following dream of a thirty-three-year-old practical man reveals another aspect of the anima. This man had developed his sensation qualities, perhaps by default, and under pressure from his father, so the qualities of feeling and intuition,, while dormant in him, were probably strong. However, his early background had literally driven feelings underground, and indeed, as the dream indicates, the anima was devoid of animation! But by nature it seemed as if the traits belonging to the feminine principle existed in form, but were not recognised by him. His personality test indicated that, of the four functions, only the sensation function had really been clearly differentiated out into consciousness. In a way it had not been safe to give expression to the other functions. I believe that this is so for many males who in their essence are closely aligned with the inner world, but, due to social and family oppression, have made an adjustment in the interests of survival by developing those functions that are regarded as being more acceptable for men. Thinking and sensation are obviously the two 'approved' male functions, and in this man's case, as in so many others, he chose sensation, partly because he lacked confidence in his own thinking ability. Such men tend to become practical, able to fix things in the outer world, but often experience a constant, nagging doubt about whether this is really what they ought to be doing. This doubt has the effect of disconnecting them from the task, in a way that can leave them feeling very unfulfilled. Often they can benefit immeasurably by literally re-aligning their conscious perception of themselves and being given help to develop interests and activities that are more closely related to their basic nature, instead of that which has been imposed upon them by families and society. For men, this oppression of being streamed in a certain direction and into particular activities simply because one is a male is as great a psychological oppression as any that females have experienced. The fact that they get adequate financial rewards, power, and prestige for this oppression tends to mask it and the underlying sense of loss and sadness. Thus it is more difficult to see the oppression of males than females, because the social rewards disguise it. Inwardly there is in these men the same sense of being second-class citizens, because they often find themselves in situations in which they do not feel at ease or competent, because they are not using the functions that they are more naturally inclined towards. So the male who finds himself in engineering or building may well have an inclination for a far more aesthetic involvement in life, particularly if intuition and feeling are strong in him. The inner malaise he feels, the sense of something not quite being right will haunt him, reaching its peak around mid-life.

The dream of this thirty-three-year-old practical man just entering mid-life and facing his anima is revealing in these respects. Apart from having obvious links to the personal level of his unconscious, it is also a dream that points to the archetypal face of the anima.

I'm working in an art studio on a recumbent female form. It is a sort of statue that another artist, a male, has constructed, but has not finished off. He is a technical expert, good at working with materials and knowing their capabilities and limitations. However he seemed to lack the real feeling to finish the statue off and bring it to life.

I have just used loving care and feeling to bring the statue to life and it has actually become a living human female with all the emotional responses and human characteristics. She seems to have been neglected by everyone else in the studio. There are other women working in the studio too, but they seem to show the same lack of care that the artist did. They are all involved in being objective about their work and don't get emotionally involved.

I feel very close to the form I have created, the living woman. She needs lots of tender human warmth from others because she feels neglected and a little rejected by everyone at the studio. I suggest that she could come home with me, rather than stay at the studio over night, but then I realise the conflict that it would create with Jane, my wife, and I forget about it.

Now that she has life, everyone else is taking interest in her, but only as a work of art, not as a woman with feelings. The artist who started the work on her seems to be claiming her as his, because he had constructed her form, but I resent him for this because I feel he could never have brought her to life the way I have.

There seems to be conflict as to what should become of her and I ask her how she feels towards the artist and she replies that he made the component parts. Her attitude is that he just had the ability to piece the component parts together but would never have had the ability to provide the human warmth and feelings that were necessary to give the life that she now has. At the same time she seems to show no recognition to me of what I have done for her. She just seems overwhelmed by having been neglected and feels forlorn. I feel very tender and loving towards her, but it seems to be an admiration of the miracle I have created, rather than a love that can be consummated.

The most obvious event in this dream is the bringing to life of the previously inanimate statue. The dreamer finds himself at work on a recumbent female

187

form. As a metaphor, this is very illuminating, since recumbent, apart from meaning to lie or recline, also means inactive and idle. In this sense it captured the quality of his anima as being inactive and idle. According to the dream, it has been constructed by another male, technically competent. This other male could be one of two factors. At the first level it represents a shadow figure of the dreamer, perhaps referring to his outer sensate qualities, which render him technically competent, but devoid of a feeling connection. However, taking into account the latter part of the dream where the dreamer has a conversation with the female image about her feeling towards the artist, another, additional, possibility emerges concerning this male figure. He could represent the unconscious wishes or aspects of the underdeveloped attributes of the dreamer's father. So much communication in families is unconscious, and the dreamer's father may well have been able to assemble the appropriate components for his feminine self, but incapable of giving them life. Thus the father has not been able to 'finish off' the construction, as the dream states. In this situation a son is often unconsciously asked to complete the father's uncompleted business. In outer reality, the dreamer's father was in a profession involved with caring for others, and thus may well have had access to the component parts of his feminine self, but, caught in a role, he may not have been able to give them life, so this task was passed on to his son. As Jung says:

Nothing exerts a stronger psychic effect upon the human environment, and especially upon children, than the life which the parents have not lived.

In another place he states in unequivocal terms:

. . . children are driven unconsciously in a direction that is intended to compensate for everything that was left unfulfilled in the lives of their parents.

This unconscious direction is one explanation for the feminine form being complete within the dreamer, but inanimate. He had the components, but not the feeling, not the Eros, until the arrival of mid-life brought forth the unconscious issue. So often the arrival of mid-life brings into a man's mind the choice between continuing his father's wishes, often reflected in his occupation, and following his own inner direction.

Regardless of which way one sees the 'artist', and both ways are acceptable and not necessarily contradictory, the important part of the dream is that the dreamer brings back to life, awakens, his own recumbent anima by 'loving care and feeling'. However, while this is pleasant for the dreamer, we find that it immediately presents a problem with respect to his wife. The dreamer finds himself wanting to take the female home, but then realises that this will cause a conflict with his wife. In other words he does not know how to integrate his anima and the attendant quality of feeling within his marriage without threatening the stability of the marriage. This is the old psychological problem of how to manage the task of withdrawing projections and at the same time maintaining an outer relationship with one's partner, who has presumably carried these projections. It is valid to say that many marriages alter when projections are withdrawn, and partners often rigorously resist such withdrawal, because it very often forces them into change. Cyncial as it may sound, it is reasonably well recognised in individual therapy work, that one can assume progress is occurring when a spouse complains. The withdrawal of projections temporarily destabilises a relationship, often for the better, as it can herald a renewed level of intimacy, one not masked by projection. After all, in projecting, one is seeing only the partner one wants to see, not the one who is actually there.

So the dreamer is aware of a potential conflict regarding the integration of this reawakening or rebirth of his anima. A further, a more subtle potential conflict is also alluded to in the dream. This is the problem of ego-inflation. The dreamer twice refers to the form 'I've created'. Here, one can see the dangers of the ego presuming it is the architect of the psyche and not an artefact. Such inflation could result in an overdeveloped sentimentality in the dreamer, rather than the development of feeling. This sort of ego-inflation often seems to me to be behind the instantaneous and quasi-spiritual conversions that some men display as they parade themselves clothed in saffron robes and other personas of the feminine self. The overstatement of the feminine principle must, at the same time, point to its actual underdevelopment, since the persona is usually in an opposite position to the anima itself. If the dreamer takes this path, then the dream itself provides a warning when it points out to him that he seems to be more in admiration of the 'miracle I've created' than experiencing a love that can be consummated. This is a way of saying that if he becomes ego-inflated with the contact with his anima, then it will not be productive. Within the dream the anima herself seems to have some wisdom about this potential problem, for she refuses to give any recognition to the dreamer, and instead conveys her sense of forlornness. However, if the dreamer can heed the warning of the anima itself, then the dream can be seen as indicating the beginning of breathing life back into his psyche and freeing it from a singularly external and unimaginative spot.

At the archetypal level the dream provides an interesting parallel to a mythological story, a story that the dreamer himself was totally unaware of. It concerns Pygmalion, the legendary king of Cyprus, who was a skilful sculptor and who fell in love with a beautiful statue that he made. He gave it the name Galatea, and was so enchanted by the beauty of his own handiwork that he prayed to the goddess of love, Aphrodite, to breathe life into the cold marble. According to the story, one day Pygmalion was moved to kiss the marble lips of the statue, and at that moment Aphrodite breathed life into the carved body. As stories would have it, this one is no exception, Pygmalion married Galatea.

The parallels between the stories are striking, and serve to point out the universal nature of archetypal patterns that transcend both time and culture. Here, in Melbourne, Australia, in 1986, we find Pygmalion alive and well and Aphrodite still at work.

The two preceding dreams highlight the themes of neglect of the anima image, a neglect that is tantamount to having lost contact with the soul. The action and state of the anima image is fundamentally representative of the state of the dreamer's contact with his soul, his psyche, or his imaginal realm. In neglecting this, he is failing to realise that life is a metaphor, an 'as if' experience. Consequently, he becomes either earthbound in the body of the material world, or dry and sulphurised in the barrenness of mind alone.

The remainder of this chapter will focus briefly on two dreams that demonstrate positive anima contacts. The first is of a thirty-five-year-old academic man, who in terms of personality types was clearly an intuitive-thinking type. He had this dream around the peak of his mid-life crisis, in which he was experiencing a distressing level of disillusion concerning the academic world and the attendant values. In short, his inner world of images was coming unhinged, and the image that had originally moved him into the academic life was no longer capable of sustaining him, because mid-life had evoked a different and new inner challenge: in his case a need to redress the imbalance in the psyche of too much air and fire, thinking and intuition, by a development of earth and water, sensation and feeling. Many people, both men and women, who singularly pursue an intellectual life exhibit the same imbalance, hence the sense of them often being 'airy fairy' or 'up in the air' or 'all theory'. The lack within their psyche is a lack of water and earth, often manifesting itself as a lack of compassion and empathy, along with any underlying level of emotional immaturity. Anyone who has witnessed the circus of a faculty meeting will be in no doubt as to the level of emotional maturity!

The dream captures the unconscious stirrings within the dreamer to find alternative ways of dealing with his inner conflict other than his old traditional way. One wonders whether he had the dream straight after a faculty meeting, which has some tribal qualities similar to those of the dream!

I was inside a house with a number of white people, there had been some sort of disturbance with a group of Aborigines who were gathering together outside, a type of tribal gathering.

In the dream I think I was a teenage child, a large father type figure was closing the door and indicating very forcibly that the best way to deal with troublesome blacks was to lock them out, ignore them and they would go away.

The Aborigines in the meantime were chanting in some ritualistic tribal way (a grieving ceremony?). I felt some discomfort in how to deal with them although I don't think I saw them as hostile.

After a period of time Elizabeth K. appeared and suggested that the best way of dealing with the situation was to go outside and form two circles, an inner one commencing with the whites in this circle and an outer one formed by the Aborigines. Then after discussion she suggested that the circles swap over and the inner became the outer. This process would then continue until satisfactory negotiations had occurred.

The dream opens with the dreamer finding himself inside a house with a number of white people and with a disturbance outside. The 'inside' could be seen as representing his ego-conscious view of himself, contained and restricted and surrounded only by

192

familiar ideas; that is, other white people. It is outside his conscious awareness, where his aboriginal self is causing a disturbance. The dreamer's own association to the Aborigines was predominantly one of uncertainty, an unknowing, yet feeling a sense of awe and mystery about them as a people. He was also struck by the antiquity of their culture, their ancient wisdom, and their attachment and respect for the earth. Thus the images of the Aborigines was seen to be a reference to this man's own inner, but as yet unrecognised, ancient wisdom, wisdom that seemed to lie in the collective unconscious. Indeed, the very word 'Aborgine' confirms this, since it is derived from the Latin words *ab*, meaning 'from', and *origine*, 'the beginning'. For the dreamer it was a type of wisdom and knowledge that stood in stark contrast to his 'white people' knowledge, which consisted entirely of intellectual knowledge, orderly, predictable, and publishable in proper professional journals. As so often happens, major transitions in our lives stir the deeper levels of the psyche, the more archaic levels, the aboriginal level in white man. But in his rush to indiscriminately embrace intellectual knowledge, the white man has rejected this other way of knowing, the beauty and the majesty of the dreamtime, in short, like this dreamer, he has lost contact with his aboriginal self.

It is interesting then to note when he might have lost it, presumably around teenage years, since he perceives himself in the dream as a teenager. The father image, the image of outer authority, the senex figure, the values of the masculine world, indicates the best way to deal with the 'troublesome blacks was to lock them out'. How poignant this dream is, not just for this individual man, but as a statement of how the white man's masculine values in Australia have literally dealt with the Aboriginal people by 'locking them out', ignoring them and raping their land in the pursuit of externally valuable minerals. At the individual level, the dreamer's lack of feeling and adherence to the masculine values of his culture can be seen as dominating the first half of his life, the true heroic ego in pursuit of dragons and any other images that threaten the prevailing order.

As if to confirm this loss of contact, the Aborigines in the dream engage in a form of ritualistic chanting, and the dreamer finds himself querying whether it is a type of 'grieving ceremony'. As they have been locked out for some twenty years, the image of a grieving ceremony seems an apt one. The dreamer himself was, at the time of the dream, experiencing a sense of depression, a symptomatic expression of grief. At the time, he had no idea that it was his aboriginal self he was grieving for, he thought it was due to a lack of promotion in his current academic position!

But his unconscious mind had other ideas, and we find that as a consequence of not feeling comfortable dealing with them in the old way, some help appears in the form of a female companion, Elizabeth K. He recognised her in the dream as a friend of his, whom he described as being a very 'earthy, feeling sort of person'. A perfect personal anima image for this man, who needed to develop his sensation and feeling aspects. As a female image in this dream she displays a sensitive and creative knowledge of how to solve the conflict. In essence, this is firstly to go outside, for the dreamer to step outside the safety of his 'white' knowledge, his conscious position, and actually to face the Aborigines. The method for solving the conflict that the anima image provides is basically one of negotiation via interchanging circles. In other words, by allowing an ebb and flow, an interchange in positions of his ego-conscious self and his unconscious mind. This would suggest a lack of defensiveness, resulting in integration without fusion of over-identification. This reminds me of a saying of Jung's:

Consciousness and unconsciousness do not make a whole when one of them is suppressed and injured by the other. If they must contend, let it at least be a fair fight with equal rights on both sides.

The final dream to be discussed in this chapter is a dream that once again picks up the theme of neglect of the anima, but in a different manner from the previous dream. It is the dream of a thirty-one-year-old man involved in the building industry, whose personality was complex, since he had developed both his intuitive and sensation functions, which left feeling and thinking in the relatively inferior, or underdeveloped, positions. This pattern of personality development, the development of opposites, has often struck me as the pattern that characterises highly creative people, such as artists. They need the imagination and vision that comes with intuition, but at the same time they need the practical and technical skills that are included in the sensation function. It is therefore not surprising that they would experience much tension, creative tension, as they struggle to hold an image and give it external form or expression. The latter step inevitably seems to fall short of the image and the very execution of the act can be a source of feelings of loss.

In this man's case, he had strongly developed his outer, technical skills, and was very competent in all manner of building and construction. These were attributes and skills that had been passed on from his father, who had been his sole parent from the age of twelve, when the dreamer's mother had died. So, for all of his adolescence, a powerful period of identity formation, he had not had any access to or experience of females or the feminine attributes. Thus his sensation quality, while creative, because of his intuition, was nevertheless underdeveloped in its feminine face. In other words, his sensation function was bogged down in masculine values and equipment, and his psyche was yearning for the sensual/feeling

195

experience. The loss of his mother had, it seems, been a critical loss in this respect, since she may well have cultivated this inner, or feminine, aspect of the sensation function. Here, then, is the man's dream:

In my car at a camping ground with a group of people. I didn't like the front of the caravan park and suggest that we can go up the back where there is some lovely bush where we will also have access from a side road. We drive through the park, up and over some rough ground and out onto a narrow treed strip between a road and a creek gully. Try to decide where to camp. Here in the centre is a little narrow. We can go up the hill where it will be a little noisier, or down further into the gully. I walk down into the gully, it becomes quite dark. Somebody is camping there. This lady has been here by herself for a very long time. She is dirty and ragged, but underneath happy and pretty. I share some food with her, she takes it and then throws it into the fire (more as a matter of course than any dislike). As I'm walking back I notice how intricately and well made are her small animal cages. She has made traps and animal runs out of small sticks and some sort of string, obviously very competent.

He finds himself at a camping ground with a group of people, but decides to move because he does not like the front of the caravan park. This scene conjures up images of crowds, business, out front, public, etc., whereas his needs in the dream were for the bush, wilderness, and a side road, rather than a main road. Thus the dream might be seen to be referring to the dreamer's need to drop out of the main stream of life, to pursue a more secluded spot in life, to withdraw from business. This decision to retreat, then, involves him going over some rough ground. Often the withdrawal of oneself from an active, external life precipitates a period of going over rough ground within oneself, since mania and hyperactivity are classic defences against sad and depressing feelings, 'the rough ground' inside. Then he finds himself unable to decide where to camp, with three possible options. It is interesting to note that these options emerge only after he has travelled across the rough ground. In other words, withdrawal from the outer world for a while, from the front of the caravan park and facing inner feelings, rough as they may be, leads him to having a choice of where to camp. Without the yearning for solitude and his willingness to traverse the rough ground, the question of options would not have occurred for this man. Reflection, then, becomes possible by withdrawal from the outer world.

Where he finds himself, in the centre, is too narrow — a reflection on where he currently finds himself in life. The narrowness has been brought about by the overly masculine qualities of his sensation function, the tying down to tasks and purposefulness that narrow and restrict one's conscious awareness. Alternatively, to go up the hill entails enduring noise, the noise perhaps of thinking and thoughts, its 'up' implies into one's head. Finally, he decides to descend the gully, in which both the descending quality and the darkness remind one of Hades, the underworld, the unconscious. This decision proves a critical one, since it is in this gully he comes across the female camper, who has been camping by herself for a very long time. This is obviously an anima image that he comes across in the gully of his psyche. However, as we see from the dream, she is an unusual image. Firstly, she likes or prefers solitude, and her life involves an engagement with the animal kingdom, setting traps and building runs. The dreamer admires the intricate cages and is obviously admiring of her bushcraft competence. Further, despite her appearance of neglect, unlike other anima and animus images we have discussed, she is not sad or forlorn or emaciated. On the contrary, he sees her as being underneath happy and pretty, happy presumably where she lives in the solitude of her bush or natural setting. Is she, then, an anima image that naturally lives in the unconscious mind, in other words, an archetypal image?

It is difficult to escape the conclusion that she is of this order, since anyone familiar with Greek mythology will have seen the obvious links and parallels between this anima image and the goddess Artemis. Artemis was the twin sister of Apollo and, not only was the goddess of the moon, the feminine principle, the Yin, but also was the goddess of nature and wilderness, as well as being a huntress. Even more importantly, she was a virgin goddess, a virgin psychologically, which means she is inviolable, belongs to no one, is confined by no bond. In short, she is an archetypal image, not containable by the bonds of consciousness. According to Guthrie, Artemis represents the mystic, primitive identity of hunter and hunted. These descriptions so perfectly fit the female image in this man's dream that they necessarily point to the literal coming across the Yin quality in himself in the image of Artemis. Where else would one find her, other than in the descending gully of the psyche, after all she lives alone in the forest, it is her domain. It is also important to note that Artemis is Apollo's twin, which psychologically suggests that this feminine image in this man is not dominated by patriarchal values, but, on the contrary, pursues and expects a sibling equality with the masculine world. Thus she represents the feminine, but equal, face to this dreamer's outer masculine sensation quality. He seems to recognise this face by sharing some food with her, which she, almost ritualistically throws into the fire.

Above all else, what Artemis represents, in my view, is to reminds us of a necessary link between soul and solitude. The dreamer notes that she has been 'here by herself for a very long time'. In the noise and business of city life, requiring constant use of egos and personas, it is the wilderness and Artemis, goddess of the wilderness, who calls us back to our soul. The 'Mercurial Queen of Solitude', as she has been called, personifies and embodies the struggle to find the soul. As Arianna Stassinopoulos so eloquently says:

There is a passion behind Artemis's remoteness, but it is a passion directed not at relationships but at the search for one's self, one's soul, in solitude and separateness.

Thus the dream indicates the need within this man to continue his search for his soul, and further, that this search will be in solitude, not in the noise of the hill and the narrow confines of his present situation in which he finds himself. The dream is a clear example of this deeper realm of the psyche, the archetypal realm to which we now turn. However, before doing this, since the discussion in this chapter has so extensively dealt with soul and the role of the anima image in this search, it seems appropriate to conclude with the thoughts of Herman Hesse from *My Belief*:

Ask her who means freedom, whose name is love! Do not inquire of your intellect, do not search backwards through world history! Your soul will not blame you for having cared too little about politics, for having exerted yourself too little, hated your enemies too little, or too little fortified your frontiers. But she will perhaps blame you for so often having feared and fled her demands, but never having had time to give her, your youngest and fairest child, no time to play with her, no time to listen to her song, for often having sold her for money, betrayed her for advancement . . . you will be neurotic and a foe to life—so says your soul if you neglect me and you will be destroyed if you do not turn to me with a wholly new love and concern.

10
SELF AND BEYOND

While the poetry of T. S. Eliot has always inspired
me, as I approached this chapter my respect for the
precision of Eliot's poetry was what I was most aware
of. When one attempts to discuss the archetypal realm
of the psyche, Eliot's words, which I have already
quoted, once again seem highly appropriate:

> Words strain,
> Crack and sometimes break, under the burden,
> Under the tension, slip, slide, perish,
> Decay with imprecision, will not stay in place,
> Will not stay still

These lines capture the inability of words, which
belong to the ego-conscious level of mind, the rational
mind, to convey the archetypal level, which is the
source of all images, including words. Thus to attempt
to write about the 'Self and Beyond' is a little like
asking a light bulb to describe electricity. As has
already been discussed, the archetypes and archetypal
images reside in the collective unconscious, that realm
of the psyche that transcends our individual, separate
biographies and identities. It is that level of the psyche
that finds its origin and being in the history of man,
not the history of a particular or specific man. The

collective unconscious represents the evolutionary history of the mind, just as our bodies represent the ongoing biological evolution. In the simplest possible terms, archetypes are patterns of energy, the driving force of the psyche, the reservoir of psychic energy itself. These patterns of energy are represented in the conscious mind via images and cannot be known rationally, only experienced.

The experience of the archaic and powerful images evokes an acute awareness of that conjunction of the personal with the divine, of the transpersonal function within ourselves. Thus mythology and mythological stories are representations of the collective aspect of the human psyche and as such restore the link between man and the eternally enduring force within himself. It is this that gives the numinous quality to archetypal images. To experience this quality is to experience the existence of the objective psyche, the objective soul or spiritual reality that transcends our personal nature. Dreams having this quality are dreams that come from the collective unconscious and are dreams that we remember vividly, often for many years, because they have a peculiar energy about them. They have, in short, come from the source and are truly 'messages from the gods', revelations from the objective psyche, approached only through the living symbolic experience, not through rational thought. As Jung said of the archetype:

Not for a moment dare we succumb to the illusion that an archetype can be finally explained and disposed of. Even the best attempts at explanation are only more or less successful translations into another metaphorical language. (Indeed, language itself is only an image.) The most we can do is to dream the myth onwards and give it modern dress.

One of these 'more or less successful translations into another metaphorical language' has been the metaphor of God. In the experience of an archetypal force one finds the pattern of God, not the Christian monotheistic God, but the pattern of numinosity, the polytheism of the Greeks. As Jung reminds us, the metaphor of God as we know it, despite its relative loss of meaning, represents one archetypal pattern, the Self, the pattern of wholeness. But the archetypal patterns are far more fluid and manifold than a singular image, they represent the ground of our being, of which the striving towards wholeness is a central, but not exclusive, theme. Particular images arise from the objective psyche, from the kingdom of the gods, at a specific period in an individual's and a society's history. It then acts as a myth to live by, a guiding image, and, if connected to consciously, it provides energy and meaning at times of transition. It is as if at crisis periods in our lives we dig deep into the history of our species for knowledge and psychic truths that will direct the continuance of the journey towards wholeness by providing an appropriate myth.

As we know from Jung, the world of dreams describes a situation in terms of psychic inner truths, and as such are a vital avenue for discovering mythical understanding, discovering images and plots of our inner story. One obvious way of working through and overcoming the problem of frozen images that have already been discussed is to seek the renewal to be found in and derived from archetypal images. It follows, therefore, that it is at times of transition that we most need to renew ourselves and reconnect to the source of energy. This reconnection occurs when we are able to confront and consciously relate to the appropriate myth or archetypal image. In the context of the preceding discussion it is worth reflecting on one of Jung's definitions of dreams:

The dream is a little hidden door in the innermost and most secret recesses of the soul, opening into that cosmic night which was psyche long before there was any ego-consciousness, and which will remain psyche no matter how far our ego-

202

consciousness extends . . . All consciousness separates; but in dreams we put on the likeness of that more universal, truer, more eternal man dwelling in the darkness of the primordial night.

The following dream of a man at the mid-life transition adequately demonstrates the existence of this 'little hidden door' within us. It is important to note that the dreamer, a thirty-seven-year-old man, was completely unaware of Jungian or any other depth psychology. Since leaving school at the age of sixteen years, he had worked in the world of banking and finance, and the existence of archetypes, wholeness, Self, or whatever had not entered his conscious mind. He was referred to me by his local family medical practitioner for assistance with feelings of depression, which were associated with an acute mid-life transition. As is my custom, I inquired about any dreams that he may have had, and he informed me that he had vivid dreams, but had dismissed them as 'weird', implying nonsensical. Given the previous discussion on anima and its role in mid-life, this dream can be seen as a fine example of the archetypal face of the anima.

The dream began with four families and their children in a large meadow surrounded by a high wooden fence.

Inside the meadow the families existed in a style similar to the Garden of Eden with animals and birds of all kinds existing in peaceful co-existence. The animals were recognisable but different to their modern counterparts, with the lion for example being bright yellow with long curly locks instead of a mane and having three large toes.

I decided I wanted to see what was on the other side of the fence but none of the adults had any desire to investigate as all their needs were provided in the meadow.

All the children however wanted to see on the other side of the fence so we set off.

When we scaled the fence and climbed over the ground opened up swallowing all the children and myself into the bowels of the earth. We landed in a large cavern with underground caves and rivers flowing in all directions. In the centre of this cavern stood a tall woman dressed in a white shift reminiscent of a Greek goddess.

Although I cannot remember her face she was someone I had known all my life and she said I had to lead the children to safety and that she would accompany us on our journey. The children and I seemed to spend an eternity following rivers and caves in an effort to return to the surface and our meadow.

Finally we followed a very large river which started to rise to the surface however we became aware then that this river flowed into the ocean. We were trapped and the tide started to come in and engulf our cave. As we tried to swim out of the cave the woman from the cave led us into a large bubble which closed over and rose to the surface of the ocean.

Inside the bubble was a large stone altar with a crucifix in the middle of the altar. To our immediate left was a man facing the ocean with his back to myself and the children and to me he was Christ. He said the children and I would only be able to leave the bubble with the help of the woman from the cave as she was the only person who knew the secret of the bubble. Christ continued and said that if she did not wish to help us we would be eaten by a whale which we could now see approaching the bubble with its mouth open.

The figure of Christ faded and I asked the woman to help us. She agreed and called us all to the altar, placed her right hand, arm outstretched, against the centre of the crucifix. Instantly, the bubble opened and we fell through the bubble and all landed including the woman in the meadow we had set out from.

It was as if time had stood still as no one seemed to notice we had been away. As I turned to tell the other

*adults about our journey I noticed that the woman
from the cave had disappeared. Life returned to
normal in the meadow.*

To discuss this dream adequately would almost
warrant a book in its own right, since it is both very
rich and complex. Moreover, it has that sense of
awe about it that I think is so characteristic of
archetypal dreams, and I have included it primarily
in order to establish the sense of awe. One is left
wondering who it is that is doing the dreaming or
imagining, since in conscious life the dreamer had not
connected to the world of archetypes. It also establishes itself as an archetypal or 'big dream', as the
primitive tribesman would call it, because it so
markedly deviates from ordinary, everyday symbols.
We can see in this dream the 'opening into that cosmic
night' that Jung spoke of. Quite clearly the dream transcends the dreamer's personal life experience and so
the effect of such dreams is usually powerful.

The context that surrounded this dream was the
man's loss of direction in mid-life, a direction that had
predominantly been set in action by his father, an
image or myth that he had now outgrown. One of
the consequences of the heroic myth that moves most
men in the first half of life is that they become successful at the cost of a severe repression of their inner
development and awareness of the unconscious mind.
This dream, then, is almost an epic journey into the
unconscious, Dante accompanied by Beatrice through
the caverns of the unconscious mind. He, in the
dream, clearly wanted to see what was on the other
side of the fence, to look beyond the materialistic
Garden of Eden and its attendant state of psychological innocence. Despite his conscious attitude, his soul
was yearning for the journey into Hades, and only
the child part of himself wanted to accompany him.
The children perhaps represent the spontaneous, new
growth, imaginative and playful aspects of the
dreamer. The 'adults' were happy and contented

where they were, just as the 'adult' parts of himself did not want to explore the inner world. In many ways this scene can be seen as a senex-puer dilemma, with the old order not wanting to change contrasted to the puer or youthful parts of himself, which were seeking change. The female figure, the lady of the caves, is clearly symbolising an archetypal figure, although at the same time the dreamer finds himself saying that, although he cannot remember her face, she was 'someone I had known all my life.'

Without going into precise details, two or three themes stand out in this dream. While there no doubt exists many different possible meanings in this dream from fear of incest and swallowing by the mother, through to a deep spiritual yearning, the awesome quality transcends any particular interpretation. Thus my comments are, in the main, only pointers to further possible meanings, since as Jung warned us, we cannot finally explain an archetype away. The dream signifies to me the powerful unconscious forces at work within this man, the powerful opposite forces to his conscious attitude. Inherent in this power is the danger of being swamped or drowned by the unconscious as he finds himself in the large river that joins the sea. This can be seen as akin to the individual identity being submerged or invaded by the vastness of the collective unconscious itself. Indeed, it is only through the help of the woman, who obviously lives in the caves, the archetypal anima, that this drowning is avoided. She manages this rescue in an interesting way; that is, she closes them in a bubble, which then rises to the surface of the ocean. In other words it floats on the great sea of unconsciousness. The bubble reminds me of the hermetic vessel of the alchemists, the well-sealed vessel within which the alchemical work or opus took place. Indeed, being well sealed was vital to the alchemists, as indeed being contained is for us in our inner journey into the unconscious mind. The alternative is to be swamped by the unconscious forces, to lose the boundary between our ego-conscious self and the vastness of the unconscious sea. This state is more commonly recognised as psychosis. So his archetypal anima, the ancient woman within him, knows that he must be contained if he is to avoid destroying himself. The bubble then provides most of the remaining action of the dream, including the spiritual aspects, with the appearance of the Christ image.

In outer life the man professed no particular religious beliefs, and thus the figure of Christ is not one that he would have expected to appear in his dream. Within Jungian psychology, Christ is frequently seen as an archetypal symbol of Self. In this sense the Self, the numinous figure within this man, directs him and advises him on how to be rescued. It is as if the dreamer is not yet ready for the deeper meaning of his mid-life transition, since panic and fear of being devoured enter the dream at this point. Alternatively, one could say that by being contained he comes into contact with his deeper self and, at this point in time, that was all he needed to know, to recognise that he had a 'Christ' within himself.

The approaching whale immediately conjures up the biblical story of Jonah and the whale, which within Jungian terms is often referred to as the 'night sea-journey or crossing'. This relates to the journey through the unconscious by focusing on the sun being swallowed at sunset by the sea and reappearing at sunrise in the east as a transformed hero. In other words it is seen as a myth, referring to exploring the unconscious mind. It can also be seen as a fear of being devoured by the mother, a theme that so often appears in fairy-tales, where children are devoured by a witch, dragon, etc. A major task at mid-life is to separate the feminine self from the mother image, and in this dream we can see that the anima is playing a vital role in this struggle, since she agrees to help the dreamer to escape. The action she chooses to use in effecting the escape is mysterious, and one can only assume it refers to some form of crucifixion or death of a particular conscious attitude of the dreamer. It perhaps also refers to the possible spiritual journey that may lie ahead of the dreamer. Obviously the lady from the caves stayed where she lived, in the deep unconscious, as an archetypal image must, since she disappears when the dreamer finds himself back in the meadow. Such is the nature of the archetypes that they cannot be made conscious as such, but we can become aware of their presence within our psyche.

Indeed, whatever one makes of this dream, the important point is, and was for the dreamer, the awareness that he was not alone in his psychic house, even if life did return to normal in the meadow. The effect of this awareness is to relativise the ego and remind the dreamer that we are constantly moved by deep forces within ourselves, despite the ego's assertions of supremacy. In this sense, simply meeting the dream is enough, since this is an act of meeting ourselves and participating in the ongoing journey towards wholeness. With this man, he came at the time of mid-life because he had forgotten the symbolic language, and thereby was in danger of invasion from his unconscious mind.

As I have mentioned several times, archetypal dreams seem to occur at major transition points in our lives, and therefore we ought not to expect them to occur frequently. One of the mistakes I have observed in people interested in Jungian psychology is their unrealistic expectations about such dreams and the associated tendency to dismiss more seemingly mundane and ordinary dreams. This attitude really reflects an ego-inflation that one is so special that the only dreams occurring will be archetypal ones. On the other hand, it can also reflect a defensive attitude against the less acceptable aspects of oneself and a tendency therefore to engage in archetypal reductionism in order to avoid negative feelings and attitudes.

These comments aside, it is nevertheless valid to assert that major transitions do tend to evoke big dreams. Such events as birth, marriage, separation, and death are all capable of evoking such dreams. In so doing they reconnect us to the history of the species in dealing with these events and establish the events in a broader and, by implication, deeper perspective. The following dream of a man in his early thirties occurred a few days after his father's death, and therefore points to both the personal and archetypal issues involved. It is most common for people to have a dream shortly after the death of a parent or any other significant person, since this is registered in the psyche as a major transition and, in the case of parents, it is the transition into now being the first generation. As previously discussed, the death of a parent often also prefaces the commencement of mid-life. It is as if our parents' dying on the outside provided the stimulus for questioning their living presence in our inner images, myths, and sense of identity. This dream reflects many of these issues.

Dad had returned from hospital and seems to be rehabilitated. I am re-installing him in the dining room downstairs. I have fed him and am putting the paintings back on the wall when the frame of one of them breaks in my hand. It crumbles. I am surprised at how I have let him come back and am submitting to his requests, unquestioningly. He just lies in bed and expects it all to happen as he requests. He doesn't seem to be concerned about the painting.

I seem to be watching some cartoon-fantasy. There is a jester-type figure who is able to extend his arms out to his sides and then just curl up as though he is doing forward roles in the air (I misspelt rolls this way unintentionally when I first wrote the dream out, but seems to be an interesting slip). He is able to stay extended in the air like this indefinitely, just spinning inexplicably. He and an obviously evil character are talking together and the jester says that he is going to the palace.

The scene is now the palace. The queen is there with a lady in waiting and He-man from Masters of the Universe is there as Prince Adam. Suddenly this spinning character appears and at first the queen is amused thinking that he has just come to entertain her, but a male voice says 'He's come through all the alarms. We must be in danger'. At that instant the spinning character, while spinning, casts spiders web over everything which even prevents Prince Adam from turning into He-man to combat him. Then a huge mouth appears in the chamber. It is open and we can see down the open throat. Everything in the palace is in danger of being sucked into the mouth and consumed unless forces can be mobilised to stop the spinning man.

This dream quite clearly falls into two parts, the first being personal and the other archetypal. As a dream, it shows the not-uncommon phenomenon of a dream including both realms or levels of the psyche. So in the first section we have the dreamer's personal unconscious response to his father's death. Here we can see that the major theme is a *status quo* one, a return to how the situation was before his father's death. In outer life the dreamer was actually involved in physically caring for his ill father prior to his death. The dream opens with the specific comment that 'I am re-installing him in the dining room', which was where, in outer life, the father had been living. Yet his father's death had given him a choice between simply continuing on as if his father were alive, inside him, unchanged, and grasping the opportunity to change and embrace new growth. The dream then makes an interesting comment: all is proceeding as if nothing has changed, when suddenly the frame of one of the paintings crumbles in his hand. The effect of this, in the dream, is to make the dreamer aware that he has let his father come back into his life and is unquestioningly submitting to him. The frame crumbling is a very precise image, it does not break, he does not drop it, it does not simply come apart, it clearly 'crumbles'. Using the dreamer's own association, this was seen as the old framework crumbling, the old way of relating, the old way of relating crumbling. In the dreamer's own words, he said: 'At this point I realise that I am just putting that part of me back in the old familiar spot without asking myself any questions about it.' It is in the framework crumbling, as he attempts to restore things to the way they were, that the dreamer is given the opportunity to choose change. This is reflected in the dream by the immediate change of scene and level in the dream.

The second segment, the archetypal segment, commences when the dreamer finds himself watching a cartoon or fantasy of some sort. As has so often been mentioned, the location in a dream, or setting, tends to point to the parallel phenomenon in the dreamer's psyche. So in being a cartoon-fantasy, we can suspect that the action is taking place at the level of fantasy, a way of indicating that where he can find his own inner jester is in his imaginal world. The dreamer himself associated the cartoon image with the quality of animation, 'something that brings life, puts soul to what would appear to be lifeless figures and characters'. Further, his personal association to the jester-like figure was a memory of himself, much younger, perhaps around eight years of age, when he used to do somersaults in the water, just as the jester was doing in the air. Psychologically this association perhaps points to the time when the dreamer was more animated and playful and less under the thumb of a very dominant and authoritarian father. At the archetypal level the jester figure can be seen as a Hermes type of figure, the trickster god, who also acts as a messenger between consciousness and unconsciousness. The overriding quality of this particular jester image is energy: in the dreamer's own words

211

he is 'full of energy, a veritable ball of it'. Symbolically one could see that where he could re-energise himself is by paying attention to and watching his fantasies, his own inner cartoons or animated images. Thus this level of the dream tends to indicate an approach that the dreamer might take in dealing with the loss of his father. In terms we have spoken of before, the dream may well be indicating to 'stick to the image'.

The jester then does something unexpected: he tells an 'obviously evil character' that he is going to the palace, a royal superior place above the ordinary, an archetypal place within his psyche. However, it seems a puzzle why he should tell an 'obviously evil character'. From discussion with the dreamer, it emerged by way of active imagination that the jester, or spinning man, as he came to call him, was going to the palace to overthrow the old regime. The evil man obviously does not object to this, and one is left wondering whether his evilness lies in his acquiescence. In conscious life the dreamer, through his negative early experiences, had repressed his positive side, and hence the shadow consisted of positive, affirming attributes. Within this context it becomes feasible to see the 'obviously evil man' as the dreamer's shadow, whom he needs to inform of the impending change, otherwise the dream will evoke the positive shadow and concomitant anxiety. By informing the shadow in advance, the dream is indicating to the dreamer a mechanism for avoiding the anxiety that may well come with a change in the old order. As was previously discussed, anxiety comes from the unfamiliar and for this man to experience his positive, affirming side, to affirm his own identity instead of being submissive to his father would be an unfamiliar experience, and therefore one that would evoke considerable anxiety.

The scene then shifts to the palace, which the dreamer saw as representing the reigning order, which in his case would be the archetypal pattern of submission, not assertion. In sharing the dream he also expanded on the three characters he found at the palace. He saw all of them as lifeless, almost in suspended animation. He described them interacting with one another, but in a mechanistic, lifeless manner. Then once again the hiatus word 'suddenly' appears in the dream, and this 'suddenly' heralds in the jester to the palace, energy into the old order. The queen, while at first amused, is then warned by a male voice of danger: 'He's come through all the alarms. We must be in danger.' This voice is another aspect of the dreamer, perhaps a negative shadow, who resists change and, if he got control, would take the dreamer back to the beginning scene, where he would once again unquestioningly follow his father's orders. Getting through the alarms is somewhat akin to getting through the psychological defences, which act as alarms against invasions from the unconscious mind. The effect on the spinning character of this warning is dramatic, he instantly spins a web over everything: in short, he binds them all. Thus, what potentially might have energised the old order and led to change now seemingly becomes destructive when thwarted by the male voice. It is such a powerful web that Prince Adam cannot transform himself into He-man and free them. It is strong enough even to bind the hero.

The web could be seen as the web of illusion, which binds the characters in such a way that they are in danger of being swallowed by the huge mouth that then appears. Here again we find this interesting archetypal theme of devouring, but in this instance, instead of a whale, or a mother, I think it is more constructive to see the parallel between this mouth and the mythological figure of Saturn or Kronos. The god Kronos had been warned that one of his children would overthrow him, and in order to prevent this he swallowed each of them at birth. Symbolically this

213

can be seen as referring to the old order, Kronos, swallowing all new growth; that is, change. Such a parallel is obviously relevant within the context of this dream. The link to the web seems to me to be that the dreamer may create an illusion of change by changing house, car, job, or whatever, but not really embracing the energy of change associated with the jester or Hermes character, which would involve an overthrow of the senex or old order. As with any individual, an illusion of change has the effect of simply increasing the chances of being swallowed back into the old order. Thus the dream can be seen as highlighting, for the dreamer, the archetypal struggle between change and the *status quo*, between senex and puer. It further highlights the powerful role of the male voice, or shadow, who perceives the renewal of energy as attack. In summary, this dream reflects both the personal level for the dreamer of his conflict in dealing with his father's death and the attending possibilities of change, and at the same time captures the archetypal issues concerning change.

The final dream that I wish to share in this book is perhaps appropriately one that still remains somewhat of a mystery. It is as if, despite whatever understanding we have of dreams, it takes us only into deeper and more complex dreams that defy ready understanding, if not understanding at all. I think that it is as vital to see this side of dreaming as it is to see the side of understanding. A dream not understood, with the correct attitude towards the dream, can be, in my opinion, just as powerful as one that is understood. This is because it stands as a monumental reminder that the psyche is unfathomable, it has no limits, it is never completely knowable, only constantly approachable. The dream in question is that of a thirty-seven-year-old Australian woman, who had the dream while visiting Zürich, in Jung's homeland, Switzerland.

214

I am seated amongst ancient, hewn, large, granite stone blocks. In front of me is a narrow wall— about 3 to 4 feet in width which is also made of stone. But across it is a strip of porcelain about 4 to 6 inches high. I am told to enter a state of meditation staring at this wall and as I do so, my images will appear on it.

After what seems a long time, symbols/images begin to appear, slowly emerging from the wall. The strip of porcelain has now divided itself into three smaller tiles.

On the first tile a figure of an old man, cloaked in an ancient white robe appears, with a bright yellow halo. He is facing towards my right (his left), side on view, and behind him are three markings of pastel colours—blue, mauve and pink. The style of the drawing reminds me of Giotto's style.

A voice says solemnly 'Regard the halo', as I hold the tile in my hand after taking it off the wall.

On the second, middle tile, a symbol of a cross appears (Ankh cross).

On the third tablet, another figure-symbol begins to take shape but I either can't recall it or I must have woken up. I sense it was a snake . . . but as I woke I wasn't sure whether it was me imagining it a snake or whether a snake had actually appeared or begun to appear.

Upon reading this dream one is immediately struck by its unusual symbolism and sense of mystery. It also has that numinous quality, the quality that suggests a 'message from the gods'. In this sense it is a fine example of an archetypal dream and a potent reminder that psyche is composed of more than ego. This 'reminder' is in its own right a source of healing for modern times, since if observed and engaged in it relativises the ego and realigns us with the depth and breadth of our psychological being. The 'forgetting' of this other dimension, beyond rationality, beyond consciousness, is the source of much of our ills, since in this 'forgetting', as has so often been discussed, lies the loss of our soul or imaginal capacity. Life as a solely literal event is a life devoid of meaning, richness, and a sense of awe. In short it is a life characterised by the oppressive burden of the outer world and its problems.

This dream so clearly belongs to that realm of psyche beyond ego, and to engage in it, to let it dream us, is to participate in it. In doing this, one finds soul. In this spirit, what struck me and the group in which the dream was discussed was that it seemed to be about spiritual matters. The dreamer herself felt that the setting reminded her of Macchu Picchu, where she had visited some four years previously. It was an ancient Peruvian city in the Andes discovered only in 1911 and thought to be a cradle of traditional Inca civilisation. A profusion of feminine ornaments has been found there, and this has been thought to verify that Macchu Picchu may have been the final home of the priestesses of the Inca Sun God. However, at a symbolic level, it suggests that this ancient culture may well have been a predominantly feminine one, one in which Ying values were dominant. The dreamer herself had very strong feelings about the Spanish conquest and destruction of the Inca civilisation, and these feelings were linked to her negative attitude towards Christianity. In short, she identified in the dream with the Incas as victims of orthodox Christianity's destructiveness. This association, the location of the dream in the ruins of the Inca civilisation, and the conflict between two different religious systems throws some possible light on the dream itself. Since, as we have seen before, physical location of a dream tends to establish psychological location within the dream. From this it becomes possible to link the feeling that the dream is to do with spiritual matters to the more specific issue of spiritual conflict within the dreamer, a conflict that existed for her between two different religious attitudes. This is obviously an old and ancient issue, a conflict that transcends the personal biography of this particular individual dreamer. The 'ancient, hewn, large, granite stone blocks' suggestive of Stonehenge tell us of the age of the conflict. It is the conflict between the masculine, Yang and legalistic form of Christianity, and the feminine, Yin, feeling basis that has been so actively destroyed by orthodox Christianity. The sense of rules, logic, and laws versus feelings, compassion, mystery, and respect for the inner world. In short, the conflict is concerning the domination of the exoteric face of Christianity over the esoteric.

The dreamer is told in the dream to enter a state of meditation. She related that the voice was distinctly a strong male voice, which she had heard in previous dreams. A possible link or association that comes to my mind is the relationship between the voice and the Hindu concept of Chakras. The fifth Chakra is *visuddha*, the throat centre, which is associated with ether and ephemeral quality that this implies. Jung, in an extensive discussion of the symbolism of the Hindu concept of Chakras, sees them as symbolic expressions of complex psychic facts, with ascending Chakras being representative of higher levels of consciousness energised by Kundalini. In discussing the throat Chakra and its attendant quality of ether, he sees this as symbolic of psychical as opposed to physical reality, since ether is a most volatile element, a metaphor for the limits or end of physical matter. This limit or end of the physical reality and consequently the seat of psychic reality is to be found in the symbolic location of the *visuddha* Chakra in the throat. Jung says of this Chakra:

> . . . psychical facts are the reality in *visuddha*
> . . . we are beyond the air we breath, we are reaching into the remote future of mankind, or of ourselves.

Thus this Chakra symbolically represents the reality

of imagination and the transition from literality to the imaginal. The Hindus located it in the throat, and, as it is from here that we speak, it can also be said that when a man speaks from *visuddha*, he could be seen as speaking psychic truths.

To return to the dream, it becomes possible to say that the voice the dreamer hears is the voice of the higher Self, speaking a psychological truth, which is what gives the voice its commanding and compelling quality. This 'truth' is perhaps the highlighting for the dreamer of her spiritual conflict and therefore it commands her to meditate on it. The result is that the first tile is of an old man, who reminded the dreamer of Giotto's style. According to Gombrich, Giotto was the genius who broke the spell of Byzantine conservatism in art by rediscovering the technique of creating the illusion of depth on a flat surface. More specifically, much of Giotto's paintings were of strictly religious themes, and thus the dreamer's association to the style of painting may also refer to the beginning of a new era in her religious beliefs, the beginning of creating 'depth on a flat surface'. The voice specifically commands the dreamer to 'regard the halo'. She understood the 'regard' to mean to have regard for it, or, in other words, to look at it. According to Cirlot, a halo is 'a visual expression of irradiating, supernatural force, or, sometimes, more simply, of intellectual energy in its mystic aspect'.

Within the Christian tradition the halo is simply associated with holiness, within the eastern tradition with auras, but in all instances the link is to spirituality. It is therefore interesting that the dreamer is told 'regard the halo', to give heed to it, and not any other aspect of the image. This could be seen as telling her to pay attention to the mystical or esoteric face of Christianity, not the old masculine form. That the halo is yellow or gold can be seen as corresponding to the mystical aspects of the sun, which links the symbol back to the dreamer's association of the setting with Macchu Picchu.

The three markings of the pastel colours, which can be seen as belonging closely together as colours, remained unclear to the dreamer. If one takes the predominant theme of blue, then Cirlot, discussing this colour says, 'Blue (the attribute of Jupiter and Juno as god and goddess of heaven) stands for religious feeling, devotion and innocence.' Here we find the theme of religion again emerging, and it is further sustained by the colour of red, which is often seen as the life-giving principle. Mauve can be seen as a colour in transition between red and blue, and perhaps reflects the transition going on within the dreamer between the old religious beliefs and her emerging spiritual renewal . . . her inner Giotto at work.

The meditation upon the first tile can now perhaps be seen as a direction to the dreamer to reflect upon her inner conflict regarding her spiritual awareness. The second tile she describes as a symbol of a cross, but more specifically it was not the Christian cross, but an Ankh, the ancient Egyptian cross and symbol of immortality and eternity. The dreamer herself was unable to amplify this symbol, however one could see it as an indication that eternal and immortal truths may follow from the meditation upon the inner spiritual conflict. The transition from outer Christianity, which the dreamer had rejected, to the inner, mystical face, may lead to an awareness of aspects of immortality. Following the dark night of the soul, purgation, the mystics tell us that the morning light of new intelligence comes, the illumination. The third phase in the mystical path, the rubedo stage in alchemy, is the union or red of contemplative love. Is this perhaps why the third tile remains blank? She inadvertently calls this tile a 'tablet'. The snake is perhaps suggestive of the process of death and rebirth, the theme of immortality and life beyond physical death. As was stated in the beginning of the discussion of this dream, there are aspects of it that remain a mystery, as indeed are the issues that it seems to be pointing towards. But if soul is imagination, then it is dreams like this that serve to remind us of possibilities beyond death and in the words of Wordsworth's 'Ode, Intimations of Immortality':

Our birth is but a sleep and a forgetting:
The Soul that rises with us, our life's star,
Hath had elsewhere its setting,
And cometh from afar.

11
A PRAGMATIST'S EPILOGUE

In a book that has been concerned almost exclusively with the mercurial qualities of soul, it seems apt, albeit perhaps ironic, to finish with a chapter on salt. No doubt some readers will have already found themselves thinking that the entire contents need to be taken with a grain of salt! Little would they realise the wisdom of their thoughts. However, the salt I am referring to is the alchemists' salt, which they term sophic salt, philosophical salt, to distinguish it from common salt. So the salt to be added is a metaphorical salt, that third aspect of the alchemist's *tria prima*.

As has already been mentioned, within the alchemical tradition one can see sulphur as symbolic of mind, mercury of soul, and salt of body. Thus, having explored the ever-moving and volatile aspects of dreams, it is now time to add some body, some factual, 'real' information. Hence this chapter is entitled 'A Pragmatist's Epilogue'.

James Hillman, in a brilliant discussion on alchemical salt, says:

> Salt gives what one has in one's head a worth among people: tangible value on earth . . . to salt

or earth one's winged speculations is to express them with a common touch.

The 'tangible value on earth' for dreams often revolves around the task of trying to remember them, since it is very rare for me not to be asked 'How can I remember my dreams?' Equally common are the questions that people ask when starting work on their dreams regarding the nature of dreams, their frequency, colour, extent, etc., etc. Thus this final chapter is concerned with earthing the world of dreams by focusing upon these issues. However, by so doing, in attempting to earth dreaming, I am at the same time aware that one of the qualities of salt is that it fixes things, preserves them to the point of fixity, and thus what I have to say ought not to be seen as a set of fixed, over-salted 'rules', but rather as a fluid set of guidelines and of suggestions. In this context, the words of Hillman again provide a rich insight into the problem of possible fixation.

> The dosage of salt is an art: it must be taken *cum grano salis*, not corrosive, bitter irony and biting sarcasm or fixed immortal dogma, but the deft touch which brings out the' flavour.

Just as we know that excessive salt causes a hardening of the arteries, so also excessive facts and information can cause damage to the flow of dreams. Nevertheless, the necessary requirement is that we actually remember the dream in the first place, so that the art, as Hillman suggests, lies in the 'deft touch' of facts or salt and not in a deluge.

Far too many dream books suffer from an excess of salt in so far as they provide fixed definitions of symbols and, as a consequence, equally fixed interpretations. I hope that this book has unequivocally established my view that such fixed views do indeed harden the arteries of dreams and reduce the psychological circulation, thereby damaging one's soul or imaginal capacity. The following questions and all too brief answers are representative of questions I have repeatedly been asked. There is no suggestion on my part that the list is either exhaustive or comprehensive, but I hope it provides some guidelines.

Does everyone dream?

This must be the most common question asked, even if it is framed in the negative by some people when they say 'I never dream'. The answer is that every adult dreams, with the first period of dreaming occurring some 90 minutes after we fall asleep. This period lasts for approximately 5–10 minutes. The evidence for this is from laboratory studies, where the eyes of people asleep have been observed to move rapidly. This has been termed Rapid Eye Movement or REM for short. When the subjects are awakened during REM sleep they invariably report a dream. It is assumed that the sleep cycle continues in 90-minute segments, with the dream period getting progressively longer until just before we wake, when it can be as long as 40 minutes. Therefore we can conclude that the average amount of time spent dreaming each night by most people is round about 2 hours, or approximately 20–25 per cent of actual sleeping time.

Why do some people remember dreams and not others?

This is a complex question to which there is no clearcut answer. It has been assumed that repression, the unwillingness to face or know our dreams, is what accounts for variations in recall or remembering ability. While I am sure this plays a very major role, I doubt if this is the only reason. However, the importance of repression is demonstrated by the fact that people who cannot remember dreams are very often those who want to avoid unpleasant and anxiety-provoking experiences in their normal waking life. I think another possible, but as yet unproven, explanation lies in personality differences. And Jung's classification of individuals into extroverts and introverts may be relevant here. Extroverts by nature are more attached to the outer world, their energies flow out into the world, and therefore they are not very inwardly directed. Introverts, on the contrary, are mainly inwardly directed and therefore more likely to be receptive to and aware of dreams, leading to a more efficient recall.

It is also possible that personality variations account for the intensity and detail of dreams. Obviously the more detailed and intense a dream is, the greater are the chances of recalling it. It seems logical that there is a better chance of recalling an emotionally long dream, for example, than a vague, bland, unexciting one. From my experience, contrary to expectations, I have found that introverted-sensation-type people tend to have vivid dreams, and are extremely good at recalling them when their attention is directed towards the world of dreams. Perhaps the explanation lies in the fact that, being predominantly sensation, they are astute observers of detail, and being in addition introverted they are aware of the inner world. The combination probably leads to very detailed dreams, since they have a wealth of factual data to draw upon during the night.

Is it true that certain foods increase dreaming?
There is a popular belief that we have bad dreams because of something bad we have eaten. Alternatively, certain foods, such as blue cheese, are assumed to increase the richness of dreams. There is at present little experimental data relating to the role of food in dreams and dreaming. A possible explanation for the experience of food-related dreams may be the disturbance of sleep resulting from indigestion. Physical discomfort may well periodically awaken us, and thereby break into the REM phases of the sleep cycle, where we are more likely to remember a dream, because we would at that time either be having it, or have just had it.

What are the effects of drugs and alcohol on dreams?
Although the research data on dreams is not conclu-
sive, there seems to be a general consensus that both
stimulants and sedatives, if taken over a long period
of time, will diminish the amount and intensity of
dreams. One wonders what the long-term effects are
on the well-being of individuals who deprive themselves of Rapid Eye Movement sleep and dreams by
taking stimulants and sedatives over long periods of
time.

Do we dream in colour or black and white?
My impression is that most dreamers have some
colour in their dreams and particularly vivid colour
is often an important clue to the dream, since it can
be seen as one way of intensifying an image. Patricia
Garfield provides a very thoughtful and extensive
discussion of colour, based on her own research, and
she concludes that colour is far more likely to appear
in dreams after several hours of sleep. A possible
explanation for this is that either we have more intense
dreams later in the sleep cycle, or, alternatively, the
colour fades from those dreams we have earlier in the
night.

Why do we have recurring dreams?
The phenomenon of the same dream repeating itself
seems quite common. The simple explanation is that
the dream keeps repeating itself because we have not
understood it, and thus the issue it is attending to
remains unaltered.

*What are nightmares and how do they differ from
dreams?*
The answer is that nightmare are dreams, but they
are specifically severe anxiety dreams that wake us
up with a fright. It is possible that nightmares literally wake us up to ourselves when we are persistently
refusing to face something.

Are there dreams that come true? that is, prophetic dreams?

In my experience there are such dreams, although I think they are relatively rare. At a simple level, some dreams appear to 'come true', since the dream itself is a true symbolic depiction of a real-life situation of the dreamer's. But, as to the more specific quality of prophetic dreams, I see no reason why these should not exist. The unconscious mind is not contained by the normal constraints of time and space and, therefore, we may well be able to anticipate events in the worlds of dreams. The same could be said of telepathic dreams. My personal experience is that, around the theme of death, telepathic dreams are perhaps far more common than we want to believe. The experience that I have had regularly reported to me is that of dreaming that somebody is ill or dying, and then some time later discovering that the dream coincided with the actual physical death of that person. However, it is very important to reassert that I think that far more often the theme of death in a dream is a symbolic expression of the loss of some attribute or quality within ourselves that we associated with the person we dreamed of. Yet, on the question of telepathic dreams, Jung has some interesting thoughts:

> The authenticity of this phenomenon can no longer be disputed today. It is, of course, very simple to deny its existence without examining the evidence . . . Certain people are particularly sensitive in this respect and often have telepathically influenced dreams . . . The phenomenon undoubtedly exists, but the theory of it does not seem to me so simple.

Are dreams wish-fulfilling?

Within the theme of this book, the answer can only be the broad one: that dreams are one way in which we can become aware of ourselves and expand our consciousness, and, in this sense, they fulfil the wish to become oneself. As to fulfilling specific wishes, I suspect that the answer is that we are often compelled towards completing the images in our psyche, like a moth to the light, and, in this way, dreams and dream images may well be wish-fulfilling.

Is working on your dreams dangerous?
The answer is clearly No, so long as one remembers that dreaming is a symbolic, metaphorical language and not a literal language. If we take dreams too literally, then not only are we denying ourselves an opportunity for self-knowledge, but at the same time we are risking mental disturbance by losing contact with the outer world of everyday life. A preoccupation with dreams to the exclusion of everyday responsibility is just as disturbed and destructive an activity as a refusal to attend to the inner world at all. A further danger in working with dreams lies in our over-intellectualising them and being obsessed with 'working them out'. Strong thinking types are prone to this and, in so doing, they suffer further loss of their soul, since they blacken and tarnish the images by the excessive sulphur of thinking. Behind this obsession to 'work it out' is very often fear and anxiety and a desire to control life and render it predictable. Thus there is no danger in a dream *per se*, or, in dream work, the danger lies in our attitude towards the dream. It is my hope that this present book has contributed towards an understanding of the attitudes that facilitate our working with dreams, which must in themselves stand as a remarkable source of knowledge about ourselves.

SUGGESTIONS FOR REMEMBERING AND RECORDING DREAMS
Obviously, before you can work with your dreams, you must first have the material to work on, and for this you need to keep a dream diary. This allows an on-going record of your dream world, and enhances

the capacity to understand a dream, because it places a single dream within the context of others. Any one dream in isolation is very difficult to understand, a little like taking one painting of an artist and trying to draw conclusions about the style, motivation, message, etc. Clearly, keeping a dream diary, and remembering dreams are related, and the following suggestions are all intended to aid this process:

1. First and foremost, you must have a receptive attitude towards dreams. Before going to sleep, it·is useful to suggest to yourself several times over that you are going to have a dream and that you are going to remember it. This attitude of receptiveness is absolutely critical, a necessary incubation ritual, an attitude that people who reject and ignore their inner world find very difficult to hold. Naturally, as a consequence of this, they rarely remember their dreams.

2. Always keep a pen and pencil beside your bed, along with a small bedside lamp. This will allow you to jot down the dream images during the night, and will aid your recall of the dream in the morning.

3. Better still is to have a small tape-recorder, preferably voice-activated, beside your bed and record your dreams during the night. This is a particularly effective technique for people who are experiencing difficulty in recalling dreams upon waking.

4. As a general rule, applying to waking up during the night or in the morning, it is advisable not to open your eyes suddenly or jolt yourself too strongly into the awakened state. This sudden awakening seems to have the effect of shaking the dream images loose and you then experience the frustrating feeling of knowing that you've had a dream, knowing it is there, but not begin able to recall it. I think it is useful to lie absolutely still when one wakes up and ask yourself the question, 'Did I have a dream last night?' Then it is helpful to imagine your mind as a television set,

and wait for it to warm up to see if any pictures are coming. If so, then quickly run through the entire dream, still with your eyes closed, before getting up to write it.

5. When recording a dream, it is preferable to simply write down or report as much of the detail as possible, suspending your critical faculties, and ignoring whether it makes sense or not. If you allow yourself to evaluate the dream, then you will experience a loss of detail and possibly a loss of the dream altogether. The first and foremost task is simply to get it down, not evaluate it.

6. If you experience consistent difficulty in recalling a dream, then there are several simple techniques you might try. The first is to alter your sleep pattern, go to bed a little earlier and wake up at a different time. This sometimes has the effect of intervening in the sleep cycle at a different place, closer to REM sleep. The farther you are away from REM sleep in the sleep cycle when you wake up, the more difficult it is to remember the dream.

Some dream scholars suggest a more stoic routine of setting an alarm to go off approximately two hours after going to sleep. The theory behind this is that you increase your chances of waking during the first REM period. There is little doubt that dream recall is richest and most detailed immediately after a REM sleep period, so it is well worth experimenting with the sleep cycle.

7. In my experience, difficulty in remembering dreams often coincides with excessively busy periods in one's life. It is as if we do not even have time to dream and, perhaps through physical tiredness, we spend less actual time in REM sleep. At the psychological level, I suspect that excessive business takes us outside of ourselves, predominantly into the literal world, and these are the times when we forget the symbolic inner world. Busy periods may be unavoidable (although I suspect much of it is of our own

creation) and one technique that can help is to meditate, or do some relaxation before going to bed. This has the effect of returning us to the inner world and thereby cultivating an appropriate climate in which to hear a dream. It also clears the mind of much of the day's refuse and anxieties.

8. Another technique that I have found has helped people who are experiencing difficulties in remembering dreams is to read a novel before going to bed. Unlike boring, flat, and unimaginative technical literature, this provides the psyche with some images that it may be able to use in constructing a dream. Films can often provide the same sort of material.

9. Many people have reported that they have richer dreams on holiday. There are probably several factors behind this, but the effect is that they can recall the dream more readily simply because they are more vivid. No doubt the alteration of the daily routine, changes in sleep pattern, and changes of external environment all contribute to the increased intensity of the dream. A change in physical location often produces a change in psychic space.

10. Finally, it is not only important actually to write the dreams down, but of equal importance is to record the dreams in a substantial and attractive book. Having dreams on sheets of loose paper does not convey a serious, committed attitude towards dreams and this dismissiveness impairs recall. It is useful to write the dream down on one side of the page and your random associations on the other. These ought to include any event, feelings, people, of the previous day, along with anything else that comes into your head in relation to the dream. Just trust the seemingly random thoughts and let the dream come to you. After all, you dreamed it, so somewhere you know what it means. What else are dreams, in the final analysis, than messages from ourselves to ourselves?

I can think of no more appropriate way of concluding than by quoting the thoughts of Carl Jung, whose writings, along with those of James Hillman, have been such a powerful and sustaining source of inspiration throughout the writing of this book.

In the last analysis, most of our difficulties come from losing contact with our instincts, with the age-old unforgotten wisdom stored up in us. And where do we make contact with this old man in us? In our dreams.

SOURCES

The publication details for Jung's *Collected Works* cited in these notes are:
C. G. Jung, *Collected Works*, edited by Sir Herbert Read, Michael Fordham, Gerhard Adler, and William McGuire, and translated by R. F. C. Hull (except for volume 2, which was translated by L. Stein in collaboration with Diana Riviere), Bollingen Series XX, Princeton University Press, Princeton, and Routledge & Kegan Paul, London, 1954-79.

Chapter 1 Setting the Scene
1   Ernest Jones (ed.), *The Life and Work of Sigmund Freud*, Basic Books, New York, 1961, p. 234.
4   Erich Fromm, *The Forgotten Language*, Grove Press, New York, 1957, p. 7.
5   Synesius of Cyrene, 'On Dreams', trans. Isaac Myer, in R. Wood (ed.), *World of Dreams: an anthology*, Random House, New York, 1947, and discussed in Fromm, op. cit. pp. 132, 133.
5   Max Zeller, *The Dream—The Vision of the Night*, Analytical Psychology Club of Los Angeles, 1975, p. 183.

6   Fromm, op. cit. p. 140.
7   James Hillman, *Insearch: psychology and religion*, Spring Publications, Dallas, 1967, p. 57.
8   James Hillman, *Loose Ends*, Spring Publications, Dallas, 1978, p. 3.
12   Hillman, *Insearch*, p. 30.
12   James Hillman, *Healing Fiction*, Station Hill, New York, 1983, p. 46.
15   Zeller, op. cit.

Chapter 2   Dreams through Time
18   Gunnar Landtman, 'The Kiwai Papuans of British New Guinea' in R. Wood (ed.), *World of Dreams: an anthology*, Random House, New York, and discussed in Erich Fromm, *The Forgotten Language*, Grove Press, New York, 1957, p. 110.
18   Kilton Stewart, 'Dream Theory in Malaya', ch. 9 in Charles Tart (ed.) *Altered States of Consciousness*, Anchor/Doubleday, New York, 1972, pp. 161–70.
19   Patricia Garfield, *Creative Dreaming*, Ballantine Books, New York, 1974, pp. 84–9.
20   Mary Ann Mattoon, *Understanding Dreams*, Spring Publications, Dallas, 1984, p. 40.
20   James Hillman, *Healing Fiction*, Station Hill, New York, 1983, p. 23.
20   T. C. McCluhan, *Touch the Earth*, Promontory Press, New York, 1971. p. 30, and discussed in John Sanford, *Dreams and Healing*, Paulist Press, New York, 1978, p. 6.
21   Ibid. p. 7.
26   *The Odyssey*, trans. E. V.Rieu, Penguin Classics, Harmondsworth, 1956, pp. 102–3.
27   Mary Watkins, *Waking Dreams*, Spring Publications, Dallas, 1984, p. 24.
29   C. A. Meier, 'The Dream in Ancient Greece and its Use in Temple Cures', in G. Grunebaum

& R. Caillois (eds), *The Dream and Human Society*, Northwestern University Press, Evanston, 1966, p. 313, quoted in Watkins, op. cit. p. 27.

29   Plato, *The Republic*, trans. B. Jowett, quoted in Fromm, op.cit. p. 119.

30   Aristotle, 'De Somnis' (On Dreams), in R. McKeon (ed.), *The Basic Works of Aristotle*, Random House, New York, 1941, pp. 618–25, quoted in Fromm, op. cit. pp. 121–2.

31   James Hillman, *Re-Visioning Psychology*, Harper & Row, New York, 1975, p. 23.

31   C. G. Jung, *Collected Works*, vol. 6, para 78.

31   Ibid. vol. 11, para. 889.

31   H. McCurdy, 'The History of Dream Theories', in *Psychol. Review*, 53 (1946) 225–33.

32   Artemidorus, *The Interpretation of Dreams: Oneirocritica*, trans. R. J. White, Noyes Press, Parkridge, NJ, 1975.

32   McCurdy, op. cit.

33   Artemidorus, op. cit. trans, R. J. White, and quoted in M. Ullman and N. Zimmerman, *Working with Dreams*, Hutchinson, London, pp. 41–2.

33   Quoted in Fromm, op. cit. p. 126.

35   Synesius of Cyrene, 'On Dreams', trans. Isaac Myer, in R. Wood (ed.), *World of Dreams: an anthology*, Random House, New York, 1947, and discussed in Fromm, op. cit. p. 131.

35   Jung, op. cit, vol. 12, p. 360, note 98.

36   Arnold Mindell, *Dreambody: the body's role in revealing the Self*, Routledge & Kegan Paul, London, 1984.

36   James A. Hall, *Clinical Uses of Dreams: Jungian interpretations and enactments*, Grune & Stratton, New York, 1977, pp. 10–15.

Chapter 3   The Modern Era: Freud and Jung
38   *The Complete Psychological Works of Sigmund*

Freud (Standard Edition), Hogarth Press, London, vol. 15, 1961, p. 87.
40 Sigmund Freud, *The Interpretation of Dreams*, Allen & Unwin, London, 1954, p. 240.
40 Ibid. p. 136.
43 C. G. Jung, *Collected Works*, vol. 18, para, 464.
44 M. Ullman & N. Zimmerman, *Working with Dreams*, Hutchinson, London, 1983, p. 56.
44 Jung, op. cit. vol. 16, para. 86.
44 Ibid. para. 318.
45 Peter O'Connor, *Understanding Jung, Understanding Yourself*, Methuen Haynes, Sydney, 1985.
49 *Age* (newspaper), Melbourne, Australia, May 1985.
51 Jung, op. cit. vol. 16, para, 330.
51 Ibid. vol. 18, para 507.
54 Ibid. vol. 8, para 505.
55 *Encyclopaedic World Dictionary*, Hamlyn, London, 1971.

Chapter 4   Image, Soul, and Dreaming
57 C. G. Jung, *Collected Works*, vol. 13, para. 75.
58 James Hillman, *Insearch: psychology and religion*, Spring Publications, Dallas, 1967, p. 41.
58 James Hillman, *Suicide and the Soul*, Spring Publications, Dallas, 1978, p. 46.
59 Peter A. O'Connor, *Understanding the Mid-life Crisis*, Sun Books, Melbourne, 1981.
60 James Hillman, *Healing Fiction*, Station Hill, New York, 1983, p. 74.
60 Hillman, *Insearch*, p. 43.
62 Ibid. p. 65.
62 Hillman, *Suicide and the Soul*, p. 46.
62 Hillman, *Healing Fiction*, p. 56.
63 James Hillman, *Archetypal Psychology: a brief account*, Spring Publications, Dallas, p. 1983, pp. 26-7.

64 Ibid. p. 42.
64 James Hillman, 'Further Notes on Images',
    Spring, 1978, p. 171.
64 Edward Casey, 'Toward an Archetypal Imagi-
    nation', *Spring*, 1974, pp. 1–32.
64 Hillman, op. cit. p. 7.
65 Jung, op. cit. vol. 12, para. 400.
65 Henry Corbin, 'Mundus Imaginalis or the Imagi-
    nary and the Imaginal', *Spring*, 1972, pp. 7–15.
65 Roberts Avens, *Imagination is Reality*, Spring
    Publications, Dallas, 1980, p. 33.
65 Jung, op. cit. vol. 14, para. 753.
66 Ibid. vol. 6, para. 745.
66 Ibid.
66 James Hillman, *Re-Visioning Psychology*,
    Harper & Row, New York, 1975, p. 23.
66 Jung, op. cit. vol. 8, para, 618.
66 Ibid. vol. 6, para. 78.
67 James Hillman, 'Peaks and Vales', in *Puer
    Papers*, Spring Publications, Dallas, 1979,
    p. 56.
68 Dalai Lama, quoted in Hillman, op. cit. (I have
    used abstracts from this letter. The entire
    letter is quoted in Hillman's article, p. 59.)
71 Bruno Bettelheim, *Freud and Man's Soul*,
    Flamingo, London, 1985.
71 Ibid. p. 36.
71 Ibid. p. 77.
72 Freud, quoted in Bettelheim, op. cit. p. 35.

Chapter 5 Meeting the Dream
75 Aristotle, 'De Somnis' (On Dreams), in R.
    McKeon (ed.) *The Basic Works of Aristotle*,
    Random House, New York, 1941, p. 620.
75 C. G. Jung, *Collected Works*, vol. 9, paras 265,
    143.
77 C. G. Jung, 'Psychological Interpretation of
    Children's Dreams. Notes on lectures,
    Autumn-Winter, 1938-1939', edited by Lillian

Frey and Raymond Scharf, trans. Mary
Foote, with C. Brunner (mimeographed), and
quoted in Mary Ann Mattoon, *Understanding Dreams*, Spring Publications, Dallas,
1984, p. 106.

78   St Bernaud of Clairvaux, quoted in James
      Hillman, *Insearch: psychology and religion*,
      Spring Publications, Dallas, 1967, p. 23.
78   James A. Hall, *Jungian Dream Interpretation:
      a handbook of theory and practice*, Inner City
      Books, Toronto, 1983, p. 37.
80   Patricia Berry, 'Approach to the Dream', *Spring*,
      1974, p. 64.
80   Calvin S. Hall, *The Meaning of Dreams*,
      McGraw-Hill, New York, 1966, p. 88.
81   T. S. Eliot, 'Burnt Norton', in *Collected Poems
      1909-1935*, Faber & Faber, London, 1936,
      p. 190.
81   James Hillman, 'Further Notes on Images',
      Spring, 1978, p. 173.
81   Jung, *Collected Works*, vol. 17, para. 189.
82   Ibid. vol. 17, para. 162.
87   Ibid. vol. 8, para. 533.
88   Ibid. vol. 18, para. 200.
89   Hillman, *Insearch*, p. 57.
89   Jung. op. cit. vol. 10, para. 320.
91   T. S. Eliot, *East Coker*, Faber & Faber, London,
      1940, p. 11.
91   James Hillman, 'An Inquiry into Image', *Spring*,
      1977, p. 82.
92   Hillman, *Insearch*, p. 61.
93   Hillman, 'Further Notes on Images', p. 156.
94   Ibid. pp. 176-8.
95   Ibid. p. 180.
95   Robert Grinnell, quoted in ibid. p. 181.
96   Hillman, op. cit. p. 182.

Chapter 6   A Map for the Journey
99   James Hillman, *Insearch: psychology and*

religion, Spring Publications, Dallas, 1967, pp. 66.

99   Roberts Avens, *Imagination is Reality*, Spring Publications, Dallas, 1980.

99   Patricia Berry, 'An Approach to the Dream', *Spring*, 1974, p. 67.

101 C. G. Jung, *Memories, Dreams and Reflections*, Collins and Routledge & Kegan Paul, London, 1963, p. 189.

101 C. G. Jung, *Collected Works*, vol. 11, para. 769.

102 Ibid. vol. 12, para. 44.

102 Marie-Louise von Franz, *C. G. Jung: his myth in our time*, Little, Brown, Boston/Toronto, 1975, p. 73.

103 Ibid. p. 74.

109 P. W. Martin, *Experiment in Depth*, Routledge & Kegan Paul, London, 1955, p. 78.

110 Peter O'Connor, *Understanding Jung, Understanding Yourself*, Methuen Haynes, Sydney, 1985 (especially ch. 4).

122 Jung, op. cit. vol. 9, part 2, paras 45–6.

122 Edward C. Whitmont, *The Symbolic Quest*, Princeton University Press, Princeton, 1978, pp. 260.

123 Jung. op. cit. vol. 16, para. 469.

124 Linda Fierz-David, 'Frauen als Weckerinnen Seelischen Lebens', in *Kulturelle Bedeutung der Komplexen Psychologie*, Springer, Berlin, 1935, p. 490.

124 *I Ching or Book of Changes*, trans. R. Wilhelm and C. F. Baynes, Bollingen Foundation/Princeton University Press, Princeton, 1950, p. 9.

129 Emma Jung, *Anima and Animus*, Spring Publications, Dallas, 1978, p. 79.

130 James Hillman, 'Anima', *Spring*, 1973, p. 100.

131 Ibid.

132 Emma Jung, op. cit. p. 82.

Chapter 7   Shadows in the Night
134 C. G. Jung, *The Visions Seminar*, Spring Publications, Dallas, 1976, Book 1, p. 213.
134 Ibid.
135 Ibid. p. 211.
136 C. G. Jung, *Shadow, Animus and Anima*, Analytical Psychological Club, New York, 1950, quoted in Maria F. Mahoney, *The Meaning in Dreams and Dreaming*, Citadel Press, Secaucus, NJ, 1980, p. 108.
142 Quoted in Bruno Bettelheim, *Freud and Man's Soul*, Flamingo, 1985, p. 62.
144 J. E. Cirlot, *A Dictionary of Symbols*, Routledge & Kegan Paul, London, 2nd ed. 1971, p. 53.
146 C. G. Jung, *Collected Works*, vol. 11, para 140.

Chapter 8   The Man of Your Dreams—Animus
158 James Hillman, *Insearch: psychology and religion*, Spring Publications, Dallas, 1967, p. 65 .
167 C. G. Jung, *Collected Works*, vol. 16, para. 304.
168 C. S. Hall, 'Representation of the Laboratory Setting in Dreams', *J. Nervous Disorders*, 144 (1967) pp. 198-206.
176 Jung, op. cit. vol 13, para. 397.

Chapter 9   The Woman of Your Dreams—Anima
179 C. G. Jung, *Collected Works*, vol. 7, paras 114–15.
182 Ibid. vol. 12, para. 53.
182 C. G. Jung, *Dream Analysis: notes of the seminar given in 1928–1930*, ed. William McGuire, Princeton University Press, Princeton, 1984, p. 217.

188   C. G. Jung, *Collected Works*, vol. 15, para. 4.
188   Ibid. vol. 17, para. 328.
190   H. A. Guerber, *The Myths of Greece and Rome*, Harrap, London, rev. ed. 1952, p. 72.
195   Jung, op. cit. vol. 9, part 1, para. 522.
198   W. K. C. Guthrie, *The Greeks and their Gods*, Beacon Press, Boston, p. 100.
199   Arianna Stassinopoulos & Beny Roloff, *The Gods of Greece*, Weidenfeld & Nicholson, London, 1983, p. 70.
199   Herman Hesse, *My Belief*, trans. Denren Lindley, Jonathan Cape, London, 1976; also quoted in Stassinopoulos, op. cit. p. 75.

Chapter 10   Self and Beyond
200   T. S. Eliot, 'Burnt Norton', in *Collected Poems, 1909–1935*, Faber & Faber, London, 1936, p. 190.
201   C. G. Jung, *Collected Works*, vol. 9, part 1, para. 271.
202   Ibid. vol. 10, para, 304.
217   C. G. Jung, 'Commentary on Kundalini Yoga', *Spring*, 1975, pp. 1–34 and 1976, pp. 1–31.
217   Ibid. 1976, p. 16.
218   E. H. Gombrich, *The Story of Art*, Phaidon, London, 14th ed. 1984, pp. 150-1.
218   J. E. Cirlot, *A Dictionary of Symbols*, Routledge & Kegan Paul, London, 1962, p. 135.
219   Ibid. p. 54.

Chapter 11   A Pragmatist's Epilogue
221   James Hillman, 'Salt: a chapter in alchemical psychology', in *Images of the Untouched*, ed. J. Stroud and G. Thomas, Spring Publications, Dallas, 1982, p. 127.
222   Ibid. p. 132.
225   Patricia Garfield, *Creative Dreaming*, Ballantine Books, New York, 1974 , p. 231.

226 C. G. Jung, *Collected Works*, vol. 8. para. 503.
231 'Roosevelt "Great" is Jung's Analysis', in *New York Times*, 4 Oct. 1936, quoted in *C. G. Jung Speaking: interviews and encounters*, ed. William McGuire and R. F. C. Hull, in Bollingen Series XCVIII, Princeton, 1977, p. 89.

Index

Aboriginal dreamtime, 192–4
Abraham, Karl, 47, 92, 131
Achilles heel, Greek myth, 115, 116
alchemy/alchemists, 34, 35, 36, 70, 97, 110, 125; and *imagination*, 65; *see also* depression; dream examples; mercury; salt; sulphur; Wilhelm, Richard
American Indians, 20–1
American Psychoanalytical Movement, 72
anima, specifically (woman), 130, 177–99
animus, specifically (man), 156–76
anima/animus, 50, 99, 110, 116–17, 120–33, 156, 160, 161; *see also* dream examples;psyche; shadow
anxiety & allied ills, 8, 76, 79, 90–1, 119, 137, 227; *see also* depression; mental health
Apollo, 8, 116; Temple of Delphi, 8
Aquinas, Saint Thomas, 35–6
archetypal forces, 120, 123, 124, 127, 129; *see also* anima/animus; shadow; Yin/Yang
Aristotle, Greek philosopher, 30, 31, 35, 75, 93; *Parva Naturalia*, 30
Aristotelian image, 57
Artemidorus, Roman dream-theorist, 29, 31–3, 34, 82; *The Interpretation of Dreams*

(*Oneirocritica*), 31
Artemis, Mercurial Queen of Solitude, 198–9
Asclepius, Greek god of healing, 5, 7, 8; cult of, 26–7, 28, 29; sanctuaries of, 28, 38, 73, 90
Aserinsky, sleep research (1953), 3
Ashanti tribesmen, Africa, 18
astral-travelling belief, 18
Augustine, Saint, Bishop of Hippo, 34–5; location of soul, 61
Aurora Consurgens, see Aquinas, Thomas
Avens, Roberts, 65; *Imagination as Reality*, 99

Bacon, Roger, 13th century philosopher, 61; location of soul, 61
Bartholomew of England, 13th century Franciscan monk, 35
behaviourism, 8, 11
Bernard of Clairvaux, Saint, *Nosce Te ipsum*, 78
Berry, Patricia, 80, 88, 95, 99
Bettelheim, Bruno, American psychoanalyst, 71, 72, 73
Bishop of Ptolemais, *see* Synesius of Cyrene
Blake, William, quoted, 16
Buber, Martin, 125
Burghölzli Mental Hospital, Zurich, 45, 60
Byzantium (A.D.869), 66

Casey, Edward, 64
Chakra, *see* Jung
chemical language, 34
Christianity, 25, 165, 167,

170, 201-2, 218; *see also* Clement
Cirlot, J.E.,144, 218
Clement, Roman christian, 2nd century A.D., 34
colours — blue, mauve, red, 219; yellow, 127, 144; *see also* dreams
computers, 70
Corbin, Henry, 65, 75
counselling, 10-11, 73; *see also* dream examples
'cures' to psychological problems, 10, 11, 12, 15

Dalai Lama of Tibet, *see* Goullart, Peter
depression (and the soul), 63, 64, 106, 115, 137, 160, 178, 179; *see also* anxiety; mental health
Doolittle, Hilda (H.D.), poet, 71
dreams: action in, 30, 138; analogies in, 93; approach to interpretation, 75-97; archetypal, 47, 49; belief/disbelief in, 2; benefit from recording dreams, 28; biblical references to, 6, 7, 21-2, 32; categories of, 17; church's resistance to, 34, 35, 66-7; circumstances related to, 32; colours in, 225 (*see also* colours); compensatory law, 51, 55, 82, 103-4, 106, 110, 117; danger in 'working out', 227; demonic or divine, 36 (*see also* church's resistance); drug-alcohol effect on, 224-5; examples of, interpretation, 6, 12-14, 22-5; 33, 47-8, 51-2,

53-5, 82, 83-5, 96, 106, 127-9, 137-55, 158-76, 180-200, 203; food influence on, 224; free association (Freud), 41, 42; healing by, 8, 29, 38, 50, 52, 64, 65, 73, 152; history of, middle ages, 66-7; as images, 57, 75, 80, 81, 88; interrogating for meaning of, 77-8; in mid-life crisis, 179-80; prophetic, 23, 225-6; in psychotherapy field, 12; recall of, 4, 223-4 (*see also* Jung; symbolic language); recording of, suggestions for, 227-30; recurring, 225; symbolic language of, 2, 114; telepathic, 226; theory/practice, 87, 104; theory of (*see also* Artemidorus); therapy groups, P. O'Connor, 73-4, 149, 150, 152, 154; time spent in, 223; through time, 17-37, 90; true or false, 36-7, 38, 43; wish fulfilment, 40, 42, 55-6, 73, 104, 110, 226; *see also* Aquinas, Bettelheim; Clement; earth dreaming; Freud; Hall, Hesiod, Homer, images; Jung; Lucretius; mercury; nightmares; salt; soul; sulphur
earth dreaming, 222
ego, 4, 16, 27, 28, 90, 106, 107, 121-3, 190; *see also* Freud; Jung; psyche; Whitmont
Eliot, Thomas S., poet, 81, 91, 200

243

Emerald Table of Hermes,
quoted, 154
Epidaurus, Greece, 27
Eros, 175, 177, 189
extroverts/introverts, *see*
Jung

fairy tales as insight, 3
feeling/thinking, 112–13,
115, 117, 118, 120, 131,
132, 153, 165; *see also*
Jung, Fierz-David, Linda,
124
Franz, von, Marie-Louise,
102–3
Freud, Sigmund, 1, 11, 29,
31, 34, 57, 72–3, 81;
clinical work, 39, 56; on
the ego, 122; *Future of
an Illusion*, 72–3; and
images, 67; *Interpretation
of Dreams*, 1, 72;
*Question of Lay
Analysis*, 72–3; on the
shadow, 109; theory of
dreams, 38–56, 61, 71,
77; *see also* Bettelheim;
Doolittle; Jung
Fromm, Erich, 4, 6

Galen, location of soul, 61
Garfield, Patricia, 19
Gate of Horn, *see* Homer
Gate of Ivory, *see* Homer
Gombrich, E.H., 218
Gore, Father Brian, 166,
167, 168
Goullart, Peter, 14th Dalai
Lama, 68, 70
Greece, classical references
to, 20, 25–33; *see also*
myths/mythology
Grinnell, Robert, 95
Guthrie W.K.C., 199

Hades, 59, 61, 107, 116,
121–2, 176, 205

Halaks, *see* Senoi tribe
Hall, Calvin, 80
Hall, James, 78, 168;
Clinical Uses of Dreams,
36
hallucinogenic drugs, 122
Hesiod, *The Thegony*, 26
Hesse, Herman, *My Belief*,
199
Hillman, James (Jungian
analyst), 7, 8, 12, 20, 31,
34, 58, 60, 66, 88; his
techniques, 94–5; *quoted*:
58, 62, 63, 64, 66, 67, 81,
89, 91, 92, 95, 96, 99,
130–1, 158, 221–2; *see
also* myths, soul
Hippocrates, location of
soul, 61
Homer, *The Odyssey*, 26,
34, 37, 44

identity crisis, 160
images as problems, 12, 16,
19, 30; archetypal, 46,
50, 102, 127, 129, 201,
202; *see also* dream
examples; Jung; Islamic
view on
imaginal world, 10, 57,
64–5, 102, 112; *see also*
Paracelsus
imagination, 9, 10, 31, 34,
36, 63, 64, 75, 114;
active, 93; symbol of,
described, 69
individuation, 10, 106, 116,
122, 176; Jung's
interpretation, 8, 34, 52,
102, 125
inferior functions, 114, 115,
116, 117, 119, 120, 126,
129; development of, 171;
identification of, 118; in
men, 132, 178; *see also*
dream examples; mid-life
crisis

inner world, the, 5, 35, 36,
71, 98, 102, 106, 178,
227, 229
Interpretation of Dreams,
see Freud, Sigmund
intuition/perception, 111,
114, 115, 117, 118, 131
Islamic view on images, 65

Job, Book of, Old
Testament, 6–7, 22
Jung, Carl Gustav, 2, 7, 8,
11, 20, 31, 34, 40, 65,
88–9; on anima/animus
(1930s), 129–30; on the
archetype, 201; on the
Chakra, 217; on children,
188; comparison with
Freud, 40, 41, 42, 43, 44;
consciousness/unconsc-
iousness, 195; definition
of dreams, 202–3; on the
ego, 122, 176;
extroverts/introverts
classification, 223–4;
function of dreams, 50;
on healing, 176; on
images, 64, 65–6, 75, 82,
102, 202; and *imaginatio,*
65; *Memories, Dreams*
and Reflections, 104;
psychological theories,
97, 100; types, 110;
reaction to *Secret of*
Golden Flower, 101; his
Red Book, 101; on the
shadow, 134–6, 145–6, on
telepathic dreams, 226;
theoretical ideas on
anima-animus, 120;
theory on dreams, 44,
57–8, 76, 79, 87, 99, 167,
230; thinking/feeling
framework, 112
Jung, Emma, 129, 132

Kierkegaard, Sören, 146; on

vocation, 156
Kiwai of Papua New
Guinea, 18, 59, 60
Klein, M., 11
Kleitman, sleep research,
1953,
Landtman, G.,
anthropologist, 18, 59
literalism, 8, 9, 10, 11, 31,
65, 67, 77, 98; destroyer
of meaning 79, 178; *see*
also Freud; Jung;
Lucretius; mid-life crisis
logic v reason, 2, 3
Lucretius, Greek
philosopher, 31
McCurdy, H., 31, 32
Martin, P.W., 109
materialism, 1, 67
Mattoon, Mary Ann, 20
Meier, C.A., authority on
ancient healing rites, 29
mental health, 38, 39, 45,
59, 60, 72, 73; *see also*
anxiety; Jung;
psychoanalysis; soul
mercury (soul), 69, 70, 71,
103, 221
'messages from the Gods',
20–5, 33, 38, 46, 57, 201
metaphors, 71, 75, 76, 91,
103; metaphorical quality
of dreams, 77, 79, 81, 86,
88, 92, 95, 96, 108, 188;
metaphorical language,
201
Middle Ages, 25, 31, 36, 66
mid-life crisis, 51, 59, 84,
118, 156–7, 160, 166,
176, 178–9, 189; *see also*
dream examples
mind, 71, 78; *see also*
sulphur
Mindell, Arnold,
Dreambody, 36
Mysteries of Isis, 28
mythology/myths/ images,

P.W.
sleep, 3, 34, 39, 40;
  research into 3, 40; *see
  also* Aserinsky; Kleitman;
  REM
Socrates, Greek
  philosopher, 29
soul, the, 34, 54–74, 91, 93,
  96, 97, 101, 102, 157;
  description of, 59–61,
  99–100; and immortality,
  103; in orthodox religion,
  66–7; *see also* alchemists;
  American Indians;
  anima/animus; Avens,
  Roberts; Bettelheim;
  depression; Doolittle,
  Hilda; dreams (groups);
  Fierz-David, Linda;
  Goullart, Peter; Hesse,
  Herman; Hillman, James;
  Kierkegaardian vocation;
  mercury; psyche;
  psychological types;
  spirit; tactile therapies
spirit, the, 61, 64, 65, 66,
  68, 71, 97, 99; *see also*
  soul
spiritual life forces, 19, 20
Stassinopoulos, Arianna,
  199
Stewart, Kilton,
  anthropologist, 18–19
sulphur (mind), 69, 70, 71,
  76, 221, 227
superior functions, 113, 118,
  119, 165
symbolic language, 4, 5, 32,
  41, 46, 104, 227

symbols, 16, 41, 46, 47,
  58–9, 61, 64, 201
Synesius of Cyrene, Bishop
  of Ptolemais, 5, 35

tactile therapies, 67–8
Talmud, 81
Theseus/Pirithous, Greek
  myth, 121
thinking, *see*
  feeling/thinking

Ullman, Montague, 44; *see
  also* Zimmerman, Nan
unconscious mind/world, 2,
  11, 22, 37, 39, 59–60,
  122–3, 206; collective -,
  45, 46, 48, 120, 121, 127,
  201; *see also* Freud's
  theory of dreams; Hades;
  Hillman, James; Jung,
  Carl; soul

Watkins, Mary, 27
Whitmont, E.C., on the ego,
  122
Wilhelm, Richard,
  translator, 101, 124
wish-fulfilment, *see* dreams
Wordsworth, William,
  *Intimations of
  Immortality*, 219–20

Ying/Yang, 68, 110, 124–6,
  132, 148, 149, 177, 216,
  217

Zeller, Max, 5–6, 15
Zimmerman, Nan, 44; *see
  also* Ullman, Montague

247